New Dramatists 2000

About New Dramatists

Founded in 1949 by a playwright, Michaela O'Harra, New Dramatists is a unique resource for the American theater. The company is dedicated to the playwright and serves as an artistic home, a research and development center, and a national writers' colony. The company finds and nurtures new talent through a competitive, membership selection process and a seven-year playwright development program tailored to the writers' individual needs.

New Dramatists gives writers the tools that they need—time, generous theater space, a pool of talented and experienced actors and directors, writing equipment, meeting space, and a gifted peer community—to grow artistically and strengthen their commitment to theater. The company augments this central focus on artistic growth through programs that advocate and distribute each writer's work to theater producers, through grants and fellowships, international exchanges, and with annual playwriting retreats in Lake Placid, New York, and Key West, Florida.

Writers pay nothing to join and participate in New Dramatists. The program is made possible through contributions from the theater and entertainment community. In return for this gift of time and resources, member playwrights write and create new works for the theater. The company organizes an average of seventy-five readings and workshops of new plays and musicals by its members each season.

Member playwrights and alumni have won ten Pulitzer Prizes, including the 2000 Pulitzer Prize for Drama to alumnus Donald Margulies, twenty Tony Awards, fifty Obie Awards, seventeen Drama Desk Awards, and ten Susan Smith Blackburn Awards.

New Dramatists' founding artists and producers committee included Michaela O'Harra, Howard Lindsay, Russel Crouse, Richard Rodgers, Oscar Hammerstein 2nd, John Golden, Moss Hart, Maxwell Anderson, John Wharton, and Elmer Rice.

New Dramatists

2000

Best Plays by the
Graduating Class

Edited by Todd London,
Artistic Director

CONTEMPORARY PLAYWRIGHTS SERIES

A Smith and Kraus Book

A Smith and Kraus Book
Published by Smith and Kraus, Inc.
177 Lyme Road, Hanover, NH 03755
www.SmithKraus.com

Manufactured in the United States of America

Cover and Text Design by Julia Hill Gignoux, Freedom Hill Design

First Edition: August 2001
10 9 8 7 6 5 4 3 2 1

ISBN 1-57525-269-4
Contemporary Playwrights Series
ISSN 1067-9510

Contents

Preface
Robert Anderson
vii

Introduction
Todd London
xi

Exchange at the Café Mimosa
Oana-Maria Cajal
1

Coaticook
Lenora Champagne
45

Landscape of Desire
Barry Jay Kaplan
67

Carry the Tiger to the Mountain
Cherylene Lee
119

Acapulco
Jacquelyn Reingold
165

A Shoe Is Not a Question
Kelly Stuart
225

2000–2001 MEMBER PLAYWRIGHTS

Luis Alfaro

Mark Bazzone

Neena Beber

John Belluso

Deborah Baley Brevoort

Carlyle Brown

Bridget Carpenter

Lonnie Carter

Kia Corthron

Nilo Cruz

Gordon Dahlquist

Lisa D'Amour

Herman Daniel Farrell III

Catherine Filloux

Stephanie Fleischmann

Karl Gajdusek

Anne García-Romero

Melissa James Gibson

Keith Glover

Silvia Gonzalez S.

David Greenspan

Karen Hartman

Julie Hébert

Sander Hicks

Arlene Hutton

Honour Kane

David Lindsay-Abaire

Dmitry Lipkin

Ruth Margraff

Rogelio Martinez

Murray Mednick

Alejandro Morales

Lynn Nottage

Kate Robin

Edwin Sanchez

Octavio Solis

Diana Son

Caridad Svich

Dominic Taylor

Edgar Nkosi White

Doug Wright

Chay Yew

Paul Zimet

Preface

There's a sign over my desk that reads, "Nobody asked you to be a playwright." I put it there almost forty years ago to stop my bitching.

Although the message is still lamentably true — talented playwrights are wooed by television and movie producers, but rarely hear "How are you doing?" from theater producers — there was a time, soon after we all came back from World War II, when people were asking us to be playwrights.

The honorable and venerable Theatre Guild had a group of young playwrights meeting under the guidance of John Gassner and Theresa Helburn. Theatre Incorporated, a new producing firm, gathered some of us with Theodore Apstein keeping order. The American Theater Wing, which had been so active during the war with projects such as The Stage Door Canteen, set up a whole "academy" where they sponsored refresher courses for returning veterans.

Mary Hunter, who was the academic head of this Professional Training Program, approached me to teach the playwriting courses. Barely a playwright myself (I had had one off-Broadway production), I started the courses and taught myself and a fair number of other young playwrights. I can still see myself rushing into class full of enthusiasm about what I had just found out that morning about writing plays.

Distinguished guests such as Howard Lindsay, Elia Kazan, Arthur Miller, and Moss Hart came to share their experiences and wisdom with us. And once a week the students' plays were read aloud by a group of neophyte actors including Eileen Heckart, Jean Stapleton, and Harry Belafonte. The Wing also received free tickets to the theater.

At the same time a young playwright, Michaela O'Harra, with one Broadway production to her credit, felt the theater industry itself should offer some "growing ground for *all* qualified new dramatists." Since Howard Lindsay had been extraordinarily supportive of my program at The Theatre Wing, I suggested to Michaela that she solicit his advice and hlep. Her passion for the idea was contagious, and she persuaded Howard to become the godfather of her venture.

And so with the support of Howard Lindsay and Russel Crouse, The Dramatists Guild, The Playwrights Company, Richard Rodgers and Oscar Hammerstein, and John Golden, the New Dramatists was started in 1949.

For some years the dedicated Michaela ran the organization almost single-handedly, with occasional help from other New Dramatists like Eva Wolas. Our office was the small cloakroom in the Hudson Theatre (owned by Lindsay and Crouse), and we met in a large, dimly lit conference room five flights up at the top of the theater. There, week after week, we neophytes gathered to listen to the likes of Lindsay, Robert Sherwood, Maxwell Anderson, Elia Kazan, S.M. Behrman, Moss Hart, and others. Those early New Dramatists eager for every word included William Inge, Paddy Chayefsky, William Gibson, Horton Foote, Joe Kramm, Ronald Alexander, and Sumner Locke Elliot among oth-ers. They would, in due time, return to talk to new generations of New Dramatists including James Goldman, Michael Stewart, Max Wilk, Joe Masteroff, Arnold Schulman, Jack Gelber, Lanford Wilson, who would in due time . . .

When someone had a play ready, he or she would read it to us and bravely listen to the comments. Thanks to the producers, we went to the theater free. We felt appreciated.

Over the years we grew out of the cloakroom to the offices in City Center with Michaela still firmly at the helm but aided now by such administrators as the late George Hamlin and the casting and production wizard, Robert Colson.

Now we have our own building, an old church, which contains two the-aters and is located on the same block as the old church housing the Actors Studio. (It's a nice picture, the playwrights and actors developing side by side.) The nature of the group has shifted over the years. The playwrights are more sophisticated, many of them having had productions in regional, Broadway, off- and off-off-Broadway theaters.

The New Dramatists is still a place for talented playwrights to develop, to grow, and to work in a theater with fine actors and directors with no pro-duction pressures. In the years since New Dramatists was founded, many valu-able nurturing grounds have sprung up around the country. All are doing notable work. The New Dramatists, however, is unique. Upon admittance, the writer becomes a member for seven years — seven years to hear his or her plays read, see them workshopped, listen, learn from others, see theater, enjoy the support and companionship of other playwrights and the services of a trained staff of people who are there to help the playwright grow and develop.

There is no charge for all this. The only requirements are talent and a willingness to pursue a goal.

We point with pride to the work of the member playwrights who over the years have shared their talents, wisdom, and caring and who have emerged — if not Pulitzer Prize–winners, as ten of our members have — at least to a better understanding of their art and craft.

Robert Anderson
Member Playwright, Original Class Member
New Dramatists Board of Directors

Introduction

THE EVOLUTION OF A PLAYWRIGHT

What makes a playwright? How does an artist grow?

This is not a test. If it were, anyone attempting to answer these unanswerable questions would fail or, at best, go home with an incomplete. The making of an artist — any artist — is one of the compelling mysteries of being human. We can follow the course of a life's work, track its influences, analyze the writing in light of everything we know about the writer's psychology, culture, and intentions. Still, however exhaustive or precise our maps, we end up in a country with no name, whose borders change more rapidly than a nation at war with itself.

Maybe each playwright's body of work is its own evolving map, with its own topography, mines, tributary sources, roads leading who knows where. Maybe the only feature common to all writer-maps is the legend at the bottom, blotted out by a coffee spill. Without a readable key, how can we determine scale or distinguish a major artery from an off-ramp?

We can't. Even looking backward, over the corpus a writer leaves behind, we can't make absolute sense of his or her trajectory. Shakespeare — that great example — stands, amidst our interpretive attempts to know him, as the premier Rorschach test. Check out the infinite (and ever-growing) listings under "Shakespeare, lives of. . ." The history of dramatic literature reinforces this mystery at every turn. One writer seems to grow in a straight line, headed, in almost logical progression, for a pinnacle or crowning achievement. Another settles in early, discovers a singular voice and goes with it, until, in a lunatic late-career leap, she or he throws it all out and hurtles into the unknown — with a dream play, expressionist epic, the unrecognizable. Still others start out with a bang and then seem to die early, long time no see, before, as if out of a fallow period that crosses generations, they re-emerge, newborn and fully formed. Everywhere you look you find every kind of career: wunderkinds, late bloomers, one-play marvels, lifetime achievers.

This anthology — the first of what will be an annual publication — is no exception. Its organizing principle offers little help on how to read the plays herein. These six extraordinary writers hold only one thing in common: They've all come to the end of their membership at New Dramatists, the nation's oldest center for the support and development of playwrights. Seven years ago they began a journey of self-cultivation in the company of the forty or more playwrights that make up this writing community at any given moment. Now that journey is done. Because New Dramatists tailors its "program" to the expressed needs of each individual writer — because, in other words, the writers determine and drive their own development here, selecting what plays to work on when and how — there's no set course, no shared progression. Again, no map.

And no common profile. Consider the writers whose plays you're about to read. Oana-Maria Cajal comes from postwar Romania, Lenora Champagne from rural Louisiana, Kelly Stuart from the suburbs of Los Angeles, and Jacquelyn Reingold from the heart of Manhattan. Their training, too, has no common thread. Barry Jay Kaplan was trained as a novelist and wrote several commercially successful novels before turning to playwriting. Cherylene Lee, who began as a child performer on stage and in movies, was educated as a geologist/paleontologist and designed wastewater systems on the road to writing for the theater. Champagne ventured into playwriting from doctoral studies, French-language scholarship, and performance art. They are the products of different generations and influences with wildly varied artistic concerns. Even within a single body of writing, you can find this wild variety.

So, how did we choose which play would "represent" these writers' fruition since 1993? First and foremost, we did what we always do at New Dramatists: We let the playwrights decide for themselves. With feedback from the editor and publishers, the authors selected the plays they wanted the world to know them by at this moment in their writing lives. Their reasons were personal, artistic, professional, and idiosyncratic. As such, they, too, will remain mysterious.

Our job at New Dramatists is to nourish the development of the playwright, not merely the play. Naturally, then, I'm somewhat skeptical about anyone's ability to draw conclusions about the vision and capabilities of a writer on the basis of a single script. To improve the odds, we've surrounded each play with biographical information and the testimony of artists familiar with the playwright's work. In the next few paragraphs, I'll try to add some context, too, to flesh out the portrait of the artist behind the play.

Barry Jay Kaplan's *Landscape of Desire* tackles the subject of a writer's development head on. It's the dramatic equivalent of a *bildungsroman*, portrait of a novelist (playwright?) as a young man. *Landscape* occupies a central, important place in Barry's oeuvre, even as, on the surface, it bears little resemblance to his other work. On one hand, the triptych of scenes that make up *Landscape* provides a central, dramatic statement of two of Barry's preoccupations: gay sexuality and the corruption of — I'm not sure what to call it — love or desire, or maybe the more embracing "promise." Each of these scenes begins with a kind of pure ambition or desire (though these diminish from act to act) and each culminates in a corruption, betrayal, or degradation of that desire. Barry's writing doesn't celebrate gay sexuality or culture so much as place it in the context of heterosexual America and calculate the damage on the individual. *Landscape*'s portrayal of the publicly closeted (read sell-out) movie star foreshadows his musical, *Rock and Roy*, about the toll of Rock Hudson's secret life. On the other hand, while a few of his plays draw on the autobiographical, this play *feels* like autobiography; the ambition-dreams and betrayals that mark the periods of the central character's growth as a novelist have long teased me into drawing connections to the playwright's own evolution. Also, there's a directness, an everyday-language quality to the dialogue here that differs from some of his other dramatic work. I'm thinking of the terse, fraught prose of *Bananas and Water*, a devastating play about the reunion of two brothers at the deathbed of their brutal father, or his most recent play, *A Beautiful White Room*, which plumbs one man's descent into a world of pornography, drugs, and murder in an elliptical, fragmented style that unfolds like a nightmare.

Barry Jay Kaplan's "landscape" is primarily psychological, familial, and sexual; his characters are, in many ways, their own worst enemies. He raises social and political questions secondarily: What is the place of the artist in America? What is the place of the gay man? How do we survive self-sabotage — art, ideals, humanity intact — in a world that inspires it? By contrast, Cherylene Lee's plays begin with the political and with the typically American conflict of ethnic identity. *Carry the Tiger to the Mountain*, Cherylene's contribution to this collection, dramatizes a true-life event: the 1982 murder of Vincent Chin, a young Chinese-American beaten to death by two Detroit autoworkers who thought he was Japanese. A snapshot of middle America at a moment when its industrial center felt most threatened by Japanese imports, *Carry the Tiger* begins with a cultural collision — albeit a mistaken one — and uses it to probe not only racism and injustice (the killers get off with a judicial slap on the wrist and no prison time) but also heritage, assimilation, and identity. (In a happy reversal of history, this play became the centerpiece of a Governor's civil rights initiative and national forum on racial justice in West Virginia, where it was commissioned and produced by the Contemporary American Theatre

Festival.) Wisely, Cherylene moves in two directions at once, toward the political and the personal. Here, she personalizes her documentary subject by focusing on the transformation of Lily Chin, Vincent's old-world mother, as grieving mother becomes civil rights activist and spokeswoman.

If I had to argue *Carry the Tiger*'s place in Cherylene's work-to-date, I'd say it's a crystallization play, one that brings together careerlong obsessions in a defining way. East and West meet here — as they do in all her work — at the hyphen that binds Chinese-American. As in *Arthur and Leila*, which locates a socialite woman and her ne'er-do-well brother among their family heirlooms, or *Knock Off Balance*, which pits a Hollywood talent agent against a successful relative from Hong Kong, or the (just possibly) autobiographical *Lost Vegas Acts*, about three women, formerly a Las Vegas sister-act, struggling through their adult lives — Cherylene's scientific eye is trained on the place of heritage or legacy in a changing world, a world of cultural connection and ethnic collision. Even her theatrical traditions collide in *Carry the Tiger*, as American popular music and the ancient martial art Tai Chi come together to make a new-old whole.

Oana-Maria Cajal might also be called a political playwright, though her methods couldn't be farther from those of Cherylene, because what strikes you first is not the politics — not the content — but the unmitigated strangeness of her world. It's an unfamiliar world, even to the people who populate her plays. They are Eastern-European refugees, immigrants, tourists, people with scant memory of the past, who've left lives behind without ever arriving anywhere; they are strange strangers in transit through strange lands, who've missed (and keep missing) the boat. Reading her collected work, you can feel the influence of Chekhov, her countryman Ionesco, and, especially, Beckett, but you also feel the ways she's extended and politicized those influences. In *Waiting for Godot to Leave,* Oana takes the seminal Beckett work a step further; Godot — like every indulgent, arbitrary conqueror — overstays his welcome, adding inertia to injury. Oana reinvents the absurd with a lot of help from the Soviet Empire, before and after. Hers is the wacky, sad, political vaudeville of our dwindling century.

Oana can write in several languages — Rumanian, French, English — but her characters speak a common tongue. I think of it as Oana-Lingua. It's the idiom of the absurd — that wry, achy, alienated comic dialect in which phrases sever from their meanings and words always miss their mark. Missing, in all its meanings, may well be the essential condition of her plays, regardless of differences in tone. Content — what's in the boxes? — is a missing piece in the absurdist farce of *Exchange at Café Mimosa*, which unfolds like an espionage thriller where sentences ricochet around the hotel settings, instead of bullets, and clues lead to nothing. Even the ubiquitous reptiles — goofy-ominous reminders of Ionesco's raging *Rhinoceroses* — are, to mix animal metaphors, red herrings. Homeland is missing from the haunted, polyglot refugee camp in *The Enduring Legend of Marinka Pinka and Tommy Atomic*, just as pieces of the past are missing from her exquisite memory play, *Love in the Shadow of the Umbrella Bamboo*.

Sketched out this way, these writers' creative terrain might seem sensible and coherent, but I offer these outlines tentatively, aware that for every connection drawn, there's left a piece sticking out, an example that doesn't want to fit. For all that overlaps in a playwright's work, there is at least as much that veers, leaps, play-by-play, in precipitous, unexpected ways. Jacquelyn Reingold's body of work is a lesson in change of direction.

Her stylistic shifts from piece to piece make a twisted plot of her career. There's the absurd sexual romp of *Tunnel of Love* — the brief picaresque of a woman in search of the vagina she was born without. Next to that, place the breathtaking simplicity of *Dear Kenneth Blake* — a romance between a Cambodian refugee and a homeless man, set in the field of an organic farm. From there to *Girl Gone* — an urban mystery about grief and identity — you must travel to the sexual underworld, a world of strippers, violence, and disappearance. Whichever way you turn, you'll discover no two plays that are the same; each one makes its own world. *Acapulco*, anthologized here, goes yet another way. It's built like a late-'60s Broadway comedy but turns genre upside-down, unsettles it by taking seriously what these comedies avoided: dawning consciousness of blacks and women in middle-class American life. In it, Jackie marries her flair for comedy and her drive to dig around in the painful human truths from which the comedy springs.

So, what is the vision connecting these disparate works? Again, it's a slippery assessment, but I'd single out three features common to Jackie's plays (aside from the givens of intelligence, wit, and craft). On a thematic level, the terror of intimacy excites her work; it's the raw nerve her very human dramas and comedies exposé. Further, her particular gifts include a talent for empathy, that quality essential for any dramatist — to enter other lives and souls — but which Jackie possesses in spades. She burrows in her characters' skins and perspectives, even when she mocks the people she's created with her own brand of wicked humor. Finally, this work shares a deep, reflexive theatrical sense — it lives in the theater, belongs there, is theatrical to its bones.

Lenora Champagne, represented here by *Coaticook*, is always stretching the boundaries of what we call "theater." She began her career — and is still well-known — as a performance artist, especially for solo performances that are poetic monologue-movement pieces. Sometimes, during the course of her years at New Dramatists, it seemed as though she were testing the waters of playwriting, or, more accurately, putting playwriting to the test. Could the dramatic form contain — as her performances could — the detail, the intricacy, the mutable, layered, impressionistic quality of life at its most finely tuned. In other words, how can one make plays that match poetry or lyric in their ability to compress feeling and express life as it changes. Her one-woman exploration of motherhood, *Wants*, became a three-woman play: three women alone in three homes — as though the solo artist could take the best from the worlds of poetry, performance art, and playwriting by splitting herself, casting three where there had been one. Her extensive work with music, specifically in the cyberspace opera, *The Singing*, written with Daniel Levy, extended this search and found a perfect connector in the through-sung musical form. The opera's story, too, provided a canvas for Lenora's fascination with want, longing, and loss; in this modern-day Orpheus retelling, a computer coder creates a virtual world and enters cyberspace. His wife goes in after him to bring him home; while his parents, the press, a televangelist, and a trio of military, C.I.A. and medical specialists maneuver to influence the outcome. The power of the human voice, the personal lyric, compression in form and impression in substance — these are the stuff of Lenora's creations.

In that context, *Coaticook* feels almost like an aberration. A play with realistic characters, situations, horrible events, everyday anguish — almost straightforward for an experimental artist of her stripe. But maybe it's not that unlikely. Many of her concerns are here: the complicated, even devastating effects of domestic life on a woman who isn't fit for it; the outsider — in this case a young Eskimo man — uprooted from his heritage and destroyed without roots. And formally the attempt at compression is here, too — eliminating everything unnecessary and leaving only essential, heightened interaction, in ways reminiscent of that great influence, Maria Irene Fornes. Because her sensibilities are so attuned to change, they make us aware of what change deprives us of, what we lose. *Coaticook* is a harsh, lyrical portrait of this loss.

As Lenora's perceptions focus on the interior life, Kelly Stuart's eye is trained — with deadly, demonic aim — on the life of society. Kelly can write with extraordinary ease in many styles — recent work mines sources as diverse as Balzac, true crime novels, and the Oresteia — and whatever she sees, she satirizes with a wit that's as bright as it is ruthless. In *Demonology*, a young mother enters into the bizarre wasteland of (male) corporate America, joining a formula manufacturer as a secretarial temp. Her ingenuous attempts to succeed parallel an outbreak of surreal, serial sabotage at the company. Her boss, meanwhile, finds out that she's expressing breast milk for her baby and begins stealing the milk — replacing it with creamer — and secretly, addictively drinking it. *The Secret Life of Spiders*, set in 1830's Paris, introduces another innocent to what one children's book author might call "a terrible, horrible, no-good, really bad" world, a world of social rank and rank society — a world of, well, spiders, not unlike twenty-first-century Hollywood, in whose shadow Kelly lives. The innocent — a man obsessed with creating fabric from the silk of spiders — literally swallows the values of society, until, through a bizarre plot-twist that enables him to have all that he desires, his desire (just as literally) eats him alive. This — I think of it as gothic satire — is Kelly's way.

A Shoe Is Not a Question (one of my favorite titles), while less fervid and gothic — though she wreaks pleasant havoc on the Orpheus myth and the fashion industry — is a satire every bit as imaginative and bold. Once again she pits an innocent, this time an almost supernaturally flexible yoga instructor, against an aging, incestuous clique of friends. Her naïve belief in the ideas of love, honesty, trust, and the like leads her in over her New-Age head, because, of course, people are not to be trusted. Even the rosy past is not to be trusted. Only, I think, Kelly Stuart can be trusted — to shame the smug, needle the foolish, and subvert all that's exploitive, greedy, narcissistic, and fatuous in this great, lousy world. With Kelly, as with all of the writers in print here, it's impossible to know where her career will career next. Wherever she turns her gaze, though, we should be afraid, very afraid.

It's been a joy and an honor to work beside these writers during their years at New Dramatists, and I've no doubt that the joy will last as they continue on their singular, mysterious ways. Now the treat is yours. This guided tour is over; it's time to read the plays. You'll find your own way, map or no.

Todd London
Artistic Director
New Dramatists

Exchange at Café Mimosa

Oana-Maria Cajal

The Man from the Sandwich Islands in a Gourd Helmet

INTRODUCTION
by Mac Wellman

Oana's plays are quite extraordinary for many reasons, but what tickles me the most is that she may be the only true, living and practicing Surrealist playwright in the country. Her experimentalism is no mere surface game or gimmickry, but springs from a profound examination of the sources of human drama, and the materials of our cultural condition.

THE AUTHOR

Oana-Maria Cajal was born in Bucharest, Romania. She received her M.F.A. degree in Theatre and Cinema Studies from Bucharest's Institute of Theatre Arts and Cinematography in 1977. In 1980, upon receiving a grant from the American Critics Association, Oana immigrated to the United States. While attending the Ph.D. Theatre Criticism program at New York's City University, Oana's emphasis turned to playwriting. She then moved to California where she received her M.F.A. in playwriting. In 1986 her first play, *Eastern European Tetralogy,* was nominated by the San Diego Theatre Critics Circle as best new play. Oana is a recipient of the National Endowment for the Arts playwriting Fellowship for 1989. In the summer of 1990, Oana traveled back to Romania where she experienced firsthand the violent events that occurred in Bucharest on the thirteenth, fourteenth, and fifteenth of June. These experiences gave rise to her play, *The Almond Seller.* Oana is a member of the Dramatists Guild, The Romanian-American Academy for the Arts and Sciences, and she was awarded a Fulbright Scholarship in 1994. *Berlin, Berlin* has received productions from the Mandell Weiss Center for Performing Arts (La Jolla, California), Workhouse Theatre in New York, and Brandeis University. *The Enduring Legend of Marinka Pinka and Tommy Atommic* was part of SummerNite Festival in Chicago in 1999. *Waiting for Godot to Leave* was produced in 2001 at Immigrants Theatre Project, in New York. *Exchange at Café Mimosa* was workshopped at the American Repertory Theatre in Cambridge, produced at the Workhouse and most recently at The Perishable Theatre, Providence, Rhode Island. Presently, Oana resides in Montreál, Canada.

CHARACTERS

HERR LEOPOLD VON RUPPERSTAHL: His indoor hobby: skull painting.

MARIE-LOUISE: His wife. Very aware of her beautiful hands.

PETER BROWN: Wears comfortable shoes.

JUNE: His wife, sexually frustrated.

THE MAN FROM THE SANDWICH ISLANDS IN A GOURD HELMET: He knows everything.

THE TAXI DRIVER, THE WAITER, THE BELLBOY: Played by the same actor.

THE PARROT

OTHER PEOPLE IN THE HOTEL: THE WOMAN IN THE WHITE DRESS

THE MAN IN A DARK SUIT

THE LITTLE SPOILED BOY

HIS AUNT

A MAN WITH AN ALLERGY

THE CHINESE MAN

NATIVE BOY WITH GUITAR AND NOTEBOOK

THE TWO BOXES: Identical

REPTILES

THE PLACE OF THE EXCHANGE

Hotel Mimosa, Tropical Island, Neutral Territory.

WEATHER CONDITIONS

Hot and humid.

SCENES

Europe

Milwaukee

On the Plane

In the Taxi

In the Elevator

In the Browns' Room

In the Rupperstahls' Room

In the Browns' Room

In the Middle of the Night

Breakfast

In the Rupperstahls' Room

Lunch

In the Browns' Room

A Walk on the Beach

In the Men's Restroom

In the Ladies' Room

Grammar in a Nutshell

The Exchange

The Woman in a White Dress

Native Boy with a Guitar

EXCHANGE AT CAFÉ MIMOSA

EUROPE

Supertitle: Herr Rupperstahl's Castle. Bach's Missa Solemnis.
Lights up.
Marie-Louise and Leopold von Ruppersthal enter from opposite directions. They walk toward each other. The phone starts ringing loudly from the other room.

MARIE-LOUISE: What could this be?

LEOPOLD: Undoubtedly, the phone, Marie-Louise.

MARIE-LOUISE: Is there no one to answer it?

LEOPOLD: It is Sunday, Marie-Louise. The servants have the day off.

MARIE-LOUISE: Dear me, why do men have such a ridiculous repulsion for answering the phone?

LEOPOLD: If you are referring to myself, Marie-Louise, allow me to say that this is not true. I distinctly remember answering the phone at least five times in the last month. *(Pause.)* And each time someone was ringing for you! Your mother, in fact. *(Lifts Marie-Louise's skirt.)*

MARIE-LOUISE: Leopold!

LEOPOLD: Ah, well, I suppose I shall answer it. Are you taking any calls?

MARIE-LOUISE: Only if it's my mother.

LEOPOLD: As you wish. *(Exits.)*

(The phone stops ringing. Marie-Louise stares into the audience trying to listen to Leopold's voice from the other room. It is impossible to make out the words. Leopold enters. He is thunderstruck.)

LEOPOLD: Marie-Louise!

MARIE-LOUISE: My mother is dead!

LEOPOLD: No! It's nothing like that. *(Pause.)* Marie-Louise! This is undoubtedly the most uncommon thing that has ever occurred to me . . . to us. *(Pause.)* Quite extraordinary!
(Blackout.)

MILWAUKEE

Supertitle: Milwaukee. The Brown's townhouse.
TV on.
Lights up.
Peter and June simultaneously enter from opposite directions. The phone starts ringing.

JUNE: Should we get it?
PETER: I thought we weren't home.
JUNE: I am not. You are.
PETER: *(Pause.)* I thought we both weren't.
JUNE: O.K.
PETER: I don't know . . .
JUNE: Then get it.
PETER: It's probably for you.
JUNE: I don't think so.
PETER: Nobody calls me at home.
JUNE: You might as well get it.
PETER: O.K.
JUNE: I am not home.
PETER: O.K.
    (Peter exits. June stares into the audience concentrating to hear Peter's voice. Nothing can be understood. Peter enters. He is flabbergasted.)
PETER: June! *(Pause.)* June! *(Pause.)* June!
JUNE: Who was it?
PETER: I just can't believe it! You won't believe it! Nobody will believe it!
JUNE: What is it?
PETER: It's . . . June! They have chosen me!
    (Blackout.)

ON THE PLANE (a)

Herr Ruppersthal and his wife are seated facing stage left. She is wearing an ostrich feather hat. He is reading a book on Henry the Eighth.

LEOPOLD: *(Pause.)* Marie-Louise! What would you say if I were to have you executed?

MARIE-LOUISE: *(Startled.)* LEOPOLD!

LEOPOLD: Henry the Eighth!

MARIE-LOUISE: A murderer, no doubt.

LEOPOLD: He only gave the order, Marie-Louise.

MARIE-LOUISE: Exactly.

LEOPOLD: Still, it is quite fascinating to think that few words can . . .

VOICE-OVER: Ladies and gentlemen, we are now only fifteen minutes away from our destination. We ask you to please return to your seats and fasten your seatbelts. Thank you.

MARIE-LOUISE: Dear me, my throat is awfully dry.

LEOPOLD: Ah, well! I'll ring for some water.

MARIE-LOUISE: It is not that.

LEOPOLD: You are afraid, Marie-Louise.

MARIE-LOUISE: That horrible box.

LEOPOLD: Marie-Louise, control yourself.

MARIE-LOUISE: There is something sinister about it.

LEOPOLD: The box looks perfectly ordinary.

MARIE-LOUISE: That is just it. It looks too perfectly ordinary.

LEOPOLD: Under those circumstances nothing can be left to chance.

MARIE-LOUISE: Somehow, not knowing what is inside. . . Oh, I must know, don't you see?

LEOPOLD: I have PRECISE INSTRUCTIONS, Marie-Louise. I was chosen from millions. Marie-Louise, the future of a whole world depends on me.

MARIE-LOUISE: I am your wife, Leopold.

LEOPOLD: I know that, Marie-Louise.

MARIE-LOUISE: You simply must tell me. Tell me!

LEOPOLD: *(Tense.)* You are extremely nervous, Marie-Louise.

MARIE-LOUISE: I am going to get sick!

LEOPOLD: Marie-Louise! *(Pause.)* You know I can't see you THAT nervous. You know what it does to me. You know what must happen then.
(The stare at each other. Pause. Blackout.)

ON THE PLANE

Mr. Brown and his wife are seated facing stage right. They both are wearing headphones. Their eyes are closed. Pause. Restlessly, June is stretching her arms and accidentally punches Mr. Brown in the nose.

PETER: June!

JUNE: Oh! I'm sorry. Let me look, Honey.

> *(She tries to look at his face.)*

PETER: For God's sake!

JUNE: I'm sorry, Honey. It was your nose, wasn't it?

PETER: You punched me in the nose, for God's sake!

JUNE: Did I hit your nose, Honey?

PETER: June! I am trying to listen to something. Would you relax, please . . .

JUNE: You are too nervous, Honey. You should try to relax. *(Pause.)* *(Takes her headphones off. Stares at Peter.)*

> Peter! *(Louder.)* Peter!
>
> *(Takes his headphones off.)*

PETER: For God's sake, June.

JUNE: I am your wife, Peter.

PETER: The instructions are precise, you know that.

JUNE: You must know what's inside that box. . .

PETER: I was chosen from millions, Honey. I have a huge responsibility.

JUNE: Why you?

PETER: For God's sake!

VOICE-OVER: Ladies and gentlemen, we are now only sixteen minutes away from our destination. We ask you to please return to your seats and fasten your seatbelts. Thank you.

JUNE: I have to use the bathroom.

PETER: *(Stands.)* Go ahead, Honey.

JUNE: *(Sits.)* I better wait.

PETER: You have plenty of time, Honey.

JUNE: I'm O.K.

PETER: *(Pause.)* My stomach feels funny.

JUNE: I have never seen you so nervous.

PETER: June!

JUNE: You shouldn't get so nervous.

PETER: Because I am a man. Is that it?

JUNE: Relax. The sweat went through your jacket.

PETER: I am sorry if I disappoint you again.

JUNE: You are all wet, Honey.

PETER: Stop it!

> *(They stare at each other.)*
>
> *(Blackout.)*

IN THE TAXI (a)

*Leopold and Marie-Louise are seated facing stage left with the box between
them. Street noise. The taxi driver is humming a popular song. He smokes.
Leopold and Marie-Louise look out the window.*

MARIE-LOUISE: Quite an unusual place. Would you agree, Leopold?

LEOPOLD: *(Pause.)* The rain is getting quite heavy.

MARIE-LOUISE: I am still shaking.

LEOPOLD: It was an accident, Marie-Louise.

MARIE-LOUISE: To see those repulsive reptiles running around loose! In an airport!

LEOPOLD: The shipment spilled accidentally, Marie-Louise.

MARIE-LOUISE: I could swear they got loose just when we were passing by.

LEOPOLD: Nonsense, Marie-Louise. *(Pause.)* Fortunately the box is intact. No
reptiles got to it.

MARIE-LOUISE: How could they? You covered it with your own body. *(Pause.)*
What is in it, Leopold?

LEOPOLD: Marie-Louise!

THE TAXI DRIVER: English?

LEOPOLD: Pardon?

THE TAXI DRIVER: English?

LEOPOLD: No, we only *speak* English.

THE TAXI DRIVER: Me also. A little. Good language, huh? *(Pause.)* You sure we
want to go to the Hotel Mimosa?

LEOPOLD: Yes, that is our destination.

THE TAXI DRIVER: Other nice hotels here . . .

LEOPOLD: Thank you, but our reservations have been made in advance.

THE TAXI DRIVER: Huh! If you sincerely wish . . .

MARIE-LOUISE: The man is warning us of something, Leopold!

LEOPOLD: It is simply talk, Marie-Louise.

THE TAXI DRIVER: Big box you carry with you, huh?

LEOPOLD: Yes, it is a big box.

THE TAXI DRIVER: Gift, huh?

MARIE-LOUISE: *(Alarmed.)* Leopold!

LEOPOLD: Shhh! *(To the Taxi Driver.)* Yes, I suppose you could call it a gift.
(Pause.) Are we almost there?

THE TAXI DRIVER: Huh? . . . *(Pause.)* Almost . . .

MARIE-LOUISE: Look! Leopold!

LEOPOLD: Where?

MARIE-LOUISE: A reptile just ran around that corner.

LEOPOLD: *(With controlled anger.)* You have to stop this, Marie-Louise.
   (Blackout.)

IN THE TAXI (b)

*Peter and June are seated facing stage left, with the box between them.
The taxi driver is humming a popular song. He smokes. Peter and June
look out the window. Pause.*

JUNE: The streets are empty.

PETER: Because of the rain. *(Pause.)* Are you okay, honey?

JUNE: How do you think that happened?

PETER: A poor quality container, I suppose.

JUNE: It's not everyday a shipment of reptiles is flown overseas.

PETER: It will take a while to catch all of them.

JUNE: If they can . . .

THE TAXI DRIVER: English, huh?

PETER: Do you speak English?

THE TAXI DRIVER: Only small talk.

PETER: Actually, if you don't mind, I am a nonsmoker and my wife just quit.

THE TAXI DRIVER: I don't mind.

PETER: Thank you.

THE TAXI DRIVER: No problem. *(Continues to smoke.)*

JUNE: *(To Peter.)* He didn't understand.

PETER: For God's sake, June. I don't feel like arguing with a taxi driver on a
   foreign island.

THE TAXI DRIVER: Everybody go to Hotel Mimosa today.

PETER: Our reservations were made for us in advance.

THE TAXI DRIVER: No problem. *(Pause.)* You got box too, huh?

PETER: Yeah . . .

THE TAXI DRIVER: Different people got same box. I took them.

PETER: *(To June.)* I guess the others got here before us. June, what is it?

JUNE: *(Staring.)* I could swear I saw a reptile in one of those windows.

PETER: Honey . . . *(Puts his arm around her.)*

JUNE: Don't . . .
   (Blackout.)

IN THE ELEVATOR (GOING DOWN)

Hotel Mimosa
Leopold with the box, Marie-Louise, the little spoiled boy and his aunt
are facing the audience. The little spoiled boy is picking his nose. His
aunt is trying to make him behave.

MARIE-LOUISE: Dear me, this elevator is dreadfully dusty.
LEOPOLD: Apparently it isn't used much. There are only two floors.
MARIE-LOUISE: I really hope they will give us another room.
LEOPOLD: All the rooms have the same view, Marie-Louise.
LITTLE SPOILED BOY: *(In a fit.)* No! No! No!
  ˶ *(The elevator stops. Pause.)*
MARIE-LOUISE: Why doesn't the door open?
  (They stare into the audience. Pause. Surprisingly, the door opens behind them
  toward upstage. The woman in a white dress, the man in a dark blue suit,
  June, Mr. Brown carrying his box, and the bellboy carrying their suitcases
  are waiting to take the elevator. Leopold, Marie-Louise, the little boy, and
  his aunt exit. At the same time, the woman in the white dress slaps the man
  in the dark blue suit in the face. She then runs away. The man runs after
  her. Entering the elevator, Peter brushes against Marie-Louise by mistake.)
PETER: Sorry!
MARIE-LOUISE: Excuse me!
  (Peter, June, the bellboy enter the elevator.)

IN THE ELEVATOR (GOING UP)

JUNE: Did you notice that pompous hat?
PETER: She's cute though.
JUNE: Could they be . . . ?
PETER: It's possible.
JUNE: God, look at this dust.
PETER: Let's be positive, June.
  (Lights go off. Complete darkness.)
PETER: For God's sake!
JUNE: Let's be positive, Dear.
PETER: I cannot take your sarcasm now, June.
PETER: Does this happen often?

JUNE: How would I know?

PETER: I was talking to the bellhop.

JUNE: He doesn't speak English. *(Pause.)*

PETER: For God's sake, June.

JUNE: *(Pause.)* Try to act natural.

PETER: You're tickling me!

JUNE: Unwind, Honey. You know what the book says.

PETER: We are not alone, Honey.

JUNE: He doesn't speak English.

> *(Lights go up. Elevator starts.)*

A VOICE FROM DOWNSTAIRS: Is everything all right?

PETER: *(Yells.)* We are fine. *(Pause.)*

JUNE: I wouldn't say that. Our sex life is a mess.

PETER: What if he speaks English?

JUNE: He is not a spy, if that is what you're afraid of.

PETER: I am afraid of many things, June, and this is a kind of fear I have never experienced before.

JUNE: It all boils down to sex.

> *(The elevator stops. The doors open. Peter and June exit. Pause. The man from the Sandwich Islands enters the elevator. The door closes.)*

IN THE BROWNS' ROOM

PETER: Did you see that man?

JUNE: What man?

PETER: The man that just got into the elevator.

JUNE: Oh, him . . .

PETER: Did he look all right to you?

JUNE: Relax, Peter.

> *(Peter tries to decide where he should put the box. He looks under the bed. A reptile shows up at the window. They don't notice it.)*

JUNE: I don't think it's a good idea to ignore it.

> *(Peter does not respond.)*

JUNE: I am talking about IT, Peter.

PETER: *(Pause.)* You know, June, there are more important things than sex.

JUNE: The box, I suppose.

PETER: As a matter of fact, yes. *(Pause.)* Hand me my travel kit, please.

(June throws his kit out the window. The reptile disappears to avoid being hit.)

PETER: I don't want to have a fight, June. I doubt, under the circumstances, that I could manage a fair fight. *(Pause.)* I'll go downstairs to get my kit. Try to relax. *(Exits, leaves the door open.)*

(June undresses.)

(Leopold and Marie-Louise enter. Leopold carries the box.)

LEOPOLD: *(Surprised.)* Oh! I apologize. I guess we have the wrong room.

JUNE: *(Covering herself.)* That's O.K.

LEOPOLD: *(Interested in June's body.)* Please, accept our apologies.

JUNE: It's O.K.

LEOPOLD: We are terribly sorry.

(Marie-Louise pulls Leopold out of the room.)

LEOPOLD: The wrong room. *(Exits with Marie-Louise.)*

IN THE RUPPERSTHALS' ROOM

LEOPOLD: *(Looks around.)* These rooms are absolutely identical. *(Pause.)* Imagine, to catch the American naked.

MARIE-LOUISE: Extremely wide hips.

LEOPOLD: Ah, well, Marie-Louise, I think she is a splendid woman. *(Looks for a safe place for the box.)*

MARIE-LOUISE: Dear me, you are simply pathetic. Do you remember what my mother used to say? "How could you marry this man, Marie-Louise? He is simply pathetic." She, of course, referred also to your habit of painting skulls.

LEOPOLD: Painting skulls is an extremely honorable hobby. Not habit, Marie-Louise. Allow me to say that, please.

MARIE-LOUISE: You weren't exactly in a hurry to get out of the American's room. Another hobby of yours, I suppose . . .

LEOPOLD: Good heavens! I was only trying to locate their box.

MARIE-LOUISE: Dear me, the profundity of your motive is overwhelming.

LEOPOLD: I think you will agree, Marie-Louise, that under the circumstances there are more important things than sex.

MARIE-LOUISE: *(Starts to undress.)* The exchange, of course.

LEOPOLD: Absolutely.

(Pause. A reptile shows up at the window.)

LEOPOLD: *(Calls room service.)* Room service? Yes, we would like a bottle of your best champagne sent up to our room . . . ah, well . . . that will have to do . . .

MARIE-LOUISE: My hands are awfully dry . . .

LEOPOLD: *(Casually.)* Let's not forget that your mother was a maid.

MARIE-LOUISE: *(Casually.)* So was your great grandmother.

LEOPOLD: You are very much mistaken, Marie-Louise. It is well established that my family is descendent of the Count of Franconia.

MARIE-LOUISE: It is also a common fact that your great grandfather committed that scandalous mesalliance with that little Italian cocotte. *(Pause.)* Have you seen my soie écru negligee?

(Marie-Louise is walking around seductively, almost naked.)

LEOPOLD: Come here ma tourterelle. *(Tries to grab her.)*

(Marie starts running around with Leopold after her. The following text is delivered simultaneously. It is a game they have played before.)

MARIE-LOUISE: Que nous arrivera-t-il?

Que nous arrivera-t-il?

Que nous arrivera-t-il pas?

Que nous arrivera-t-il?

Que nous arrivera-t-il pas?

Que nous arrivera-t-il?

Que nous arrivera-t-il pas?

LEOPOLD: Kommen Sie her!

Ich bin krank!

Ich habe mich verrirt!

Kommen Sie her!

Ich bin krank!

Ich habe mich verrirt!

Ich bin krank!

(Leopold catches Marie-Louise. Another reptile shows up at the window. A knock at the door.)

MARIE-LOUISE: Merde!

LEOPOLD: *(Moves the box out of sight.)* Come in!

(The waiter bringing the champagne and the native boy with the guitar enter. The native boy starts playing.)

LEOPOLD: *(To the native boy.)* No, no, thank you very much, but right now we are very tired, no, no . . . . *(To the waiter.)* Please tell him that it is not necessary . . .

MARIE-LOUISE: Oh, let him play, darling.

(The boy sees the reptile. Stops singing. Exits in a hurry. The waiter follows him, shaking his head disapprovingly.)

MARIE-LOUISE: *(To Leopold.)* You scared him off.

(Voices are overheard next door. Leopold and Marie-Louise listen.)

MARIE-LOUISE: The Americans . . .

LEOPOLD: Come here, my little pigeon.

MARIE-LOUISE: Shhh! I want to listen.

(The voices become louder. The overheard text will be amplified through the p.a. system.)

PETER: *Would you like to do it now?*

JUNE: *I don't know. Would you?*

PETER: *I don't know if it's the right moment.*

JUNE: *I don't know either.*

PETER: *Maybe we should.*

JUNE: *You think so?*

PETER: *What do you think?*

JUNE: *I don't know.*

PETER: *We are tired and all that.*

JUNE: *Then let's not do it.*

PETER: *On the other hand, who knows if we'll have time tomorrow?*

JUNE: *I wanted to do it in the elevator, but you didn't.*

PETER: *For God's sake, June. The bellhop was there.*

JUNE: *He didn't speak English.*

PETER: *Are you aware that you choose to have it only when external factors would make it totally impossible.*

JUNE: *That's not it. I only try to make it happen in other than routine and familiar surroundings.*

PETER: *Let's not get into this discussion now.*

JUNE: *O.K.*

PETER: *Let's do it now. It will help release some of the tension.*

JUNE: *I don't know. Now, just doesn't seem right.*

PETER: *Well, if both of us don't agree, there's really no point.*

JUNE: *Why? You really wanted it?*

PETER: *I guess.*

JUNE: *Me, too, I suppose.*

PETER: *All of a sudden I am really tired.*

JUNE: *Me too. (Pause.)*

PETER: *Good night, Honey.*

JUNE: *Good night.*

LEOPOLD: I wonder what they meant by all that?

MARIE-LOUISE: I don't know, but it sounded most scientific.

LEOPOLD: *(Grabs her.)* Come here, ma tourterelle.

   (Blackout.)

IN THE BROWNS' ROOM

June turns a night light on.

PETER: What is it?

JUNE: I hear voices.

PETER: Must be the Germans.

JUNE: She must be French.

PETER: She doesn't look French to me.

JUNE: Shhh! I am trying to listen.

   (Overheard voices from the room next door. Marie-Louise and Leopold are making love. Their alternated text will be amplified through the p.a. system. Supertitles are projected with the translation.)

MARIE-LOUISE: *(Romantic, sensuous tonality.)*

TEXT	SUPERTITLES
Papa est à la poste	*My father is at the Post Office*
Paul est à la banque	*Paul is at the bank*
Marie est à l'ecole	*Mary is at school*
Maman est à l'eglise	*My mother is at church*
Je vais au cinema	*I am going to the movies*
Je vais au park	*I am going to the park*
Je vais au concert	*I am going to the concert*
Le livre est grand	*This book is big*
Le chat n'est pas grand	*The cat is not big*
Le telephone n'est pas grand	*The telephone is not large*
L'oiseau n'est pas grand	*The bird is not big*
La montagne est grand	*The mountain is big*
La tasse est petite	*The cup is small*
Le livre est petit	*The book is small*
Le cheval est un animal	*The horse is an animal*
Le chat est un animal	*The cat is an animal*
Le chien est un animal	*The dog is an animal*
Le lion est un animal	*The lion is an animal*

| *La banane est un fruit* | The banana is a fruit |
| *Un bifteck si'l vous plait* | The beefsteak, please |

LEOPOLD: *(Passionate, forceful tonality.)*

Iishfrikadellen	*Fish croquettes*
Forelle	*Trout*
Flunder	*Flounder*
Garnelen	*Prawns*
Hecht	*Pike*
Hering	*Herring*
Hummer	*Lobster*
Jakobsmuschein	*Scallops*
Lach	*Salmon*
Kabeljau	*Cod*
Karpfen	*Carp*
Krebs	*Crab*
Scholle Plaice Seebutt	*Brill Stor Sturgeon*
Sprotten Sprats Rotbarsh	*Red sea bass*
Seezunge	*Sole*
Stint	*Smelt*
Nevnauge	*Lamprey eel*
Heilbutt	*Halibut*

PETER: What did they say?

JUNE: I didn't understand a word, but it was the most romantic sounding thing I ever heard.

PETER:; Turn the light off, Honey.

(June turns the lights off. Blackout.)

JUNE: Europeans are truly romantic. You have to give them that. *(Pause.)* Is this necessary, Peter?

PETER: It's only for one night, Honey.

JUNE: Get it out, Peter.

PETER: June, the future of the whole world depends on this box. Move over a little, Honey. That's fine. Good night, Honey.

(Long pause.)

IN THE MIDDLE OF THE NIGHT

In the dark, in the hallway. A child screams. Voices. Agitation.

THE LITTLE SPOILED BOY: Catch it! Catch it! Catch it!

VOICES: What's going on? For God's sake, what is happening?

THE LITTLE SPOILED BOY: Catch it! Catch it! Catch it!

PETER: Somebody turn a light on!

LEOPOLD: The lights don't work!

THE WAITER: Please, don't panic. Somebody is working on it right now.

MARIE-LOUISE: What kind of a hotel is this?

THE LITTLE SPOILED BOY: Catch it! Catch it! Catch it!

HIS AUNT: He thinks he saw a reptile crawling down his bed.

MARIE-LOUISE AND JUNE: A reptile?

THE VOICE OF A MADWOMAN: Reptiles! *(Horrifying laughter.)*

THE MAN FROM THE SANDWICH ISLANDS: Any cold-blood vertebrate of the class Reptilia, comprising the turtles, lizards, snakes, crocodilians and the tuatora. *(Pause.)* Loosely: any animals that crawl or creep.

THE VOICE OF A MADWOMAN: *(Whispers.)* They creep into my mind and nest there. I go about life and forget about them when all of a sudden in the middle of the night they bite me. They bite right in the heart of my dream and kill it. The snakes kill it.

PETER: What's wrong with her?

THE WAITER: She is harmless. Talking to herself.

LEOPOLD: Schizophrenia.

THE WAITER: They will come for her tomorrow morning. Puts up a fight and then goes.

THE MAN WITH THE ALLERGY: *(Sneezes.)* It's the dust. I am fed up.

THE LITTLE SPOILED BOY: Catch it! Catch it! Catch it!

HIS AUNT: Calm down dear, your aunt is going to catch it for you.

PETER: For God's sake!

> *(The lights come on. The little boy, his aunt, Marie-Louise, Leopold and Peter holding their boxes, June, the woman in the white dress, the man in the dark suit, the Chinese man, the man with an allergy, the waiter, the man from the Sandwich Islands, the native boy with the guitar are all there. Except for the man from the Sandwich Islands, the woman in the white dress and the man in the dark suit, everyone is in sleeping attire. The woman in the white dress slaps the man in the dark suit in the face and runs out. He runs after her. Everybody, except the man from the Sandwich Islands and the native boy, exits in a hurry avoiding each other's eyes.)*

THE MAN FROM THE SANDWICH ISLANDS: *(To the native boy.)* An electric light can be fixed up in a cellar or any other small storeroom with little trouble and expense. A few things have to be bought, such as the wire, bulb, and battery, but the switch can be made out of odds and ends and the whole arrangement should cost less than one dollar. The convenience of having a light in the cellar or in a dark storeroom, with a switch handy at the entrance, is obvious, and any intelligent child can fix it up. *(The native boy sleepily writes all this down.)*

BREAKFAST

Café Mimosa, the restaurant inside the hotel. In the middle there is a parrot holding a sign that reads: "Those who drink to forget have to pay in advance." The parrot will always speak into a microphone. There are few tables. Commotion offstage. The madwoman is being taken away.

THE VOICE OF A MADWOMAN: *(Offstage, loud.)* I don't want to hear your words. They are bad weeds. I can't swim through them, I can't see through them, I am afraid of them. 'Have a nice day' scares me to death! Shut up! I want to swim! Please, let me swim! *(Repeats as her voice fades away.)*

VOICE OFFSTAGE: *(Pause.)* Did you feed the parrot?

THE PARROT: Did you feed the parrot?
(The waiter brings a bag of parrot food. Puts it next to the parrot.)
(The woman in the white dress and the man in a dark suit enter and sit at a table.)
(The little spoiled boy and his aunt enter and sit at a table.)
(The man with an allergy enters and sits at a table.)
(The Chinese man enters and sits at a table.)
(Marie-Louise and Leopold, carrying the box, enter. The waiter seats them at a table.)
(The man from the Sandwich Islands and the native boy enter and sit at a table.)

LEOPOLD: *(Looks around.)* The Americans are not here yet.

THE PARROT: The Americans are not here yet.
(Leopold and Marie-Louise stare at the parrot.)

THE WAITER: It's an old bird. *(Gives them the menus.)*

LEOPOLD: We'll be ordering when the others arrive.

THE WAITER: *(In a panic, takes the menus back.)* Oh! Of course. How silly of me! Of course. I simply forgot the order of things. Excuse me, please.

LEOPOLD: That's quite all right.
(The waiter exits.)

MARIE-LOUISE: He knows something.

LEOPOLD: Only the order of things.

MARIE-LOUISE: *(Whispers.)* We should be on our guard, Leopold. We don't know how dangerous this situation might be.

LEOPOLD: Nonsense! There are plenty of people around.

THE MAN WITH AN ALLERGY: *(Sneezes.)* Now it's the rotting dates.

THE PARROT: Now it's the rotting dates.

THE CHINESE MAN: *(Says something in Chinese.)*

THE PARROT: *(Repeats.)*

MARIE-LOUISE: Oh, mon Dieu! I thought Americans had a reputation for being punctual.

(June and Peter enter. They are wearing sunglasses. Peter is carrying his box.)

THE PARROT: Oh, mon Dieu! I thought Americans have a reputation for being punctual.

(June and Peter stare at the parrot. Leopold and Marie-Louise stand up.)

LEOPOLD: Mr. Brown?

THE PARROT: Mr. Brown?

PETER: *(Takes off his sunglasses.)* Mr. Ruppersthal!

THE PARROT: Mr. Ruppersthal!

LEOPOLD: How do you do!

THE PARROT: How do you do!

PETER: You speak English! How do you do!

THE PARROT: You speak English! How do you do!

PETER: This is my wife, June.

THE PARROT: This is my wife, June.

LEOPOLD: *(Kisses June's hand.)* Enchanted.

THE PARROT: Enchanted.

(Marie-Louise nods to June.)

PETER: And this is our box.

THE PARROT: And this is our box.

LEOPOLD: Allow me to introduce my wife, Marie-Louise.

THE PARROT: Allow me to introduce my wife, Marie-Louise.

PETER AND JUNE: *(To Marie-Louise.)* Nice to meet you.

THE PARROT: Nice to meet you.

LEOPOLD: And our box.

THE PARROT: And our box.

LEOPOLD: The parrot is quite remarkable, wouldn't you say?

THE PARROT: The parrot is quite remarkable, wouldn't you say?

LEOPOLD: *(Whispers.)* Apparently he is hard of hearing so if we keep our voices down he won't be able to repeat everything.

PETER AND JUNE: Oh, good.

THE MAN WITH AN ALLERGY: *(Sneezes.)* It's the spoiled mangos.

THE PARROT: It's the spoiled mangos.

PETER: *(Whispers to Leopold.)* First I want to congratulate you for being chosen for this exchange.

LEOPOLD: I, in my turn, congratulate you. It is quite an achievement for someone as young as you are.

PETER: Also, since we have to perform in this together, I hope we'll all do our parts correctly.

JUNE: *(To Marie-Louise.)* I am half dead with stage fright, aren't you?

MARIE-LOUISE: Excuse me if I don't believe that, my Dear.

JUNE: Must be my sunglasses. *(Takes her sunglasses off.)*

PETER: The fate of the whole world depends on this and despite *(Looks around.)* the potential danger, I am sure of our success in completing our mission.

LEOPOLD: I will do my best. *(Pause.)*

PETER: I want to remind you of the right order of the events. Breakfast, lunch, a walk on the beach, dinner, martinis, café glacé.

LEOPOLD: Exactly. *(Pause.)* Shall we proceed?

THE MAN WITH AN ALLERGY: *(Sneezes.)* It's the damp bananas.

THE PARROT: It's the damp bananas.

THE CHINESE MAN: *(Says something in Chinese.)*

THE PARROT: *(Repeats.)*

PETER: Waiter!

THE PARROT: Waiter!

    (The waiter enters.)

PETER: *(To the waiter, points to the man from the Sandwich Islands, low voice.)* Who is he?

THE WAITER: He is from the Sandwich Islands. *(Low voice.)* He knows everything.

PETER AND LEOPOLD: *(Alarmed.)* Everything?

THE WAITER: *(Pause.)* Everything. There is a rumor he even knows where. . . *(Whispers in Peter's ear.)*

PETER: No!

THE WAITER: Yes!

THE PARROT: Yes!

LEOPOLD: Nonsense!

THE PARROT: Nonsense!

LEOPOLD: Shall we proceed?

PETER: I am ready.

(The waiter gives them the menus. Peter and Leopold look at June and Marie-Louise who nod in approval. Abruptly they all open their menu. They will order in a very official tone.)

MARIE-LOUISE: Café au lait et pain au chocolat.

THE PARROT: Café au lait et pain au chocolat.

JUNE: Chocolate croissant and coffee.

THE PARROT: Chocolate croissant and coffee.

PETER: Scrambled eggs and bacon.

THE PARROT: Scrambled eggs and bacon.

LEOPOLD: The Hoppel-Poppel.

THE PARROT: The Hoppel-Poppel.

THE WAITER: Would you care for some coffee?

THE PARROT: Would you care for some coffee?

ALL FOUR AT ONCE: Yes, please!

THE PARROT: Yes, please!

(The waiter exits.)

MARIE-LOUISE: I don't understand this plan at all. It seems utterly preposterous. *(To June.)* Don't you think so, my Dear?

JUNE: Well . . .

LEOPOLD: *(To Marie-Louise.)* You needn't concern yourself with that.

PETER: *(To June.)* You either.

LEOPOLD: *(To Peter.)* What could possibly happen? The plan is nonviolent.

PETER: Theoretically, yes.

THE WOMAN IN A WHITE DRESS: *(Loud.)* Shall be, was, has been . . .

THE PARROT: Shall be, was, has been . . .

THE WOMAN IN A WHITE DRESS: My life has been a blank.

THE PARROT: My life has been a blank.

(The woman in a white dress slaps the man in the dark suit and runs out. He runs after her.)

PETER: *(Pause.)* I think we should proceed with our light conversation. So, Herr Ruppersthal, what is it that you do?

LEOPOLD: Once a year I hunt red stag in Argentina. I also fish a great deal in Alaska and in Norway in the Aroy River. Of course the African Safari interests me a great deal . . . to live out in the bush, to hear the strange noises in the heart of the night, to . . . *(Forgets.)* Nevertheless, I hunt boar three times a season, killing up to 120 . . .

JUNE: *(Loud.)* And what does one do with 100 dead boar?

THE PARROT: And what does one do with 100 dead boar?

JUNE: Sorry!

MARIE-LOUISE: *(Low voice.)* Boar meat is considered something of a delicacy, my Dear.

THE CHINESE MAN: *(Says something in Chinese.)*

THE PARROT: *(Repeats.)*

THE MAN WITH AN ALLERGY: *(Sneezes.)* It's the palm trees.

THE PARROT: It's the palm trees.

LEOPOLD: In addition, I hunt pigeon and pheasant.

MARIE-LOUISE: When the weather is bad he sits by the fireplace painting skulls. I can only hope I am not going to die before him. I might end up with a wild boar hunting scene on my skull. They are disgusting.

PETER: *(To Leopold.)* I am sure you have a hard time finding skulls. They don't sell them do they?

LEOPOLD: Ah, well, there are places.

(June nervously knocks over a glass.)

PETER: *(Loud.)* For God's sake.

THE PARROT: For God's sake.

JUNE: *(Low voice.)* Sorry! We live in Milwaukee.

MARIE-LOUISE: How fascinating!

LEOPOLD: *(To Peter.)* What is your field Mr. Brown?

PETER: *(To Leopold.)* Please call me Peter. I have a business there. As a matter of fact . . . here is my card *(Gives Leopold his card.)*.

THE PARROT: Herrrre is my carrrrd.

MARIE-LOUISE: And what about you, Mrs. Brown, I hear that American women are very active.

JUNE: Oh, call me June. I work full-time on my relationship with my husband. We are trying to save our marriage.

THE LITTLE SPOILED BOY: *(Loud.)* I don't want to poop now!

THE PARROT: I don't want to poop now!

(His aunt whispers in his ear.)

JUNE: *(To Marie-Louise.)* Do you two have any children?

MARIE-LOUISE: *(Sideways glance at Leopold.)* None that I know of.

LEOPOLD: Marie-Louise!

(The woman in the white dress enters running, crosses the stage and exits. The man in the dark suit enters, looks around for her and exits running after her. Pause.)

JUNE: *(To Marie-Louise.)* What about you, Marie-Louise?

MARIE-LOUISE: Oh! *(To June, affected.)* You see my dear, I am forever busy acquiring things. I recently acquired a Louis XIV clock, a Louis XVI fireplace, a Louis XIII cabinet, a Louis XV console . . .

THE MAN WITH AN ALLERGY: *(Sneezes.)* It's the goose shit.

THE PARROT: It's the goose shit.

THE MAN FROM THE SANDWICH ISLANDS: *(To the native boy.)* A goose can live up to sixty-five years.

THE PARROT: A goose can live up to sixty-five years.

(The native boy with the guitar writes this in his book.)

PETER: *(Looks at the man from the Sandwich Islands.)* I wonder what language he speaks.

LEOPOLD: A strange language, no doubt.

JUNE: The native language, I am sure.

MARIE-LOUISE: It must be one of those tremendously obscure dialects.

THE AUNT: You are going to poop whether you want to or not.

THE PARROT: You are going to poop whether you want to or not.

(The boy and his aunt exit. The waiter covers the parrot.)

MARIE-LOUISE: Mr. Brown, Mrs. Brown, I apologize, but I have to go to my room. I suddenly lost my appetite. Leopold!

PETER AND JUNE: *(Together.)* Call me Peter. Call me June.

LEOPOLD: Ah, well. Excuse me. I must accompany my wife.

PETER: We'll see each other for lunch then.

LEOPOLD: Definitely.

(Marie-Louise and Leopold, carrying his box, exit.)

PETER: So far, so good.

JUNE: I have the feeling that any one of us could get killed at any moment.

PETER: Calm down, Honey. Do you want half a valium?

(The Chinese man touches Peter's box and says something in Chinese.)

PETER: *(Firmly, to the Chinese man.)* I am very sorry but you can't touch this.

THE CHINESE MAN: *(Says something in Chinese.)*

JUNE: *(Scared.)* Let's get out of here!

PETER: *(To the Chinese man.)* I am very sorry but I don't speak Chinese. Sorry . . .

(Peter, carrying his box, and June exit in a hurry. The Chinese man says something to the man with an allergy who doesn't understand him. The Chinese man exits.)

THE MAN WITH AN ALLERGY: *(Sneezes.)* It's the cat's ear! *(Exits.)*

THE MAN FROM THE SANDWICH ISLANDS: *(To the native boy.)* The cat's ear is a troublesome weed resembling the common dandelion. Like the dandelion, it is beautiful when in flower, unattractive when in fruit, and spreads rapidly, to the detriment of the grass in lawns and pastures. It is common in Washington and is spreading rapidly.

(The native boy writes this in his book.)

(The waiter exits.)

(The man from the islands, the native boy exit.)

(The parrot uncovers himself.)

THE PARROT: *(Pause.)* I simply can't stand the tension of feeling at one with the whole damn universe while at the same time I am a miserable bird.

(A bunch of reptiles cross the stage to soundtrack of jungle drums. Blackout.)

IN THE RUPPERSTHALS' ROOM

LEOPOLD: It will be over soon, Marie-Louise.

MARIE-LOUISE: You know, it is not required for every man and for every woman to do something great.

LEOPOLD: I was chosen, Marie-Louise. It wasn't my idea.

MARIE-LOUISE: The tension has an absolutely deadly effect on my nerves.

LEOPOLD: Turn over, Marie-Louise . . .

(Pleased, Marie-Louise turns over revealing layers of white lace from her undergarments. Leopold starts having sex with her from behind. Voices are overheard from next door.)

LEOPOLD: What are these walls made of?

MARIE-LOUISE: Shhh! The Americans . . .

(The voices become clear. The following text is amplified. During it we see Leopold and Marie-Louise making love.)

JUNE: *No, I don't think I have an orgasmic dysfunction. Maybe I am not in the mood.*

PETER: *Could something be wrong with your erogenous zones?*

JUNE: *Maybe I just cannot see myself in the position you want to see me. You know very well, in our culture the best sex is sexual intercourse in a darkened bedroom with the man on the top.*

PETER: *You know what's wrong with you, June? Performance anxiety.*

JUNE: *What about you?*

PETER: *What about me?*

JUNE: *Your performance doesn't strike me as a model of relaxation.*

PETER: *Let's just agree that our sexual scripts are different, June. What we have to do is to explore how they affect our relationship.*

JUNE: *Move over, please.*

PETER: *I can see you are not in the mood.*

JUNE: *Maybe it's this box. I don't know. This tension is driving me crazy.*

PETER: *Is this how?*

JUNE: *Don't touch me now. (Pause.) (Dreamily.) I wonder what the Europeans are doing . . .*

PETER: *You mean how are they doing it.*

JUNE: *What do you think they are doing?*

PETER: *(Angry.) For God's sake, June. She is probably playing the harp while he writes a damn sonnet in a leather-bound journal bought in Florence.*

JUNE: *Don't be sarcastic, Peter. Europeans know how to be romantic. Did you see how the Count kissed my hand? You never kiss my hand. Why don't you ever kiss my hand?*

PETER: *Hand me my travel kit, June. I need some antacids.*

PETER: *(Pause.) Why did you do it, June?*

JUNE: *What?*

PETER: *Why did you throw my kit out the window? (Pause.) I don't want to have a fight now, June. I am going to get my kit. You can go and fuck the Count if you like. If you are lucky, he might call your vagina "lily of the valley" and paint it on a skull.*

JUNE: *(Furious.) Don't talk to me like that! I bet Leopold and Marie-Louise don't shave and pee in the same bathroom at the same time. What's wrong with a little mystery? What?*

PETER: *(Exasperated.) Well I am sorry, June, that I am not The Count of Monte Cristo, I don't have grandmothers who had their heads chopped off, and I don't hunt red stag in Argentina. (Pause.) You know, it all boils down to sex.*

JUNE: *Sex! What about your mother?*

PETER: *Don't bring my mother into this. That's not fair. (Pause.) I am going to get my kit.*

(A reptile shows up in the window, watches Leopold and Marie-Louise making love for a while and exits.)

(Leopold and Marie-Louise finish having sex. Pause.)

LEOPOLD: Those Americans do talk a lot to each other. I can't quite catch the meaning of their dialogue though.

MARIE-LOUISE: Oh, I can't either, but I find it adorable.

LEOPOLD: I am a man of action, Marie-Louise.

MARIE-LOUISE: *(Dreamily.)* Frankly I admire the Americans. They are immensely open about their feelings.

LEOPOLD: *(Looking around.)* Have you seen my pistol?

MARIE-LOUISE: We never talk. Have we ever talked?

LEOPOLD: *(Looks frantically around.)* Where is my pistol?

MARIE-LOUISE: I remember when you asked me to marry you. Was that a talk?

LEOPOLD: My pistol has been stolen!

MARIE-LOUISE: I do not think you could call that a talk.

LEOPOLD: Marie-Louise!

MARIE-LOUISE: *(Startled.)* Leopold!

LEOPOLD: My pistol is missing.

MARIE-LOUISE: *(Grabs Leopold. Pause.)* I cannot stand this tension. You should not have brought me with you!

(Blackout.)

LUNCH

In the restaurant. The parrot is covered.
The little spoiled boy and his aunt enter and sit at a table. Pause.
The man with an allergy enters and sits at a table.
The woman in a white dress and the man in a dark suit enter and sit at a table.
The Chinese man enters, bows and says something to everybody present. He asks (with gestures) the man with an allergy permission to sit at his table. Sits.
Peter and June enter and sit. Peter has his box. Pause.
Marie-Louise and Leopold enter and sit. Leopold has his box.
The man from the Sandwich Islands and the native boy enter. They sit at a table so they can watch everybody else. Pause.
The waiter enters and uncovers the parrot.
The following text will be spoken into the microphone by the parrot.
The characters will act along with the lines.
At times the words anticipate their behavior.
This confuses them.

LEOPOLD: Mr. Brown . . .

PETER: Call me Peter.

LEOPOLD: Something happened. I think that my pistol has been stolen.

PETER: Waiter!

LEOPOLD: What are you doing?

PETER: We have to report this.

(The waiter enters.)

PETER: (To the waiter.) Mr. Ruppersthal is under the impression that someone has stolen his gun.

THE WAITER: I will look into it right away.

PETER: There is no need to alarm everybody.

THE WAITER: Of course. (Goes to each table and whispers in everybody's ear, except the little boy.)

LEOPOLD: Let's proceed. Marie-Louise . . .

MARIE-LOUISE: (To June.) I love your dress, is it rayon?

JUNE: No, it's 100 percent silk.

MARIE-LOUISE: Oh!

PETER: (To Leopold.) Did you rest a bit?

LEOPOLD: Ah, well . . . Yes, the beds are quite comfortable.

THE AUNT: Don't spit your food.

THE LITTLE SPOILED BOY: I hate peas.

LEOPOLD: Marie-Louise adores riding.

MARIE-LOUISE: I find horses immensely exciting.

LEOPOLD: If you asked me what the greatest thrill is in the field of sports, I would say it is watching a peregrine making a kill.

PETER: We are seeing a marriage counselor.

JUNE: Hopefully, we'll be able to make constructive changes in our behavior.
(The waiter comes over to their table.)

MARIE-LOUISE: The Fillet Saint-Pierre with leeks and caviar.

JUNE: I will have the same.

PETER: The homemade venison meatloaf.

LEOPOLD: Why not? The Hausgemachte Rehpastete, please.

PETER: What is that?

LEOPOLD: Homemade venison meatloaf.

PETER: Oh! The same dish.
(Loud crash offstage.)
(Everyone, except the little boy and the waiter, gets under their tables. Pause.)

THE WAITER: (Announcing.) A lid fell in the kitchen. It happens once in a while.
(Everyone returns to their seats.)

PETER: I would like to try the house wine.

LEOPOLD: An excellent choice, Mr. Brown.
(The waiter exits.)

PETER: Please call me Peter.

JUNE: Can I ask you a personal question?

MARIE-LOUISE: Please, Mrs. Brown . . .

JUNE: Please, call me June. Is your husband very romantic?

MARIE-LOUISE: *He had me painted by the most famous artist. What about yours?*

JUNE: *My husband originally accepted his anima, but recently he's started to reject it.*

MARIE-LOUISE: *I know what you mean, my Dear. Men are perfectly stubborn creatures. My husband is . . .*

JUNE: *Mine too.*

MARIE-LOUISE: *My husband is . . .*

JUNE: *Mine too.*

MARIE-LOUISE: *My husband is . . .*

JUNE: *Mine too.*

MARIE-LOUISE: *My husband is . . .*

JUNE: *Mine too.*

MARIE-LOUISE: *My husband has a mole on his derriere.*

JUNE: *I can't believe it. Mine too.*

MARIE-LOUISE: *Which side?*

JUNE: *Left. Yours?*

MARIE-LOUISE: *Right.*

JUNE: *Aren't all men absolutely the same?*

PETER: *What are you two talking about?*

JUNE: *Oh, woman-talk.*

PETER: *You know, I really don't like those men over there. I have a strange feeling about them.*

LEOPOLD: *Waiter!*

PETER: *What are you doing?*

(The waiter enters.)

LEOPOLD: *I am making an inquiry. (To the waiter, conspiratory tone.) Who are those two men?*

THE WAITER: *The little one is Chinese. He is very polite but nobody understands what he says. The other is a symbolist; suffers from terrible allergies. He is quite depressed most of the time.*

THE LITTLE SPOILED BOY: *I am going to kill you.*

(Everyone turns to look at the little boy momentarily.)

(The waiter exits.)

THE AUNT: *That is no way for a nice little boy to talk.*

MARIE-LOUISE: *Mrs. Brown, aren't you dying to know what is in these boxes?*

JUNE: *Call me June. Are you kidding, I would do anything to find out.*

THE AUNT: *Don't swallow! Chew!*

(The little boy spits his food.)

(The woman in white dress slaps the man in the dark suit in the face and runs out. He runs after her.)

THE AUNT: *A nice little boy doesn't swallow. He chews.*

MARIE-LOUISE: *Can't they make this idiotic parrot stop?*

JUNE: *He drives me nuts.*

PETER: *I thought he was deaf.*

LEOPOLD: *Waiter!*

(The waiter enters.)

LEOPOLD: (To the waiter.) The bird is destroying our concentration. Can you do something about it?

THE WAITER: Very well. (Covers the parrot and exits.)

(The dialogue returns to the characters. The Chinese man goes around the room asking everyone something. Nobody understands what he wants.)

PETER: (To the Chinese man.) Sorry, I don't speak Chinese. Do you, Leopold?

LEOPOLD: Not one word.

(The Chinese man goes back to his table. The man with an allergy sneezes.)

THE MAN WITH AN ALLERGY: It's the dead octopus.

LEOPOLD: (Looks at his pocket watch.) According to the plan, we two men will have to chat informally about the weather for five-and-a-half minutes.

PETER: That's right. I almost forgot.

LEOPOLD: The chat has to take place in the absence of our wives.

(Marie-Louise and June don't move.)

PETER: The chat has to take place in the absence of our wives.

(They still don't move.)

LEOPOLD: (Pause. To Peter.) Would you care to go onto the terrace?

(Peter and Leopold exit, taking the boxes with them.)

(The Chinese man follows them.)

(The man with an allergy follows them.)

(The little boy and his aunt follow them.)

(Pause.)

(Marie-Louise and June look at the man from the Sandwich Islands who returns their look.)

THE MAN FROM THE SANDWICH ISLANDS: It is true however that if a worm is halved, the head portion will produce a new tail, but, strange to say, the tail portion will also produce a tail, and not a head as we should expect. (The native boy writes this in his book.)

JUNE: (To Marie-Louise.) Aren't you just dying to know what is in those boxes?

MARIE-LOUISE: I am absolutely tired to death of not knowing what is in those boxes.

JUNE: (To Marie-Louise, about the man from the Sandwich Islands.) They say he knows everything. (Pause.)

MARIE-LOUISE: How clever you are, my Dear!

(Marie-Louise and June jump up and walk seductively over to the man from the Sandwich Islands.)

JUNE: *(To the man from the Sandwich Islands, talking slowly.)* Hello! You do know everything, don't you?

(The man from the Sandwich Islands is staring now.)

MARIE-LOUISE: Let me try. *(Talking even slower.)* What is in my husband box?

JUNE: You must tell us what you know.

THE MAN FROM THE SANDWICH ISLANDS: *(Pause.)* When we come in and out of the rain, we must dry our umbrella by opening it and placing it, handle downward, in a current of air, which will quickly dry the silk cover; but at the same time we must be careful to select a spot where the dripping water can do no harm. If we place our umbrella in the stand without drying it, the water will in turn rust the ribs and rot the cover at the end of the stick. We must always remember never to roll up our umbrella when it is at all damp.

(The native boy writes this in his book.)

JUNE: What did he say?

MARIE-LOUISE: I didn't understand a word.

JUNE: I can't believe there are still people in the world who don't speak English.

MARIE-LOUISE: These dialects are so awfully obscure!

(June and Marie-Louise return to their tables. Peter and Leopold enter with the boxes. Pause.)

PETER: *(To Leopold.)* Well, shall we meet again then for martinis?

LEOPOLD: You mean a walk on the beach.

PETER: Sorry! I got mixed up.

LEOPOLD: Allow me to refresh your memory: Breakfast, lunch, a walk on the beach, martinis, dinner, café glacé.

PETER: Got it. Thanks.

LEOPOLD: *(Gallantly kisses June's hand.)* Until then.

MARIE-LOUISE: *(To Peter.)* Au revoir!

JUNE: *(To Leopold.)* Until then. *(Exits followed by Peter with his box.)*

MARIE-LOUISE: *(To Leopold.)* You know, you didn't have to kiss the American's hand.

LEOPOLD: I am a man of the world.

MARIE-LOUISE: Yes, but she is not. *(Exits followed by Leopold with his box.)*

THE PARROT: *(Uncovers himself.)* What is all this going to add up to? I am getting a headache from repeating everybody's uninteresting words, the parrot food

is less and less flavorful, I feel ridiculous and guilty, my prostate is acting up . . . All this, and I am only a bird.
(A bunch of reptiles cross the stage. Jungle drums. Blackout.)

IN THE BROWNS' ROOM

JUNE: What did you talk about on the terrace?
PETER: The weather.
JUNE: What did he say?
PETER: *(Pause.)* We are getting closer, June.
JUNE: I know . . . I am scared to death.
PETER: Doesn't it make you horny, though?
(June throws his travel kit out the window. Flash of reptile.)
PETER: I am sorry. I didn't mean it that way. *(Pause.)* I'm going downstairs to
get my kit.
(Peter exits.)
*(Leopold enters in a silk robe with a rose in his hand. Ceremoniously hands
the rose to June.)*
LEOPOLD: *(To June.)* Madame, turn over!
(June turns. Leopold starts having sex with her from behind.)
LEOPOLD: *(In German, with English supertitles.)*

SHON	BEAUTIFUL
EINDRUCKSVOLL	IMPRESSIVE
INTERESSANT	INTERESTING
ERSTAUNLICH	AMAZING
HERRLICH	MAGNIFICENT
HERVORRAGEND	SUPERB
UBERWALTIGEND	OVERWHELMING
GOTT	GOD

*(Leopold finishes. He kisses June's hand and exits. Peter enters breathing very
heavily.)*
PETER: *(Embarrassed.)* It took me a little longer. *(Pause.)* I stopped by the
Ruppersthals' room to exchange a few words. He wasn't there, but Marie-
Louise was kind enough to show me an ostrich egg she bought in Paris.
JUNE: Oh? *(Dreamy.)* Mr. Ruppersthal just stopped by. He gave me this. *(Shows
him the rose.)* Isn't it the most beautiful rose you have ever seen? These
Europeans . . . they just know how to treat a woman.
PETER: June, maybe you should get into collecting ostrich eggs.

JUNE: Don't be silly.

PETER: *(Looks at his watch.)* O.K. Let's go.

JUNE: Where?

PETER: To walk on the beach. Thank God the rain stopped.

JUNE: Is it safe to be outside.

PETER: As safe as inside.

ON THE BEACH (IN FRONT OF THE HOTEL)

The sun is out, but it is extremely foggy. The characters walking on the beach will become visible and invisible as they come in and out of the fog. The waiter will walk around carrying a tray of refreshments.

The man in the dark suit shakes the woman in the white dress by the shoulders. They disappear into the fog. Marie-Louise and Leopold are walking toward Peter and June from opposite directions. Leopold and Peter carry their boxes.

MARIE-LOUISE: There they are! *(Waves to June and Peter.)*

JUNE: Here we are! *(Waves back.)*

MARIE-LOUISE: Isn't it magnificent?

LEOPOLD: The waves are indeed spectacular. Don't you think so, Mrs. Brown?

JUNE: Yes, they are neat!

PETER: *(To Marie-Louise.)* I didn't expect this kind of weather. It's not what they predicted.

MARIE-LOUISE: *(To Peter.)* Oh! I adore dramatic weather.

(The man with an allergy appears.)

THE MAN WITH AN ALLERGY: *(Sneezes.)* It's the oil spill! *(Disappears.)*

JUNE: *(To Peter.)* The whole thing gives me the chills.

PETER: There is no alternative, June.

LEOPOLD: Absolutely, Mrs. Brown. This walk on the beach is unavoidable.

MARIE-LOUISE: I really don't see why.

JUNE: *(To Leopold.)* Please, call me June.

LEOPOLD: June . . .

PETER: Mrs. Von Ruppersthal, I am sure you understand that there are things beyond our understanding. In any case we should be the last ones to doubt this.

MARIE-LOUISE: *(To Peter, flirtatious.)* You are making so much more sense than Leopold.

(The little boy's aunt appears.)

THE AUNT: A nice little boy won't run back and forth kicking sand and spilling water all over. Some people might get very nervous at having water poured over them. *(Disappears.)*

(A reptile appears and disappears.)

(June disappears.)

PETER: June! Where are you, Honey?

(Marie-Louise disappears.)

PETER: June! June! June!

LEOPOLD: Marie-Louise!

(Leopold disappears.)

(Peter disappears.)

JUNE'S VOICE: Peter! Peter! Peter!

MARIE-LOUISE'S VOICE: Leopold! Leopold! Leopold!

(They continue to call each other.)

(The Chinese man appears. He yells something in Chinese and disappears.)

(The man from the Sandwich Islands and the native boy appear.)

THE MAN FROM THE SANDWICH ISLANDS: *(To the native boy.)* Our eyes can see to any distance from which the light can reach them. The question *(Disappears.)* whether the light has traveled billions and billions of miles, or only half an inch makes not the slightest difference to our eyes.

(The native boy writes this in his book.)

(The woman in the white dress and the man in the dark suit appear. She slaps him in the face and runs away. He runs after her.)

PETER: Have they found your gun?

LEOPOLD: Unfortunately, not.

SCREAM: MY UMBRELLA! CATCH IT! CATCH IT!

(An umbrella flies above the stage in and out of the fog. Everyone is trying to catch it. The light is fading. They all exit running after the umbrella.)

VOICE-OVER: After a long and tiring chase, somebody finally caught the umbrella. Everyone was breathless and, even if no words were spoken, they all felt for a second, in their hearts, the joy of helping another human being; the deep gratitude for living among civilized people. Inexplicably, the next thing that everybody felt was a violent fear, a kind of premonition, causing nausea and an urgent desire to drink.

(Blackout.)

IN THE MEN'S RESTROOM

Peter enters with box. Starts peeing at a urinal. Leopold enters with box. Starts peeing at next urinal. They are a little tipsy.

PETER: Good martinis, huh, Leopold?

LEOPOLD: Do you know how a falcon kills, Peter?

PETER: Leopold, do you know . . .

LEOPOLD: The falcon kills in a snippy way, Peter . . .

PETER: Leopold . . . how different two cultures can be . . . Our cultural differences are huge, Leopold . . . *(Peeks at Leopold's penis.)*

LEOPOLD: *(Peeks at Peter's penis.)* I am not worried about it.

PETER: Most men are, Leopold. *(Pause.)* Leopold, I am going to ask you a question outside our planned conversation.

LEOPOLD: Ask me, Peter.

PETER: Leopold, were you ever concerned about the size of your penis?
(The Chinese man enters. He pees at a urinal.)

LEOPOLD: Peter, as a little boy, I shot my Swiss governess because she made a stupid Swiss joke about it. Of course, it was little. I was a little boy.

PETER: That's fascinating, Leopold! I thought that only in our culture this worry . . .
(The Chinese man peeks at both of their penises.)

THE CHINESE MAN: *(Says something in Chinese.)*

LEOPOLD: *(To the Chinese man.)* I am so sorry my good fellow, but I do not speak Chinese.

PETER: *(To the Chinese man.)* Sorry! *(Pause.)*

LEOPOLD: Anyway, yours looks normal to me, Peter.

PETER: So does yours, Leopold.

LEOPOLD: Thank you, Peter.

THE CHINESE MAN: *(Says something in Chinese and exits.)*

PETER: Not at all, Leopold. I thank you. I am awfully glad we had a chance to talk and get to know each other better. It wasn't intended perhaps, but I don't think it will affect our whole operation in any way.

LEOPOLD: *(With pathos.)* Consider me a friend.
(They shake hands and exit with their boxes. The little boy enters with a pistol. He is trying to figure out how the pistol works.)

IN THE LADIES' ROOM

Marie-Louise and June enter. They are a little tipsy.

JUNE: Marie-Louise, I am sooo sorry for spilling that on your dress . . .

MARIE-LOUISE: Oh, don't mention it, June. It happens. We are all so tense.

JUNE: Once we have dinner everything will be over.

(They enter two stalls. Their feet are visible.)

JUNE: You know, in a way, Marie-Louise, I feel very excited to be a part of such an historical moment as this.

MARIE-LOUISE: Imagine how our men must feel.

JUNE: Your husband is such a gallant man.

MARIE-LOUISE: Ah, but yours is so charmingly hairy.

JUNE: *(Giggles.)* Why, Marie-Louise, you like hairy men?

MARIE-LOUISE: Immensely.

JUNE: But yours seems hairy enough to me.

MARIE-LOUISE: Oh, you can't tell.

JUNE: The truth is that I prefer less hairy men.

MARIE-LOUISE: Then you should have my husband.

JUNE: And you mine.

(June and Marie-Louise laugh hysterically.)

(The woman in a white dress enters. She lies down on the floor.)

THE WOMAN IN A WHITE DRESS: *(Tossing desperately back and forth on the floor.)* My life has been a blank. My life is a blank. My life will be a blank. *(Repeats.)*

(The woman in a white dress stands up abruptly and exits. Marie-Louise and June exit the stalls.)

MARIE-LOUISE: I hope to God that everything is going to go according to the plan. Whatever that is.

JUNE: My legs are a little shaky.

MARIE-LOUISE: I get this strange feeling that some things are less predictable than others.

JUNE: Me too. It's weird.

(Marie-Louise and June exit. A reptile enters. The reptile enters a stall. Sits.)

GRAMMAR IN A NUTSHELL

The woman in a white dress enters the stage chased by the man in the dark suit.

THE MAN IN THE DARK SUIT: I am going to give you grammar in a nutshell once and for all! *(He manages to catch her, pins her down to the floor.)* *(The woman in a white dress tries to escape at first but gradually she starts to enjoy being so close to him. They both become increasingly aroused during his speech.)*

THE MAN IN THE DARK SUIT: *(Determined.)*

The articles are oh so wee,
These little words are A, AN, THE.
The NOUNS are names of anything
As BOOK or PLAYGROUND, BALL or RING.
PRONOUNS are used for nouns instead —
MY face, HER hand, YOUR feet, HIS head.
All adjectives just tell the kind
Of everything that we may find
As GOOD and BAD and SOFT and SWEET
RUDE, and NAUGHTY, WISE and NEAT.
While manner of ADVERBS tell
As SWEETLY, NEATLY, ILL, or WELL.
The PREPOSITIONS help each day
IN our work or AT our play.
When relationship is shown
They must do the work alone.
Good CONJUNCTIONS join together
Men AND women, plume OR feather.
INTERJECTIONS will exclaim —
OH! ALAS! AH! What a shame!
But we cannot get along
In conversation or in song
Without the VERB, the subject's fate
Expressing action, being, state.
You ARE good and I LOVE you,
Without these VERBS what would we do?

THE WOMAN IN A WHITE DRESS: *(Dreamily.)* I love you too.

THE MAN IN A DARK SUIT: *(Pause. Recovering.)* It was only an example.

(The woman in a white dress pushes him away, slaps him, and runs offstage.)

THE EXCHANGE

In the restaurant. The parrot is uncovered.
The little boy and his aunt enter and sit.
The man in the dark suit enters and sits.
The man with an allergy enters and sits.
The Chinese man enters and sits.
The man from the Sandwich Islands and the native boy enter and sit.
The waiter enters.
June and Marie-Louise enter and sit.
Leopold and Peter enter with their boxes and sit.
Long pause.

PETER: *(Low voice.)* The big moment is almost here.
LEOPOLD: *(Low voice.)* The last step. *(Loudly.)* Waiter!
   (Pause. Everyone has a sudden realization: The parrot didn't repeat! Sound of a distant gathering storm. Everyone is shocked. They all look at the parrot. The waiter enters.)
EVERYONE: Waiter!
THE WAITER: I am here! *(Doesn't understand what happens.)*
LEOPOLD: *(To the parrot.)* My name is Herr Leopold von Ruppersthal! *(Pause.)*
EVERYONE: *(To the parrot.)* My name is Herr Leopold von Ruppersthal!
THE WAITER: He didn't repeat a word!
PETER: He didn't repeat a word.
THE WAITER: *(To the parrot.)* Waiter! *(Pause.)*
LEOPOLD: Nothing!
PETER: Nothing!
THE WAITER: Nothing! This never happened before!
THE CHINESE MAN: *(Says something in Chinese.)*
THE PARROT: The noise of the falls makes constant music!
   (The waiter overwhelmed, falls on his knees.)
PETER: *(Looks around.)* Did anybody say the noise of the falls makes constant music.
THE WAITER: Nobody said that! It's a stupid thing to say!
PETER: Could it be what the Chinese man said?
THE WAITER: No! A parrot can't translate!
THE PARROT: Look! The farmer's daughters with bare arms and gowns tucked up! Catch them! Catch them! Catch them!
PETER: Everybody! Don't panic!

(Everybody gathers around Peter. The whole group is facing the parrot.)

THE PARROT: She has a lot of money.

She has a lot of nerve.

She has a purse, gloves, and a hat.

She has a skeleton, muscles ,and a brain.

Man has a pancreas, a liver, and a heart.

Man has an id, an ego, and a superego.

The tiger has stripes.

The man has shoes.

A rectangle has four sides.

A man has thirty-two teeth.

He is an idiot.

(Everyone is stupefied.)

(The woman in the white dress enters.)

LEOPOLD: The bird is making its own text!

PETER: That's impossible! These are probably words that other people said in the past!

(Sounds of an approaching tropical storm.)

JUNE: This cannot happen to us.

THE PARROT: You are only so and so at such and such an address, like thousands of other people! If a few of you are killed, what difference can it make? There are far too many people in the world!

THE WAITER: What a tragedy this whole thing is!

THE WOMAN IN A WHITE DRESS: *(Tenderly.)* The poor thing is having a breakdown!

JUNE: What about us?

PETER: We can't give up now!

LEOPOLD: We must order dinner!

PETER: *(To the waiter.)* Take our order!

THE WAITER: *(Lamenting.)* How can I? How can I?

PETER: *(Points at the man from the Sandwich Islands.)* He must know what is going on! *(To the waiter.)* You said he knows everything! *(To the man from the Sandwich Islands.)* What the hell is going on here? Say something for God's sake!

THE MAN FROM THE SANDWICH ISLANDS: *(Pause.)* When making buttonholes on thin material, baste a piece of India linen or muslin underneath where the buttonholes are to be. Then cut the button hole through both materials, and work. When finished, cut away the piece of goods underneath close to the work, and the result is a firm buttonhole.

(The native boy writes this in his book.)

(Thunder.)

THE WAITER: *(Lamenting, to Peter.)* He doesn't speak English!

PETER: I can't believe there are still people who don't speak English!

LEOPOLD: *(To Peter.)* It's useless!

PETER: *(Hysterical.)* We must order dinner!

LEOPOLD: There is nobody to take our order!

PETER: *(To the waiter.)* One more time. Take our order or I'll kill you dead. I'll have lasagna, for God's sake!

THE WAITER: How can I? How can I? *(To the parrot.)* Why in the world would he want to make his own text?

PETER: The stupid bird is going to ruin everything. The exchange is supposed to take place in a few minutes! We were supposed to have dinner and café glacé! What time it is?

LEOPOLD: It is almost time! Let's skip dinner!

PETER: *(To the waiter.)* Café glacé for four!

ALL FOUR OF THEM: *(To the waiter.)* PLEASE!

THE WAITER: How can I? How can I?

(Pause.)

THE PARROT: You can because your mother is a starfish!

(More thunder.)

THE MAN FROM THE SANDWICH ISLANDS: The starfish can do what a man cannot: It can open an oyster with its fingers! *(The native boy writes this in his book.)*

THE PARROT: A whore can open an oyster with her fingers.

THE WOMAN IN A WHITE DRESS: *(To the man in the dark suit.)* You want me to be a whore?

THE MAN IN A DARK SUIT: No, I don't want you to be a whore. I want you to learn correct English. It's my job to teach you English. You have to know English in order to marry an Englishman. *(To the others.)* She hates grammar. She slaps me for prepositions. She slaps me for verbs. She even slaps me for nouns.

THE WOMAN IN A WHITE DRESS: Do you really really want me to go to that faraway country? Do you want me to be married to an unknown man? *(To the others.)* I don't want to make love in a foreign language. I don't want to be touched in a foreign language. I want to make love in my own language. On my island. I want to be touched in my own language.

THE MAN IN THE DARK SUIT: *(To the others.)* I avoid talking to her in our own language because she needs to practice her English. It's the only way to learn a language.

JUNE AND MARIE-LOUISE: *(With emotion.)* Oh! *(They go to the woman in a white dress and hold her hands.)*

JUNE: *(To the man in a dark suit.)* How could you? Don't you believe in love?

PETER: June! This is not the moment!

THE MAN IN THE DARK SUIT: *(Exploding.)* Don't I? Don't I believe in love? *(Kisses the woman in a white dress passionately.)*

MARIE-LOUISE: *(Victoriously.)* Love triumphs! How divine!

LEOPOLD: Marie-Louise, this is not the moment!

THE MAN WITH AN ALLERGY: *(Sneezes, steps between the man in a dark suit and the woman in a white dress.)* Yes, this is not the moment! Love and poetry are ridiculous when the air on the planet is unbreathable. Yes, you give your sweetheart a flower and guess what: The flower is carcinogenic! *(Jumps on a table.)* We are poisoned every second, we are suffocating.

LEOPOLD: *(To the man with an allergy.)* My friend, your issue is valid but believe me, this is not the moment!

THE LITTLE SPOILED BOY: *(Aiming Leopold's gun at his aunt.)* I am going to kill my aunt!

LEOPOLD: My gun! *(To Peter.)* It's loaded!

PETER: Damn!

(The aunt hides behind the Chinese man.)

THE CHINESE MAN: *(Says something in Chinese to the little boy's aunt.)*

THE LITTLE BOY'S AUNT: *(To the Chinese man.)* I don't speak Chinese my good man but whatever it is, this is not the moment!

LEOPOLD: *(To the little spoiled boy.)* Little boy, this is not the moment. There are more important things now than a nice little boy killing his aunt. Come, give me the gun!

(The little spoiled boy fires the gun into the ceiling. Everybody drops to the floor.)

(Prelude of a hurricane. Wind. Lightning. Thunder.)

THE LITTLE SPOILED BOY: I am going to kill all of you!

THE WAITER: Help! Somebody help us!

(Pause.)

THE PARROT: *(Baby talk.)*

Him is his muvver's Ootsie OOh!
And muvver lub him yes she do!
Does him see de big moo moo
And the great big choo choo choo?

Watch him tiss his muvver, do.

Is him fraid ob big BOO BOO

Dat will catch him OOH! OOH! OOH!

THE AUNT: *(To the boy.)* HUNDIDO krias bow! bow! bow!

JUNE: *(To the boy.)* KATIDO krias meow! meow!

MARIE-LOUISE: *(To the boy.)* BOVIDO krias moo! moo! moo!

PETER: *(To the boy.)* KOLOMBO krias coo! coo! coo!

LEOPOLD: *(To the boy.)* SHAFIDO krias baa! baa! baa!

THE LITTLE SPOILED BOY: *(Defiantly.)* INFANO krias ma! ma! ma!

> *(Gives the gun to Leopold and runs into his aunt's arms.)*
> *(The storm breaks. Wind intensifies.)*

THE PARROT: There are two minutes left!

LEOPOLD AND PETER: There are two minutes left!

THE PARROT: Café glacé for four!

THE WAITER: Café glacé for four!

> *(The waiter exits running. Enters back with a tray of four café glacés.)*

THE PARROT: Café glacé for four!

THE WAITER: Café glacé for four!

THE PARROT: This is it!

LEOPOLD AND PETER: This is it!

> *(Peter and Leopold start to move toward each other for the exchange.)*
> *(The wind reaches a hundred miles an hour. Debris is falling down from the ceiling.)*
> *(The reptiles enter.)*
> *(Leopold and Peter try to reach each other but they have great difficulty because the reptiles, general chaotic panic, and the wind keep them apart.)*

THE PARROT: June, hand me our box!

PETER: June, hand me our box!

THE PARROT: Here's your box, Honey!

JUNE: *(Hands the box to Peter.)* Here's your box, Honey!

THE PARROT: Marie-Louise, our box!

LEOPOLD: Marie-Louise, our box!

THE PARROT: Here, my Darling!

MARIE-LOUISE: *(Hands the box to Leopold.)* Here, my Darling!

THE PARROT: Twenty-one seconds!

LEOPOLD: Twenty seconds!

PETER: Nineteen!

LEOPOLD: Eighteen!

PETER: Seventeen!

(Peter and Leopold are crawling toward each other against the wind. Everybody is watching.)

LEOPOLD: Sixteen!

THE PARROT: Five!

PETER: five!

LEOPOLD: Four!

PETER: Three!

LEOPOLD: Two!

PETER: One!

(Leopold and Peter almost reach each other.)
(Peter and Leopold each push their box for the other to catch.)
THE EXCHANGE TAKES PLACE!
(The storm stops abruptly.)

PETER AND LEOPOLD: Thank God!

THE PARROT: Thank God!

(Pause. Everyone looks at the parrot.)
(Sudden realization. The parrot is repeating again!)
(The reptiles exit quickly. Order returns. This must be verified.)

PETER: Waiter!

THE PARROT: Waiter!

JUNE: Waiter!

THE PARROT: Waiter!

MARIE-LOUISE: Waiter!

THE PARROT: Waiter!

LEOPOLD: Waiter!

THE PARROT: Waiter!

THE WAITER: Waiter!

THE PARROT: Waiter!

(The woman in a white dress slaps the man in a dark suit and runs off.)
(The Chinese man says something in Chinese. The parrot repeats.)
(Everybody, except June, Marie-Louise, Peter, and Leopold, sits down at their tables.)
(The waiter exits and enters back with a new bag of parrot food.)
(Long pause.)

MARIE-LOUISE: If you ever come to Europe . . .

JUNE: If you ever come to Milwaukee . . .

(June and Marie-Louise hug each other. Peter and Leopold shake hands vigorously.)

LEOPOLD: *(To Peter.)* It was a pleasure.

PETER: *(To Leopold.)* Did I give you my card? Let me give it to you again. Here is my card.

THE PARROT: Here is my card here is my card herrrre is my carrrrrd herrrrrrrre is my carrrrrrrrrrrd . . . *(Keeps repeating.)*
(Suddenly, an umbrella flies over the stage. The parrot stops repeating.)
(The woman in a white dress and the man in a dark suit enter chasing the umbrella.)

VOICE OFFSTAGE: Catch it! Catch it! Catch it!
(After a moment of hesitation everybody, except for the man from the Sandwich Islands, begins chasing the umbrella in perfect silence.)
(The umbrella flies above the audience and out of the theater.)
(The group runs after it.)
(The man from the Sandwich Islands gently pushes the native boy to join the group. Everyone exits the theater. Pause.)

THE MAN FROM THE SANDWICH ISLANDS: *(To the audience.)* Perhaps the most remarkable story of the effects of companionship comes from the International Bureau of Fish Propagation. The Bureau Chief has persuaded the bass in the bureau's rearing ponds to give up cannibalism, a practice long-assumed to be instinctive with these fish. He noticed that if bass are put into *weedy ponds*, they tend to become separated by the vegetation and fail to form large social groups. Some of the fish take up lodging in secluded spots and apparently develop a gangster psychology. Any small outsider unlucky enough to stray into these restricted territories gets eaten. The cannibalism does not stop when other food is thrown into the water by the fisheries men. The reason for this is that the gangsters are not able to see the food because of the intervening *weeds*. The Bureau Chief's solution was simply to clear the weeds out of the ponds before stocking them with bass. Now all the fish had to mingle. When food was thrown to them they all ate together. With everybody well fed and everybody acquainted with everybody else, nobody tried to eat anybody.
(The man from the Sandwich Islands covers the parrot.)
(Blackout.)

END OF PLAY

Coaticook

Lenora Champagne

INTRODUCTION

by Jim O'Quinn, editor-in-chief, American Theatre

Pick your pleasures: Lenora Champagne provides them generously to theater-goers lucky enough to have experienced the special brew that is her work. She is an inimitable performer (the pleasure that hooked me) of her own idio-syncratic, regionally flavored, richly human texts. She parlays the poetry and shimmer of those texts into full-fledged plays (just as flavorful, just as human). She melds her words to music. She directs plays. With each of these efforts comes the delectation of seeing things afresh, feeling things from unexpected angles, connecting the dots. She possesses that singular quality that defines an artist's contribution to the world: There's no one like her.

AUTHOR'S NOTE

In 1995 I received an N.E.A. fellowship for a two-month residency in Canada. With my six-month-old daughter and husband in tow, I spent three weeks of it in a drafty farmhouse on a sheep farm in Quebec. When we arrived, the setting was suitably bucolic, but the house was infested with flies. Robert went to work with a flyswatter, Amelie in his other arm. After a couple of days of setting out flypaper and repairing screens, the surviving flies left us, retreat-ing, I imagine, to the barn.

The house was "furnished" but lacked many things we needed. In a foray to the attic to discover stuff we could use, we found odd things — a drum set, grow lights, a baby's high chair. We put the high chair to good use, but wondered why it had been left behind. It felt like the previous occupants had left in a hurry.

One of the things they had abandoned was a black cat, who kept com-ing to us to be fed. There were many cats on the farm (two other houses on the farm were occupied), but no one wanted another one. One day a French-speaking farmer showed up for the cat — we hoped he was telling the truth when he said he was taking it to his farm — and, during our visit, I asked him about the people who had preceded us in the house. There was a boy who came there, he said, brought by his friend, a baby born to the friend's mother, a suicide in a grove of trees near the meadow. *Coaticook,* the play, is my imagined version of these events, and my response to the place as we expe-rienced it.

THE AUTHOR

In her plays and monologues, Lenora Champagne often draws on her Acadian background. A native of the French-Louisiana countryside with a doctorate in Performance Studies from NYU, she thrives on urban life but frequently writes about the dramas of women and men who live away from cities, in a more direct relationship to nature.

Champagne and composer Daniel Levy were recipients of the 1999 Richard Rodgers Award from the American Academy of Arts and Letters for *The Singing: a cyberspace opera,* which received the Frederick Loewe award the previous year. She received a Fellowship in Playwriting from the New York Foundation for the Arts in 1998 (for *Wants),* and received fellowships from the National Endowment for the Arts in 1988 (for directing), 1990 (for solo performance), and 1995 (international residency). She has been a Fellow at the MacDowell Colony five times, and she has received support from the New York State Council for the Arts, the Peg Santvoord Foundation, the Jerome Foundation, the Joyce Mertz Gilmore Foundation, and others. She has been an Artistic Associate at Classic Stage Company and Dance Theatre Workshop and teaches on the faculty of SUNY/Purchase and at New York University's Gallatin School.

Published scripts include *Dusk* (Performing Arts Journal #67) and *Wants* (Women & Performance Journal #19), together comprising *The Mama Dramas,* which premiered at Here Arts Center in January 2001. For information on her other plays and productions, which include *Isabella Dreams the New World, My Nebraska,* and *The Best Things in Life,* please use the New Dramatists web site, www.newdramatists.org.

ORIGINAL PRODUCTION

Soho Think Tank's Ice Factory 2000, Ohio Theatre, New York City. Produced by the Undermain Theatre. Directed by Katherine Owens. The cast was as follows:

Kateri Cale. . . . . Roxanne
Russell Pickering. . . . . Sam
Newton Pittman. . . . . Bruce
Suzanne Thomas. . . . . Emily
Chorus of Neighbors:*
Irma St. Paule . . . . Woman with White Hair
Lenora Champagne . . . . Woman with Country Restaurant
Bruce DuBose. . . . . Sweet Farmer with Red Cow
Richard Stack. . . . . Intellectual Farmer with Sheep
*In the Undermain production, these characters were on video.

A workshop version was presented by the Undermain at the Dallas Theatre Center as part of the Dallas Video Festival in March 2000. The play, directed by Eleanor Holdridge, was presented in New York Theatre Workshop's Just Add Water Festival 2000 with a different cast.

CHARACTERS

ROXANNE: 36, aging hippie.
SAM: 17, her son.
EMILY: 12, her daughter.
BRUCE: 18, Eskimo, Sam's friend, Roxanne's lover.

CHORUS

WOMAN WITH WHITE HAIR (French)
OLDER GENTLEMAN FARMER (English)
YOUNGER FARMER (English)
WOMAN WITH COUNTRY RESTAURANT (French)

SETTING

Coaticook is a small city in the French-Canadian province of Quebec. The play takes place in a farmhouse in the nearby countryside. All of the characters speak both English and French. Only two members of the chorus, the Woman with White Hair and the Woman with Country Restaurant, speak with French accents.

COATICOOK

WOMAN IN PARK WITH WHITE HAIR: (*She is feeding birds.*) I love animals. I come every day to feed them. Three times a day. I try to have something good for them. I'm too old for a dog, but I have a beautiful white Egyptian cat with green eyes. She loves me and my husband.

Do I have children?

Yes and no.

A boy. I adopted a boy. Eskimo. He was never right. Never French. Last year, he ran away.

(*Takes a tidbit from her bag.*)

This is a big one. It's for the squirrel.

(*Throws it. Takes out another.*)

And this last one is for him. See, this one is a cripple. Only one foot. (*She throws the tidbit,.*)

Oh! Bad! Another one got it. *Il n'y a plus!*

What? Like Saint Francis? I'm no saint. I have a mean side. I'll never be a saint.

SCENE

A farmhouse interior. Everything is green. Roxanne, wearing bathrobe, makes her way across stage with a flyswatter, swatting at flies. Emily, dropping stuff into a glass jar, sings a French song.

EMILY: *La Saint-Jean qui s'approche*
Maitresse, je m'en vais
Ou va tu ma servante
Ou va-tu habiter?
Au chateau de mon pere
Je veux m'y marier!
(Emily looks out the window.)

EMILY: Ma! Ma, come see.

ROXANNE: (*Offstage.*) I'm busy, baby.

EMILY: It's a double rainbow! All across the sky. (*Dreamily to herself.*) The rainbow ends in a field of golden wheat.

(The door opens. Sam and Bruce enter.)

SAM: Come on in. I'll take your stuff upstairs.

(Emily stares at Bruce. Sam notices.)

SAM: What you staring at? Never seen an Eskimo before?

(Bruce grins at her.)

SAM: This is my kid sister, Emily. She can be a pain, but mostly she's okay. Emily, this is Bruce. He's going to stay with us awhile. Be right back.

(Sam heads upstairs with Bruce's gear.)

EMILY: *(Pause.)* Okay.

(She turns back to the window.)

BRUCE: Can you see the rainbow from there?

EMILY: Yes.

(She moves over to make room for him to look. He joins her.)

EMILY: Are you really an Eskimo?

BRUCE: I was born one.

EMILY: Then what?

BRUCE: I was adopted by a French family in Coaticook.

EMILY: Sometimes I wish I was adopted.

ROXANNE: *(Calling out.)* Sam, did you buy flypaper? These flies are driving me nuts.

(She enters, wearing a bathrobe, wrapping her hair in a towel. She sees Bruce.)

ROXANNE: Excuse me. I wasn't expecting company.

(Sam bounds down the stairs.)

SAM: Ma, this is Bruce. The guy I was telling you about. He's going to stay with us awhile.

BRUCE: Only if it's no trouble. I can give a hand, help out around the place for my keep.

ROXANNE: *(Sizes him up.)* You can stay. Here's a flyswatter. Get to work.

SCENE

Bruce stands in the center of the room, his eyes closed, concentrating. Emily watches.

EMILY: What are you doing?

BRUCE: Attracting flies.

EMILY: Why?

BRUCE: So I can take them outside.

EMILY: Why don't you just kill them?

BRUCE: I prefer to leave that to the spider. That's her job.

EMILY: There are plenty of flies for the spiders to eat. Have you seen how fat they are?

BRUCE: The flies?

EMILY: No. The spiders.

BRUCE: When I take these flies out, you can show me.

EMILY: All right.

(She watches and waits as he concentrates. They breathe together. He opens his eyes.)

EMILY: No one else ever has time for me to show them things.

BRUCE: Time is the only thing I have.

LADY WITH RESTAURANT IN THE COUNTRY: You have to respect what you eat. Food should be happy while it's alive. Chickens and ducks have a very short life — only sixteen weeks. It's not hard to keep them happy.

We raise all our animals for the table. Some pheasants are arriving soon. And we raise capons. Ducks don't fly, unless the mother teaches them how, so we keep them in a pen outside. We don't raise animals inside. Only outside, in the summer. I don't like the smell in the barn. And it's not nice for the animals.

We had a cow, but it was mean. We brought it to a farmer, and he said we could come and get some hens for eggs. So a week later we went to get them. When my husband saw the cow, he cried. Her hair was coming off her back. Her eyes looked different; she didn't recognize us. All of the animals were standing in shit. The chickens smelled like tooth decay. I threw away their eggs for a whole month until they were chickenlike again.

SCENE

Bruce and Sam in the attic.

SAM: You line the wall with aluminum foil, like this. Use regular pots for the plants — plastic or clay, it doesn't matter. The fluorescent light is very important. That's what keeps the plant growing round the clock, day and night.

BRUCE: Doesn't it need a rest?

SAM: No, the light can stay on all the time.

BRUCE: I meant the plants.

SAM: Don't worry about it. The plants are working for you.

BRUCE: Plants are patient, and trusting. If you treat a plant well it will reward you with a rich harvest.

SAM: Look, these are yours. Take care of them however you want. Just remember that you're responsible for your percentage of weed. Agreed?

BRUCE: Sure thing.

(Sam leaves. Bruce separates and plants seeds and shoots. Emily appears.)

EMILY: What are you doing?

BRUCE: Planting.

EMILY: I can see that. Why aren't you planting outside?

BRUCE: These plants are special. They need careful attention.

EMILY: Oh.

(Sam reappears, carrying a big cooking pot, watering can, tools.)

SAM: Scram, squirt. This place is off-limits.

EMILY: What are you doing with Mama's pot?

SAM: None of your business. Now leave us alone. Go on. Get out!

BRUCE: I'll come down soon, Emily.

EMILY: All right. But it's my house, too. I can go where I want.

(She leaves.)

BRUCE: She's a sweet kid.

SAM: She's a pain. Always underfoot.

BRUCE: It's good to have a sister.

SAM: I hadn't noticed. Here, give me a hand with this.

(They pour a sack of earth into the cooking pot.)

SCENE

Emily and Roxanne shuck a mound of corn. Offstage, Sam plays a drum set.

ROXANNE: What a relief to be rid of those flies. Bruce sure has a knack with a flyswatter.

EMILY: *(Grunts/snorts.)*

ROXANNE: Stop that, Emily. It's not polite.

(Yells.) Sam! That's too loud.

EMILY: What do you expect, Ma. They're drums. You should have thought of that when you let him get them.

ROXANNE: He doesn't have to hit them so hard.

(Pause, she searches.) Where is the big pot?

EMILY: Upstairs.

ROXANNE: What's it doing there?

(Bruce enters from outside. Hovers in doorway.)

EMILY: Sam's growing something in the attic. He needed a big pot to plant it in.

ROXANNE: How am I supposed to cook the corn?

EMILY: Cut it up and boil it in lots of little pots.

(Roxanne scowls, then starts throwing small pots on the stove.)

BRUCE: Or I can build a fire and roast it outside.

EMILY: Is that what Eskimos do?

ROXANNE: Emily!

BRUCE: It's okay. I was eight years old when I was adopted. I've forgotten a lot. Now I speak the French language.

EMILY: You're still different.

(Roxanne turns around with a huge platter of corn.)

ROXANNE: You're the man here, Bruce. You decide how to cook it.

SCENE

They eat corn. Sam and Roxanne drink beer. Emily drinks root beer. Bruce doesn't drink.

SAM: I guess we'll eat well now that you're here, Bruce.

ROXANNE: Hey! I'm a good cook.

SAM: Don't get uptight, Ma. I'm just showing some appreciation.

ROXANNE: Well it *is* nice to have a man around.

EMILY: *(Grunts or snorts.)*

ROXANNE: Emily! Do that again and you'll leave the table.

(To Bruce.) It must seem quiet here after town.

BRUCE: I'm glad to be here. When Sam said I could come out here, I thought it was a good chance. Be on the farm, in the country, get away from Coaticook.

ROXANNE: *(Reaching out to touch Bruce.)* We'll do our best to make you happy, Bruce. I promise you that.

SCENE

SWEET FARMER WITH RED COW: I raise cows because I like them. When a lamb is born, it's just a little thing, like a baby, but a calf is a good 100 pounds. It's something substantial. Do you want me to call the cows for you? *(He walks off; comes back with cow.)*

This one is Red Millie. You'll never see another cow like her. She's a pet. She'll walk across the field for you to pet her. And she has to come first. She won't let any other cow come before her. No, I'll never sell Red Millie.

See the bull back there? The one with his head up? He's one now, so he's okay, but next year, when he's two, he'll be full of himself. I never keep a bull more than two years.

Those cows over there haven't calved yet, so I keep them in a separate pen. It's to protect them from coyotes. Normally, cattle can kill a coyote, but a mother cow hides the newborn and goes off to eat, and the coyote can get the calf then.

I've got two calves in the barn; one mother didn't have any milk, the other broke both hips right after she had the calf. Had to shoot her.

Have to watch out for bears. Last summer I saw a big black bear walk right across this field.

SCENE

Emily cuts paper at the kitchen table. Bruce watches.

EMILY: This is going to be a lampshade, see? A chinese lantern. Paper. The light here is too harsh. I need to make it more gentle. Softer. Nicer.

Everything here is rough. The only color is green. There are many colors in the spectrum. Red orange yellow green blue indigo violet. Though I never see indigo or violet in the rainbow, even when the other colors are bright. All those colors are in white. Black is absence. Of color. Nothing there.

Did you know that human beings can distinguish over 10,000 colors? Maybe even ten million, I forget.

There's yellow in the field outside. Goldenrod and oats. You can see it from the window. That's the only relief from green around here. And the sky. Whatever color that is when you look at it.

So I thought I'd make red lanterns. And pink. Make it festive. Bright. Gay, even. Maybe we'll have a party! What do you think?

BRUCE: Sounds good to me.

SCENE

Paper lanterns are strung in the kitchen. Music plays. Emily serves popcorn and brownies.

SAM: Way to go, Emily!

BRUCE: It was a good idea.

(Emily beams.)

ROXANNE: Anyone can pop popcorn.

SAM: Without burning it? She's got one over you there, Mom. And these brownies are goo-od.

ROXANNE: *(To Bruce.)* How did you and Sam hook up?

SAM: I told you, Ma.

ROXANNE: I want Bruce to tell me.

BRUCE: I heard him at a club in Coaticook. I liked his music. I talked to him about it.

ROXANNE: You think he's good.

BRUCE: He could be.

ROXANNE: He could go somewhere.

BRUCE: If he keeps at it.

EMILY: Oh, no! More drumming!

SAM: Shut up, squirt.

ROXANNE: Someday I'll go somewhere. Maybe soon.

EMILY: You just say that because that's what Marie-Helene does.

SAM: Who?

EMILY: That waitress Mom worked with in Montreal before we came here, the one whose father rented us this house. She has different boyfriends and travels all the time. Mom wants to be like her.

ROXANNE: I just like that she's free. She's not tied down. *(To Bruce.)* How old do you think I am?

BRUCE: I don't know. How old are you?

EMILY: Twenty-three, can't you tell?

ROXANNE: I'm thirty-six.

BRUCE: You seem young. For your age.

ROXANNE: *(Pause.)* I could go for some more adult refreshments.

EMILY: Ma! This is my party!

ROXANNE: Well, cry if you want to. Sam, don't you have some weed upstairs? Or what exactly have you been growing in the attic?

SAM: Ma, I don't think in front of Emily . . .

ROXANNE: I'm the mother here, and I decide what's what. Now get me some weed. I feel like smoking, and I'm out of cigarettes.

BRUCE: I'll go.

(He leaves. Sam follows.)

EMILY: You can't let me have anything, can you? I made this party, I planned it, I was having fun, and now you're spoiling it!

ROXANNE: Don't get in my way, Emily.

EMILY: I can see what you're doing. You're trying to make him interested in you. He's my friend. And Sam's. You better leave him alone.

ROXANNE: Don't you dare try telling me what to do.

(Sam and Bruce walk in with a huge amount of weed as Roxanne and Emily glare at one another.)

SAM: What's going on?

ROXANNE: Emily and I were just having . . . a little discussion. My goodness! What a harvest!

SAM: Bruce has the knack. This is a bumper crop.

ROXANNE: Well, let's get going. Who's got the papers?

(Emily rushes out in tears. Bruce starts out after her.)

ROXANNE: No, Bruce. Let her go.

(Roxanne stretches out on the couch and motions for Bruce to sit next to her. Somewhat reluctantly, he joins her.)

SCENE

Middle of the night. The air is hazy with marijuana smoke. An old Moody Blues recording plays ("Knights in White Satin"). Roxanne is partially disrobed, lying on the couch, passed out. Bruce lies on the floor, beer bottles at hand. A caribou, with antlers, ambles across the stage to where Bruce is lying on a mattress. The caribou nuzzles Bruce. Bruce reaches his hand out for it just as it walks away. Bruce wakes up. Emily stands where the caribou was. Bruce tries to sit up and fumbles with his pants.

EMILY: You did it with her, didn't you?

BRUCE: Yeah. I did.

EMILY: Why?

BRUCE: She's nice.

EMILY: She's pathetic. It's disgusting. You're my friend.

BRUCE: Look, you don't understand this stuff.

(Bruce drinks.)
EMILY: What do you mean?
(He doesn't reply. Keeps drinking.)
EMILY: Bruce, your coming here is the best. I never had anyone to talk to before.
(Bruce drinks.)
EMILY: Bruce?
(Bruce groans and rolls over. Emily covers him with an Indian print spread or an old quilt. She grabs a glass jar and heads outside.)

SCENE

In the yard. Dawn. Emily puts earth and feathers in a glass jar and shakes it up.

EMILY: *(Chants.) Allons Dancer*
Allons Dancer
Jamais rester pas la
Allons Dancer

Take the French and the cold,
the animals and the spirits
and shake it up, baby.
Twist and shout.
(Emily throws down the jar, shattering it. Silence.)
(Sam approaches.)
SAM: What are you doing?
EMILY: Making a spell.
SAM: Do you know how?
EMILY: I can figure it out.
SAM: Well, I hope you do.
EMILY: She made a big mistake.
SAM: I'm the one who made the mistake, bringing him here.
EMILY: No. I like him. He's good.
SAM: He's up to no good right now. I thought coming here would help him straighten out, give him something to do. I didn't count on this.
EMILY: You mean, Roxanne.
SAM: Right.
EMILY: I could kill her. He's my friend.
SAM: He was my friend. And he's with my goddamn mother.

(Emily starts to leave.)
SAM: Where are you going?
EMILY: To get another jar. I have to figure out the spell.
SAM: You do that, little sister. You do that.

SCENE

Morning. Emily gently touches Bruce. He wakes up.

EMILY: I brought you some coffee.
BRUCE: Thank you.
EMILY: You shouldn't drink so much.
BRUCE: I know.
EMILY: The cat had kittens last night.
BRUCE: Really? Busy night.
EMILY: Roxanne wants to get rid of them.
BRUCE: This is a farm. There's room for cats.
EMILY: That's what I said.
   (Roxanne walks in, with coffee and breakfast on a tray.)
ROXANNE: *(To Emily.)* Shouldn't you be getting ready for school, or something?
EMILY: It's Saturday, Ma.
BRUCE: She doesn't mean any harm . . .
ROXANNE: This is between the two of us. Emily, don't give me any trouble here,
   because I can give it back to you in spades.
BRUCE: Roxanne . . .
EMILY: It's alright, Bruce. See you later.
   (Emily leaves.)
BRUCE: What's the big deal, Roxanne? She's just a kid.
ROXANNE: You want to know what's wrong? You can't even imagine.
BRUCE: You might be surprised. Try me.
ROXANNE: Ohhhhh . . .
   (Roxanne reaches down to embrace Bruce. He gently pulls her arms away.)
BRUCE: Roxanne. What happened last night. It won't happen again.
ROXANNE: Oh? You didn't like it?
BRUCE: That's not it. It just complicates things too much. Sam is my friend . . .
   (Sam walks in.)
SAM: But you weren't thinking about that, were you?
ROXANNE: Now, Sam . . .

BRUCE: This one is between us.

SAM: Upstairs or outside?

BRUCE: Up to you.

(*Bruce and Sam face each other, hands at sides, as Roxanne looks from one to the other.*)

SCENE

Drums, bass guitar. Lights up on Sam and Bruce, improv-ing together. The drums and guitar shriek at each other, then argue, then find some way to coexist in relative harmony. Sam is good on the drums. Bruce plays a decent bass.

Sam gives a final whack. The guys breathe heavy, exhausted.

SAM: (*Holding out a drumstick.*) You want it?

BRUCE: (*Taking the drumstick from him.*) All right.

(*Bruce plays the drum. As he plays, it changes from a rock 'n' roll instrument to something ancient, mellow, deep, with resonance. He begins to chant with the drumbeats.*)

(*Emily appears in the doorway, sipping a root beer. She watches Bruce play.*)

(*Roxanne appears over Emily's shoulder.*)

(*Sam, Emily, and Roxanne watch Bruce.*)

(*Bruce ends with a final call.*)

(*Silence.*)

BRUCE: (*To Emily.*) How about a sip of that root beer?

(*Emily hands it to him.*)

BRUCE: Sometimes I want to bust out. I don't like this heat. The sun is too hot. I dream of ice floes and caribou.

EMILY: Have you ever seen a caribou?

BRUCE: I don't remember. But I dream about them all the time.

SCENE

Roxanne and Bruce on the couch. Sam sits to the side, brooding. Beer bottles and marijuana.

ROXANNE: I'm hungry.

(Bruce tries to get up to look for something.)

ROXANNE: You stay here. Sam can get it. Sam! More food.

SAM: Why don't you let your new friend get it for you?

ROXANNE: *(Coaxingly.)* Sam . . .

SAM: My name is Sam. Sam I am.

(Bruce laughs. Sam leaves the room.)

ROXANNE: I'm so hungry. I'm hungry all the time now. I can't get enough to
eat. I want meat! I'll take lamb, I'll take chicken, give me a roast and I'll
eat the whole thing. It's . . . it's a craving. I've never had one before. There's
an animal inside of me trying to gnaw its way out and I'm the teeth, I'm
the sharp claws . . .

BRUCE: Why are you telling me this?

ROXANNE: Because you're like me. You're hungry, too.

(They embrace passionately.)

SCENE

*Roxanne is throwing up offstage. We hear her retching. Emily is peeling
potatoes. Sam walks in.*

SAM: What's wrong with her?

EMILY: She's sick.

SAM: I got that.

EMILY: Heard her and Bruce yelling?

SAM: Yep.

(Roxanne drags herself to the table.)

EMILY: Want some coffee, Ma?

ROXANNE: No. Give me a soda cracker.

(Emily gives her the box. Bruce walks in. Emily and Sam look at him.)

BRUCE: Did you tell them?

EMILY: Tell us what?

ROXANNE: *(Desperately cheerful.)* Children. We're going to have a baby.

*(Roxanne rushes off to the bathroom. Sam kicks a chair over. Emily looks with
dismay at Bruce, who stares down at the floor, his fists clenched.)*

SCENE

Emily, listlessly seated at the kitchen table.
Roxanne walks in. She is visibly pregnant. They don't speak.

ROXANNE: He's gone. You might as well stop stewing about it.

EMILY: It's all thanks to you.

ROXANNE: Shell these peas for me.

> *(Emily just looks at the pile of peas Roxanne has set next to her. Goes on with her brooding.)*

EMILY: It's so boring without him. There's no one to talk to.

ROXANNE: You can talk to me.

EMILY: *(Snorts/grunts.)*

ROXANNE: Emily!

EMILY: You don't have anything that I want. You don't know anything that I can use. You're not like anyone I want to be. You're just . . . getting old.

> *(Emily storms out. Roxanne sits down where Emily was sitting. Starts to shell the peas. Then bursts into tears, lays her head on her arms on the table, and weeps.)*
>
> *(As Roxanne cries, Sam, in his room, at his drums, sings.)*

SAM: *(Sings.) I am wandrin'*
said the blind man
far from home

I am wandrin'
said the blind man
where'er I roam

Just lookin' for someplace to mend
where I can find a friend

Don't know where he comes from
or where to go
no, don't know where he comes from
or how to grow

when he tries to ease his mind
he leaves trouble behind

I can see
said the blind man
what is happ'nin to me

I can see
said the blind man
what you're doin' to me . . .

Shit. They've got me singing the blues.

SCENE

The kitchen. Roxanne is at the table. Sam bounds through the kitchen door.

SAM: He's back.
ROXANNE: What?
    (Bruce appears in the kitchen door.)
SAM: See for yourself.
    (Sam heads upstairs.)
BRUCE: Hello.
ROXANNE: This is certainly a surprise.
BRUCE: Is it?
ROXANNE: It is.
BRUCE: I couldn't stay away.
ROXANNE: You missed me? Us, I mean?
BRUCE: I kept thinking, that's gonna be my kid, and he's going to have a hell of a time. I wondered what he would look like and who would teach him the things he'll need to know.
ROXANNE: Oh.
BRUCE: And Coaticook was a drag. The old folks were not happy to see me and there was the same nothing happening there as here, only more so. I felt . . . crowded. So when Sam showed up to bring me back, he didn't have to convince me.
ROXANNE: Sam went to get you?
BRUCE: Yeah. I thought you sent him.
ROXANNE: No. No, I didn't.
BRUCE: Maybe he just has a sense for what his mother wants.

(Bruce gropes Roxanne. She gasps. He puts a hand on her breast and starts kissing her. She resists at first, then gives in. They are in a fumbling, passionate clinch when Emily walks in. She holds a jar. She drops the jar when she sees them.)
(Bruce and Roxanne jump apart.)

EMILY: Bruce! You're back!

(Emily beams at Bruce. Roxanne glares at Emily. Bruce looks from one to the other and back.)

BRUCE: Yeah. Let's celebrate.

(He goes to the fridge, opens it, takes out a beer, and downs it, in big gulps, right at the fridge, door still open. His drinking is lit by the light of the fridge.)

SCENE

Roxanne puts food on the table. Sam bumps into her on his way to his chair.

ROXANNE: OW!

(She grabs her arm where it hurts. A dark spot shows past her sleeve. Sam pushes the sleeve up.)

SAM: How did this happen?

ROXANNE: I ran into the door.

EMILY: It's turning colors, Ma. Green. Yellow. Indigo!

ROXANNE: My own personal rainbow.

(She pulls her sleeve down and turns away.)

BRUCE: I'm sorry.

(Everyone looks at him.)

ROXANNE: Bruce, leave it alone.

SAM: No, please go on. I want to hear about it. Really. I'm very interested.

EMILY: He probably just had too much to drink.

SAM: You touch her again, and you're out of here.

BRUCE: Yeah. I got it.

SAM: You're an idiot, Bruce.

ROXANNE: Sam! Sam, stop it. This isn't your concern.

SAM: He's my friend. You're my mother. I brought him here. It *is* my business.

EMILY: What can you do, Sam? Everything's changed.

ROXANNE: We can't go back to how we were before. There's a baby coming.

SAM: Oh yeah. Right. Hallelujah.

SCENE

Sound of a baby crying. Emily is cradling the baby, trying to get the bottle off the stove and into its mouth.

EMILY: *(Sings.) Hush, little baby, don't say a word*
Mama's gonna buy you a mockingbird.
And if that mockingbird don't sing
Mama's gonna buy you a diamond ring.
And if that diamond ring don't shine,
Mama's gonna buy you a bottle of wine.
(Bruce enters, bottle of beer in hand.)

BRUCE: I don't think that's how the song goes.

EMILY: He likes it. See, he stopped crying.

BRUCE: Mother's milk. Mother's milk.

(Bruce drinks the beer.)

EMILY: You shouldn't drink so much.

BRUCE: Right. Indians can't hold their alcohol.

EMILY: It makes you mean.

BRUCE: You have no idea.

(Roxanne enters.)

ROXANNE: Nursing the bottle first thing, are we? Don't you think you better be out looking for a job? We've got an extra mouth to feed.

BRUCE: Why don't you get a job, then?

ROXANNE: I've got to stay here and take care of it.

EMILY: I can do it, Ma.

ROXANNE: You give me that baby and get ready for school. *(To Bruce.)* Besides, you're the father. You're supposed to provide. None of the farms around here need an extra hand?

BRUCE: Not much need in winter. The best I can get right now is shoveling shit out of the Anglo's barn and the odd job with the sheep farmer.

ROXANNE: Take it, then, and keep looking. Of course, you should really try to finish school. Maybe you could get something better then.

BRUCE: You want me to work and go to school?

ROXANNE: Bruce. You have your whole life ahead of you.

BRUCE: Right. Some life.

(Bruce opens another beer. Drinks. Sam enters and goes over to the baby, who is in the high chair.)

SAM: Hello little baby. You cute little Eskimo half-breed. Hey, Bruce, maybe your mom will want to see her grandchild! How about it? Want to take the little bastard into Coaticook?

BRUCE: Shut up. Shut up! Just everyone shut up and leave me alone!

(He slams his fist into the wall. Hurts his hand. When Roxanne reaches for it, he hits her.)

SAM: Don't you lay a hand on Ma!

(Bruce and Sam start to fight. The baby wails.)

EMILY: Stop it! Everybody, stop it!

(The men are separated. They back into opposite corners, breathing heavily, exhausted.)

(The baby wails.)

(Bruce walks up to it, his hands opening and closing into fists. Everyone watches. Finally, he picks it up and hugs it in a big embrace, then hands it off to Emily and runs out.)

EMILY: *(Rocking the baby in her arms.)* Shh. Shh. Your Mama loves you. Your Daddy loves you. Your big sister loves you.

(Roxanne cries. Sam breathes heavily and glares at his mother.)

SCENE

A tree. Bruce walks up to it with a long length of rope. He throws the rope over a tree branch. Loops it over his neck. Climbs up into the tree. Checks his pocket before he's high up. Finds a scrap of paper and a stub of pencil. Writes a note. Reaches down to attach it with a string to a low branch. Below him, he sees an apparition. A lamb appears in the snow below the tree. A coyote approaches, lurking close to the ground. Bruce looks steadily at it. Bruce climbs higher. Leaps off a limb.

INTELLECTUAL FARMER WITH SHEEP: That goat is separated because it's under observation. There's something wrong with her foot. The goats are here to keep the coyotes away. The coyotes don't like the smell of goat.

What? Do the goats have different personalities? I'm not as sensitive to that kind of thing as other people are.

These lambs are being sold immediately. This is the Border Collie we're training. You have to keep it inside for six days so it will get attached to the place. See, we've insulated the barn. My sons and I did all this. One of my sons will live on the farm. He's a veterinarian. The other wants to work in forestry. My daughter? She travels, and works in a vegetarian restaurant in Montreal until she gets enough money to travel again.

In fifteen years the three farms adjacent to mine will all be sold. They've only got daughters. No sons.

The boy who hung himself? You heard about that? Yes, it's sad. But to be expected. He was Indian — Eskimo. You yank someone like that out of his culture . . . and there were no men around. He was dominated by women. Too many women. Too many women trying to tell him what to do.

SCENE

The farmhouse. Everything packed in suitcases, quickly, hastily. Roxanne, holding the baby, looks around her.

ROXANNE: Come on, Sam. Let's get out of here.
(She grabs a bundle and exits. Sam comes downstairs with a duffel bag, grabs a suitcase, and heads for the door.)
EMILY: *(Offstage.)* Aren't you going to take your drum set?
SAM: I won't have time for it in Coaticook. And there won't be room in the apartment. Hurry up. Ma's ready to go.
(Sam exits. Emily enters.)
EMILY: I'm taking everything that's mine.
(She stops at the kitchen table, smoothes out a scrap of paper she keeps in her purse. Reads it.)
EMILY: I was afraid I'd hurt the baby.
(She lights a match and burns the paper over the sink. She breathes deeply.)
EMILY: Good-bye, my friend. You'll never feel hurt again. I miss you. May your spirit find peace.
ROXANNE: *(Offstage.)* Emily!
EMILY: *(Softly.)* I'm coming.
(Emily closes her eyes, breathes in, breathes out, opens her eyes, and leaves.)

END OF PLAY

Landscape of Desire

Barry Jay Kaplan

For the Barretts.
And for Trist.
And for Ron.

INTRODUCTION
by Simon Callow

Like most directors and many actors, I am sent a large number of plays, and, as an openly gay man, among that large number is a high proportion of what may loosely be called gay themes. In general, these plays are poor. They cover a spectrum from the confessional to the militant, which may be useful in certain contexts; they rarely approach the theater as an art, a uniquely subtle vehicle for the expression of complex responses. The effect is of a ludicrous simplification of homosexual experience, which is quite as many-faceted, as contradictory, as fulfilling, and as frustrating as anything in its heterosexual equivalent.

It was, then, with growing excitement that I read *Landscape of Desire,* which had come into my hands via the friend of a friend; in other words, I feared the worst. But I found myself reading a gay play like no other. For a start, it was not at all clear on the surface whether it was a gay play at all. It was a rites-of-passage play, but one in which the initiation of the central character occurred by no profound insights, nor traumatic events; it consisted of a slow, indirect, and gradual awareness of which the audience became apprised obliquely. Its three acts traced — that is the word — an evolution, an emergence into the light of a sensibility that, out of a chaos of impressions and influences, begins to understand what it can and cannot encompass. This is like life, gay or straight, and its truths are conveyed with ellipsis and inference, treating its audience and its characters like grown-ups.

It is dismaying but, given its unprecedented subtlety, I suppose not altogether surprising, that the play has yet to find the production that will release it to the wider world. In my view, it demands to be done, and done soon. Barry Kaplan's is a new voice in the gay theater, as original and as quietly insistent as Proust is in another medium. His work — in particular *Landscape of Desire* — pushes forward the boundaries of both gay theater and theater itself.

Barry Jay Kaplan's plays have been produced at the McCarter Theatre in Princeton, HOME for Contemporary Theatre and Art, Playwrights Horizons, Ensemble Studio Theatre, St. Peters Church at Citicorp, Limbo, the William Rosenfield Theatre, Pelican Studio, the Lost Theatre, and the Hudson Theatre in Los

Angeles. He initiated and administered the playwright's unit at HOME for Contemporary Theatre and Art and was a founding member and playwright-in-residence of the Stonehill Theatre Project, for which he directed the New York premiere of Wendy Hammond's *Family Life*. He has taught playwriting at New Dramatists and the Playwrights Horizons Theatre School. He has also written for television (*Hill Street Blues* and HBO's *Encyclopedia*) and is the author of the screenplays *Banished* and *The Zombie Stare* as well as a dozen novels, including the best-sellers *Black Orchid* and *Biscayne*. *A Beautiful White Room* has been workshopped at New Dramatists and the Audrey Skirball-Kenis Theatre Projects in Los Angeles. *Landscape of Desire* has received readings and workshops at the Australian National Playwrights' Conference and at New Dramatists.

CAST

HOWARD: a writer (In Act I he is in his early twenties, in Act II in his late twenties, in Act III, his mid thirties).
MARGO: 37, an expatriate living in Mexico, beautiful, womanly.
JOE: 40, a writer, handsome, Margo's husband.
MINA: 38, a recent divorcée.
JACKIE: 21, a waiter, adorable.
MARTIN: 35, a psychiatrist.
ANGEL: 22, a hustler.
GAVIN: 40, a macho movie star.

SETTING

Act I: A hacienda in a secluded valley in Mexico
Act II: A studio apartment in the East Village in New York City
Act III: A bedroom on New York's Upper West Side; a Malibu beachfront house
The sets should not be realistic but suggestive. Elements of the set of Act I should appear in Act II. Elements from Acts I and II should appear in Act III.

TIME

The action of the play spans about a dozen years.

LANDSCAPE OF DESIRE

ACT I

The terrace of a hacienda in rural Mexico. There are a set of double doors up center going into the house. A long diaphanous curtain hangs in front of them, blown by a gentle breeze. A door downstage left opens onto a guest room. A low stone walls rims the terrace. When the characters look out over the audience they see the valley basin and a large lake. Margo and Joe appear, dancing to romantic Latin guitar music. Howard watches them, rapt.

HOWARD: God, they're so wonderful. So . . . smooth. I want to just . . . have them . . . I want to . . . I want to write about them but . . . it's always just so perfect just being with them . . . just watching them . . . I mean, what could I write?
(Writing.)
Story idea: A couple leaves America to live in a hacienda in a secluded valley in Mexico. He's a poet. She's his muse. "Cerise bougainvillea spills over the wall . . . "

MARGO: Look, darling. A gardenia moon.
(She leads Joe to a chair. He sits. On the table next to the chair are three glasses and an open bottle of champagne. She pours a glass and gives it to him, takes one for herself.)

JOE: May you live a thousand years.

HOWARD: Oh God, will I ever be able to be like that?

JOE: Howard! You're empty!
(He picks up the third glass and fills it. Howard goes to get it. Joe holds up the empty bottle.)

JOE: Maria! Mas champagne!

HOWARD: Por favor!

MARGO: She's sleeping.

JOE: I'll go.
(He doesn't move.)

HOWARD: I'll go.
(He doesn't move. He and Joe laugh.)

MARGO: Thank you Vladimir and Estragon.

(She gets up to get the champagne.)

JOE: Sit. Maria!

HOWARD: Por favor!

(Margo pours from another bottle of champagne for Joe and then for Howard and then sits.)

JOE: You are a paragon. Howard? Do I have the right word? Is she is a paragon?

HOWARD: I think "paragon" requires a prepositional phrase: a paragon of . . . virtue or . . .

JOE: Not that.

MARGO: I love being the object of abstract discourse.

JOE: *(Examining label on champagne.)* Not to be sold after June 26th.

HOWARD: My favorite year.

JOE: We have tickets for the bullfight in Mexico City Sunday, Howard. Do you have moral qualms?

MARGO: *(To Joe.)* Is Pepe fighting this week?
(To Howard.) I'm madly in love with a matador.

JOE: She's really in love with his bull.

MARGO: Oh you fool.

(They laugh.)

MARGO: Joseph was once a fighter, Howard. Did you know that?

HOWARD: No. Really?

MARGO: Jose O'Conner, the Irish torero. He was very brave.

HOWARD: Did you . . . kill it?

JOE: At the moment of truth, I became a vegetarian. Papa would not have been proud. *(Pause.)* Look at him, Margo. Writer boy making notes.

HOWARD: No I'm not.

MARGO: He's teasing you.

HOWARD: I know.

JOE: He is!

HOWARD: I'm hungry.

MARGO: *(Gives Howard something to eat.)* Try this.

HOWARD: What is it?

MARGO: Blood papaya.

HOWARD: Will I shrink or grow bigger?

JOE: That all depends on who you're eating it with.

MARGO: Joseph's been raving about you since the day he read your first story. This kid. This bright kid. This . . . writer.

HOWARD: Really?

JOE: Margo, was I ever this modest?

MARGO: I'd have remembered.

JOE: You know, Howie, I'm thinking of not going back. Ever.

HOWARD: Really?

JOE: Extend the sabbatical for life. Write full-time. Margo thinks I should.

MARGO: We've got the money. As long as we live here.

JOE: How does a diet of plantains and blood papaya sound to you?

HOWARD: Sounds great.

JOE: I've got a million ideas . . . nothing really worked out . . . but there's a novel. There is definitely a novel.

HOWARD: Right.

MARGO: Joseph, show Howard the book.

HOWARD: The book?

JOE: The book. The Book. The BOOK.

(He exits.)

HOWARD: The book! How great!

MARGO: I'm so proud of him.

HOWARD: Well sure. *(Pause.)* You know . . . where I come from, wives don't look like you.

MARGO: What do they look like?

HOWARD: Mmm . . . potatoes.

MARGO: And that makes me . . . what? Don't you dare say pomegranate or I'll slap your face.

HOWARD: No, you know what I mean.

MARGO: But Howard, a wife's the only thing I know how to be.

HOWARD: It just seems so . . . secondary, somehow and you seem so . . . so . . . primary. *(Pause.)* The first time I ever saw you was at that party at school. I was in Joe's workshop. I think I was still calling him Mister O'Conner. And someone told me who you were and I remember thinking, no, no, that you just couldn't be someone's . . . wife.

MARGO: Howard. Stop.

HOWARD: But I mean it.

MARGO: Howard, you're flirting with me.

HOWARD: I am?

(Joe re-enters with book.)

JOE: Written by Joseph P. O'Conner. Edited by J.P. O'Conner. Published by the J. Patrick O'Conner Press.

HOWARD: *(Opening to the first page.)* "To Mango?" What . . . ?

JOE: Mexican typesetters. They literally did not understand one fucking word. I said: "Jesus, es me vida—"

HOWARD: Oh oh.

   (*Reading.*) "To Margo, who knows whereof I speak."

MARGO: Thank you, darling. I do.

HOWARD: Read one aloud.

JOE: Oh I'm too shy.

HOWARD: Well can I—

JOE: All right. You've convinced me. (*He takes the book, opens to a page and prepares to read aloud.*) "Bobby Sox Baby Blues."

MARGO: Joseph! Of all the ones you could pick to read . . .

JOE: Are you stifling my oratory impulses? You who know whereof I speak?

MARGO: Oh go ahead. Howard, cover your ears.

JOE: (*Reading.*)

   "He met her the summer her braces came off.

   Had a Chevy, a stick shift, a beer.

   Took her out in the moonlight, down in the dark.

   Am I touching the right spot? No? Here?

   She wore saddle shoes, anklets, up further: not clear

   But he pulled and got in, more or less.

   Her anklets all bunched up, her panties all down,

   She said: 'deeper' and he thought: 'career.'

   (*Embarrassed pause.*)

HOWARD: I love that last line. "And he thought: career." Yeah.

JOE: Well I was trying to get a kind of ironic, you know . . .

MARGO: . . . twist sort of thing.

HOWARD: It's definitely ironic.

MARGO: My mother remembered those saddle shoes.

JOE: You sent her a copy?

MARGO: You told me to!

JOE: What a good girl you are.

   (*He nuzzles her, says something in her ear that makes her laugh. He turns to Howard.*)

JOE: Margo got her early training in obedience from her daddy. He liked to take her down to the basement for a good licking.

MARGO: Oh we've heard this a hundred times.

JOE: She still likes a good licking.

   (*Joe passes a lit joint to Howard.*)

JOE: Grown in the shadow of Mount Chapultepec. Fertilized with the pulverized bones of Montezuma.

   (*Howard smokes, chokes, passes it to Margo.*)

MARGO: No thanks.

JOE: I insist.

MARGO: I'd rather not.

HOWARD: Come on, Margo. For Montezuma's sake.

(Margo puffs, does not inhale, and passes it back to Joe.)

JOE: Damn! Now why is that? I've given this a lot of thought. Why is it that women don't like to get high?

MARGO: Not that we're extrapolating theories based on a single incident of a single woman . . .

JOE: It's instinctive. And you know why?

MARGO: And not that we're dealing in generalizations.

JOE: Control. Period.

MARGO: Let's go dancing. I'm going to call and see if La Fonda del Recuerdos is still open. *(To Joe.)* Darling, don't smoke anymore if you're going to drive.

JOE: I'm not going to drive. Howard, can you drive the Mercedes?

HOWARD: *(Very stoned.)* Stick shift?

MARGO: Howard is not driving.

JOE: He knew it was a stick shift.

MARGO: Darling.

JOE: Then you drive.

MARGO: I can't see at night.

JOE: If you don't want to go dancing, why don't you just say so? I'll go with Howard.

(Joe takes Howard into his arms and starts dancing.)

MARGO: I'm the one who said: Let's go dancing.

JOE: You're the one who said: Thank you darling, I do.

MARGO: Well I did. And now I don't.

JOE: I love this girl.

(He grabs her and they all dance.)

HOWARD: Would you guys adopt me?

MARGO: Oh honey . . .

HOWARD: I don't eat much.

JOE: Howard, that's the most charming thing you've said all day.

(Margo and Joe dance slowly offstage, Howard watches them as they dance off.)

HOWARD: Oh God they're so beautiful. "Mist rises . . . music as mist . . . "

(Later. Joe re-enters.)

JOE: I read your story.

HOWARD: Oh no. It's nothing. I just wrote it on the plane down.

JOE: Mm.

HOWARD: I was trying for a kind of economy of . . .

JOE: Oh well yes, it's extremely economical.

HOWARD: God I would hate to waste words.

JOE: And it doesn't sound like anyone else.

HOWARD: God I would hate to sound like anyone else.

JOE: Has anyone seen this stuff? You should send it out. Really. You should.

HOWARD: Well I sort of have, actually.

JOE: Well good. You should. You could be very successful.

HOWARD: I want it so much I'm afraid to even think about it. *(Pause.)* Although I have been planning what to wear for my first appearance on the *Tonight Show*. *(Pause.)* No. *(Pause.)* All these people keep saying I'm promising. I hate that. I mean, I love it but, you know, I hate it.

JOE: Writing, writing, writing.

HOWARD: How's your . . . ?

JOE: Well, you know. Trying to work out this novel.

HOWARD: Yeah . . .

JOE: Mi vida nueva.

HOWARD: Ole.

   (Pause.)

JOE: I'm curious, Howard.

HOWARD: What?

JOE: Is this for real?

HOWARD: What?

JOE: This "shy" thing you do.

HOWARD: I don't know what you mean.

JOE: I believe in you, boy. I'm going to be very disappointed if I turn out to be wrong.

HOWARD: You're not wrong.

JOE: But will you do things you don't want to do? Because there are going to be things you'll have to do and you won't like having to do them but you can't let things stop you. You can't let anything stop you.

HOWARD: I can't imagine what would stop me. To have my work known . . . to have people read me . . . to have them in my . . . It's everything. It's . . . Important is the wrong word. Important undersells what it is to me.

JOE: *(Passes Howard a joint.)* You know, psychologically, the drive toward success is just a manifestation of the fear of being left out of things.

HOWARD: *(Smoking.)* You mean, what John Updike really wants is to be invited to—

JOE: John Updike? Christ, Howard. Haven't you been listening to me for the past three years?

HOWARD: Oh right, right. You have problems with his imagery.

JOE: Overworked. Precious. Desperate for effect. The way he . . . tortures his words. And the whole Catholic thing . . . and the sexual overcompensation . . . Don't get me started.

HOWARD: No well I just . . .

JOE: Howard. I want to say two words to you about American literature. *(Pause.)* Norman. Mailer.

HOWARD: Well sure. Yeah.

JOE: Norman fucking Mailer. *(He takes a drink.)* There's too much fucking writing! *(Pause.)* You go into a bookstore . . . *(Pause.)* I mean . . . do they need my book? *(Pause.)* What's the point? I mean, in the largest sense, what is the fucking point?

HOWARD: Don't you think writers sort of . . . owe something to their talent?

JOE: Well of course you want to go all the way with it. You want to allow your talent full rein. You want to test it, challenge yourself, go to the edge of your . . . will . . . without embarrassment or shame or . . . *(Takes another drink.)* But basically . . . talent is worthless. Talent is a crutch. It's a trap.

HOWARD: Oh. But . . . well . . . do you mean . . . talent without discipline, without hard—

JOE: Margo thinks if a writer isn't sitting at his desk for eight hours a day he's not working.

HOWARD: But you've said discipline is—

JOE: Right. Discipline. Right. Well, hey what the hell am I doing out here having an actual life? I should be back there, harnessing my talent.
(He takes a bottle of gin and goes.)

HOWARD: "In place of loneliness . . . " No. "In place of . . . instead of . . . pain . . . " God, no. Uh . . . "Experience . . . "
(Later. Margo enters with Mina, carrying a suitcase. Howard is sitting outside the door of the guest room, pad in lap.)

MINA: Now you have to promise to tell me if I'm being a pest or if I get in your way in the slightest. I'm just going to sit on the terrace and not say a word. You don't have to pay any attention to me. Oh it's so fabulous to be here. Where's Joseph? Joseph! You swine! Joe! When are you going to fuck me?
(Margo and Mina laugh. Mina notices Howard.)
Oh! The famous writer.

HOWARD: You're right about the writer part, anyway.

MINA: Margo. Adorable. *(Takes Howard's arm.)* At last we meet. Now. Have I read anything you've written?

HOWARD: I don't know. What've you read?

(Margo laughs.)

MINA: Oh I'm not quick like they are, Howard. You'll have to go slow with me. First, I want you to tell me all about yourself. You may sum up the early chapters and go directly to your sordid initiation into sex. *(Pause.)* Pay no attention to me, Howard. I'm damaged goods. If I get out of line, call poison control. *(Pause.)* I don't know what I would've done if I wasn't able to come down. There was a constant pressure in my chest. *(Sings.)* "Heartaches by the number/Troubles by the score . . . "

(As Howard writes, Mina is telling this story to Margo.)

HOWARD: "Her husband's business goes chapter eleven. They have to move from a duplex on Riverside Drive to a one-bedroom garden apartment in New Rochelle and now she has to work in a stationery store in the mall. Her husband smokes pot and goes to AA meetings. Which is where he meets his latest little tootsie."

MINA: Oh I should be relieved he's dumping his troubles on someone else for a change. And he's getting fat. Good. Let her watch his cholesterol level, the stupid bitch. Did I say that?

MARGO: Mina, it's your vacation.

MINA: I know, I know. Relax. Let it go. *(Pause.)* Oh why are men such shits? *(Pause.)* What about you, Howard? Are you a shit? Would you ever betray someone you love? Would you ever turn your back on someone who trusted you and looked up to you and—

MARGO: Mina, why don't we drive into town with Manuel. I've got some things to pick up.

MINA: Oh Margo, are you just going to be perfect the whole time I'm here?

MARGO: Come on. Maybe you can surprise Joseph at the bookstore

MINA: What if I want to surprise Manuel instead?

(Mina and Margo exit.)

(Later. Joe enters.)

JOE: She wasn't in that bookstore three minutes when she had her tongue down my throat and was trying to lay me out on the floor.

HOWARD: What?

JOE: I have a welt from leaning into *The Collected Works of Lope de Vega!*

(Margo enters.)

MARGO: Joseph never turns down an attractive offer.

HOWARD: You don't mind?

MARGO: A kiss in a bookstore?

HOWARD: Well . . . I don't know.

JOE: I'm just trying to prove a point.

MARGO: You know, Howard. Joseph's been seen in the Hilton bar with Miss Universe.

HOWARD: Come on.

JOE: She was doing some public relations work for the American Embassy and—

MARGO: Howard. Really. Miss Universe!

HOWARD: Miss Universe . . .

MARGO: I mean . . . what would Dr. Freud say?

JOE: Margo, this is tired.

HOWARD: Really, Joe? Miss Universe?

MARGO: I know. It's a very large concept to take in.

JOE: She's a sweet kid from Bolivia. I had a drink with her. Christ.

HOWARD: But . . . Miss Universe.

MARGO: All right, all right. Enough of Miss Universe. Fuck Miss Universe. I mean, don't fuck Miss Universe.
(Laughs.)

JOE: Not that Margo is without sin. She hasn't mentioned her own little adventures.

MARGO: You don't have to discredit me to make your point.

HOWARD: I'm not being influenced.

JOE: And you believe her. Listen. Howard. I know you love her like a sister, just . . . don't be a schmuck.

MARGO: We do have two children who depend on us to be here in the morning.

JOE: I can disappear, you know.

MARGO: What's that supposed to mean?

JOE: It means: Don't think you can hold me by citing my responsibilities.

MARGO: Why are you being such a prick?

JOE: Howard, explain to this woman why I'm being such a prick.
(Joe exits.)

MARGO: He believes that he's permanently damaged by his past.

HOWARD: But look what he's done with his life! I mean . . . look where he's taken himself. Look what he's got. How can he doubt himself? How can he think he's damaged?

MARGO: Of course, it feeds his work. I mean, no writer can lead a life without pain or experience and expect to have anything to draw from.

HOWARD: But he's OK, though. I mean . . . this is what . . . you know . . . This is a writer's life, isn't it?

MARGO: Has he spoken to you?

HOWARD: About what?

MARGO: "I am not just a husband!" He's said that so many times. And now he has the time to write. I encouraged this sabbatical. But . . . I just want him to make peace with himself.

(Joe shouts from offstage: "Margo! I need you!" Margo exits.)

(Later. Mina and Howard in conversation.)

MINA: I think he's insane. I mean, clinical. He took me on a tour of his medicine cabinet. He is into some deep shit. He thinks he can still do pharmaceuticals. Christ! I'm telling you: He is not getting out of this one alive. I don't envy, Margo, I mean, Joseph is fabulous in almost every way but, you know, really . . . *(Pause.)* The thing is, it's all sex with them. That's what drew them together and that's what keeps them going. No matter how rotten everything else is, there's always that. Not everyone is so lucky. All the rest . . . it doesn't mean anything. *(Pause.)* I dated him first, you know. Hell, I introduced them. I knew what he liked. Margo and I have identical taste in men. Not to be relied on in national emergencies, I'm afraid. *(Pause.)* Are you in love with her?

HOWARD: What are you talking about?

MINA: Don't worry. You won't hurt my feelings.

HOWARD: Of course I'm not in love with her. Joe's in love with her.

MINA: Did you have a little three-way thing going?

HOWARD: No!

MINA: It's not the furthest thing from your mind though, is it? *(Pause.)* Margo says you're the new John Updike. Is that true, Howard? Are you the new John Updike?

HOWARD: Are you making fun of me?

MINA: Don't be nervous. I don't bite. *(Pause.)* On the first date. *(Pause.)* Unless I absolutely must.

HOWARD: I was just about to go to bed.

MINA: Oh you want to go to bed?

HOWARD: Uh. To sleep. Yeah.

MINA: You have a fireplace in your room. Shall I make a fire for you?

HOWARD: No! It makes me uncomfortable to go to sleep if it's still burning.

(Pause.)

MINA: *(She moves closer to him, kisses him. He doesn't respond.)* Howard. Honey. I can't do all this by myself. *(Pause.)* Now I'm embarrassed.

HOWARD: I'm sorry.

MINA: But not really sorry.

HOWARD: No! OK?

MINA: Then I'll just say "Buenos noches, senor." Oh and "Fuck you" too. *(Exits.)*

HOWARD: "I'm hunched in my chair. She turns to me, her eyes are sunflowers, monstrous, her teeth are glistening, dripping, waxen, cold. Wake up!" *(Later. Joe and Margo enter, Howard is reading it aloud to them.)*

HOWARD: "And in the end, I will break down the blank wall of my indifference and tell her the ways I love her."

MARGO: You are so talented.

HOWARD: You really like it?

MARGO: Love it. Love it. Love it. Joseph? I mean . . . the imagery . . . Joseph?

JOE: Yeah. Yeah. Absolutely. The imagery. It's not "Bobby Sox Baby Blues" but what is? *(Pause.)* I asked a question. Howie? *(Pause.)* You know, I don't even like to read anymore. I mean, they're all finished with their fucking books. And I will not finish mine. It's an ecological protest.

HOWARD: Of course you'll finish.

JOE: It suits Margo to think I will. It suits her to think I'm just having "trouble." That I'm "blocked." *(Pause.)* She'd prefer it if I was "a failed artist." Then she could console me. Then she could be understanding.

MARGO: She believes in you.

JOE: She's a wife. That's what wifes do. *(Pause.)* Still taking notes, writer boy? *(Pause.)* "Drinks too much. A second-rater on the talent circuit. A sell out . . . "

HOWARD: I never said any of that

JOE: Fuck you, writer boy.

HOWARD: Stop calling me that.

JOE: Do you want me to tell you the truth about your writing?

HOWARD: Well of course.

MARGO: Joseph.

JOE: *(Picks up what Howard was reading aloud from.)* "Cerise bougainvillea spills over the walls like a serape carelessly tossed by a woman rushing to her lover . . . " *(Looks up at Howard.)* Oh the heart quickens.

MARGO: He doesn't mean anything about your talent, Howard. I mean, the writing itself is . . . lovely . . . the imagery . . .

JOE: No one ever said the boy wasn't talented. But. Howard. Honey. You've got to get over all this romantic imagery bullshit and start to get real sex into your stuff or you're just going to be one of these professional virgins.

MARGO: Joseph, leave him alone.

JOE: I'm not questioning his talent. It has nothing to do with talent. But you need to get laid. Take my word, Howie. I've know you how many years? I love you, Howie. You know that. I wouldn't say it if I didn't love you. But until you get sex into it . . . you know what I'm saying . . . the whole thing is for shit. It's romance, for God's sake. Romance.

MARGO: Joseph—

JOE: Shut up, Margo. He doesn't need you. You can't be afraid all your life, Howie. I know what I'm talking about. I know. Jesus. A fuck is a fuck. You know what I'm saying? A fuck. A fuck. It's . . . nothing. It's just a fuck. You do it with anyone. It doesn't matter. She thinks it matters. She's fucked up. You know? You know what I'm saying? It's just a fuck. You could fuck . . . oh it doesn't matter. You can't be afraid of it. Terrible twisted things happen when you're afraid. You know what I mean, Howie? Is it clear? Is it clear yet? Hey, I love you, Howie. Howie. You know? C'mere. I love you.

MARGO: Howard?

HOWARD: It's O.K.

(He resists Joe's overture.)

JOE: Shit. Forget it. Forget I said a word.

(He gets a drink.)

MARGO: Do you have to have every drink that it occurs to you to have?

JOE: I'm Irish. It's in the genes.

MARGO: The doomed poet, part two.

JOE: Don't show off in front of the kid.

HOWARD: Hey, come on.

MARGO: You're being horrible and you're embarrassing him.

JOE: Miss Shit-upon.

MARGO: All right.

JOE: All right.

MARGO: All right.

JOE: All right!

(Exits.)

MARGO: I'm afraid.

HOWARD: What do you mean?

MARGO: That I'm going to have to leave him.

(Pause.)

But then you could have each of us to yourself. Isn't that what you really want, Howard? *(Pause.)* Why don't you and I go to Acapulco for a few

days? I won't seduce you, don't worry. *(Pause.)* Never mind. I understand.
(She starts to go.)

HOWARD: No you don't.

(Later. Margo and Mina enter and join Howard sunbathing.)

MINA: Oh God. That sun.

MARGO: Let's make a pact . . . that when we're older . . . sixty or sixty-five . . .
we'll go away together and we'll get fat and we won't do our hair. We'll
take cruises and wear orthopedic shoes and gossip and there won't be any
more men or desire or any of the whole fucking . . .

MINA: Margo . . . ?

MARGO: I'm kidding. I'm kidding. Really. Howard. Is there anything left in
that tube?

MINA: Margo, you ought to use a higher number. Fifteen at least this close to
the equator.

MARGO: I can take it.

MINA: No, it's people like you who have to worry the most. I don't want you
ending up looking like an old Moroccan handbag.
(They all laugh.)
Oh God I'm so relaxed! I just love this! I love it! Like three old girlfriends.
(Later.)

HOWARD: The bus to Mexico City comes in at seven. I should start down the
hill by six thirty.

MARGO: I hate it that you're leaving!

HOWARD: Career calls.

MARGO: You'll write? Letters?

HOWARD: Sure.

MARGO: Don't expect answers. We're in a backwater here.
(Joe enters, goes to the bar.)

MARGO: I put the lime tequila on ice, darling!

MINA: Why do you always forgive him?

MARGO: I don't always.

MINA: He was pounding on my door. I was terrified. I said: Go back to Margo!
Go sleep with your wife!

MARGO: Oh Mina, be quiet.

MINA: Margo. It's all ego. Oh forget it. I love you no matter what.
(They exit.)
*(Later. Joe puts Bruce Springsteen on loud and sings along. Howard comes
out of his room.)*

HOWARD: Could you make that lower?

JOE: *(Re: Springsteen.)* This man knows whereof he speaks.

HOWARD: Yeah. O.K. I want to go to sleep.

    (Joe sings along.)

    Joe, for Chrissakes!

    (He shuts off the music.)

    There are other people in the world.

JOE: Who are you to judge me?

HOWARD: I'm not judging you.

JOE: Yes you are. But I don't care. You're gone. Just one more person slipping away.

HOWARD: You are so full of shit.

JOE: And you . . . intense . . . sensitive. . . suffering . . . And always . . . looking.

HOWARD: You don't even know me! You have all these perceptions about me, you encourage me, you make me believe you recognize my talent but . . . it hasn't got anything to do with me. It's really all about you and how clever you are. "He's got this talented little friend, this little monkey who looks up to him and . . . and . . . " I don't even know whether to believe anything you ever said about me.

JOE: Oh I see. You mean . . . it was really . . . what . . . a projection of my own needs. Probably. Yeah. Or my own insecurities. Yeah. My own desires. What, Howard? Or do I really envy your talent? What, Howard? What's your theory?

HOWARD: I don't know. I don't know. I don't understand.

JOE: I see. Well you're probably right, Howard.

HOWARD: No. I don't know. I don't . . .

JOE: You want me to make it clear?

HOWARD: I . . . I don't know. I don't understand.

JOE: You want me to explain it to you?

HOWARD: Yes.

JOE: C'mere.

HOWARD: What for?

JOE: Don't be afraid.

HOWARD: I'm not.

JOE: Come on. C'mere. *(Joe has come close to Howard now and takes him in his arms and kisses him.)* O.K.? *(Joe backs off.)* Is it clear now?

    (Later. Margo and Joe appear as at the beginning, dancing to romantic Latin guitar music. Howard turns to look at them)

HOWARD: "Mist rises around them, music made manifest, music as mist, as magic. And I circle them, my longing so pure it pierces my heart yet leaves no blood, only tears."

MARGO: Howie? Join us? One last dance? No? Howie . . .

JOE: Howie? Honey? Once more? He's going.

MARGO: Write to us! We love you!

(Howard watches them dance for a long moment, then turns away.)

END ACT ONE

ACT TWO

A studio apartment in the West Village, dominated by a large bed. Behind it are a desk on which is a typewriter, empty Styrofoam cups, books, papers, a lamp. There are hundreds of books in piles on the floor. Howard enters from outside. He moves quickly around the room, straightening things. A few moments later the intercom buzzes. Howard presses a button on the wall.

HOWARD: Yes?

VOICE: Hi! It's me!

HOWARD: Come on up. Second floor.

(He presses the buzzer, continues straightening until he hears a knock at the door. He opens it.)

Oh hi.

VOICE: Hi.

HOWARD: I didn't think you were really going to come.

(Jackie enters.)

JACKIE: Well. Here I am.

(Howard watches Jackie as he looks the room over.)

HOWARD: My little cave.

(Jackie looks out the window.)

Northern exposure. Perfect for growing mold.

JACKIE: That other building is really close.

HOWARD: Lots of good apartments to look at. Very *Rear Window.*

JACKIE: Some guy is sitting there in his underwear.

HOWARD: Third floor?

JACKIE: Uh huh.

HOWARD: Pete.

JACKIE: You know him?

HOWARD: Huh? No. I heard someone call him that on the street so . . .

JACKIE: Maybe he watches you too.

HOWARD: Oh no. I'm invisible.

(Jackie continues his inspection of the room, notices the piles of books.)

JACKIE: You must really like to read.

HOWARD: Yeah. Books are . . . great.

JACKIE: Did you read all these?

HOWARD: Not yet.

JACKIE: Did you ever read anything by Colette? She's a French writer.

HOWARD: Yeah! Have you?

JACKIE: *Cheri.*

HOWARD: God isn't her prose incredible? Each sentence has such perfect shape. Each word is chosen with such . . .

JACKIE: Do you have any grass?

HOWARD: Oh do you want to smoke?

JACKIE: If you have.

HOWARD: Oh sure. I always have some. *(Howard finds a joint a gives it to Jackie.)* Oahu.

JACKIE: Huh?

HOWARD: Oahu. *(Re: the grass.)* Oahu. Hawaii.

JACKIE: Oh! Hawaiian!

(They pass the joint back and forth.)

HOWARD: Jackie, right?

JACKIE: Yeah. Harvey, right?

HOWARD: Howard.

JACKIE: Oh. Hi.

HOWARD: Hi. *(Pause.)* Are you still working at the Ballroom?

JACKIE: What do you mean?

HOWARD: You waited on me once.

JACKIE: Oh. Yeah. Right. Well . . . Actually, I'm going to be singing there soon. They're starting this midnight cabaret thing in the bar.

HOWARD: Oh you sing!

JACKIE: I have a whole act.

HOWARD: I'll bet you have a really sweet voice. I'll bet you sang in the church choir.

JACKIE: Saint Ignatius! How did you know?

HOWARD: I have my ways.

JACKIE: Uh huh. *Rear Window,* right?

HOWARD: I'm starving. You want something to eat?

JACKIE: No thank you.

HOWARD: Nothing?

JACKIE: I ate at the bar. That's supposedly why Gordon likes to go. Great chili, he says.

HOWARD: Would he be mad if he knew you came here?

JACKIE: Oh he's just mean and hideous to me. Really. He's like my father or something. I can never do anything by myself. Oh I don't even care. We never have any fun. All he wants to do is go to the bars.

HOWARD: When he has someone like you? Why?

JACKIE: You know what he does? He makes me go in alone and then he comes in later and watches who talks to me and then he makes me tell him what everyone said so he can have something on them. You know . . . how they come on, what they like to do, you know. Stuff. I don't know. I don't even like to think about it.

HOWARD: This sounds a little neurotic.

JACKIE: He's sick. I mean, who cares? You know? Plus, he's always sneaking these guys home when I'm not there and then completely denies it. I mean, there's these condoms everywhere and him and I aren't doing anything, period. So . . . But then if someone says hi to me in the streets, he goes crazy. He wants to know who he is, how do I know him. I mean, I don't do anything. So, you know, fuck him. *(Laughs. Re: grass.)* Oahu, huh? *(They laugh.)*

HOWARD: You're not from New York, are you?

JACKIE: Uh uh.

HOWARD: Midwest?

JACKIE: Midwest . . .

HOWARD: Let me guess. Ohio?

JACKIE: Ohio. Yeah.

HOWARD: And you sang in the church choir. And you were in the 4-H. You raised your own vegetables and there was a creek near where you lived and you fished. With your grandfather. *(Pause.)* I'm making it up.

JACKIE: Right.

HOWARD: Is your family still there?

JACKIE: Actually, my real parents were killed in this famous train crash when I was two months old . . .

HOWARD: Oh . . .

JACKIE: This woman named Jacqueline pulled me out of the train before it completely exploded. When I got adopted, they named me for her.

HOWARD: God. *(Pause.)* You know . . . I've sort of been . . . watching you.

JACKIE: When? Now?

HOWARD: For about a year.

JACKIE: Really?

HOWARD: I kept seeing you on the street all the time . . .

JACKIE: Where?

HOWARD: I don't know. Everywhere.

JACKIE: How come you didn't just come over?

HOWARD: I'm shy.

JACKIE: Oh sure. Uh huh.

HOWARD: I mean . . . I had many conversations with you in my mind in which I was extremely charming and in which you . . . but . . . Then tonight I was out getting the paper and I saw you go into the bar . . . and . . . I don't know . . . I decided I would just . . . throw caution to the wind . . . *(Pause.)*

JACKIE: Don't you just hate that place?

HOWARD: Yeah. I mean, I was never there before but . . .

JACKIE: Where do you usually go?

HOWARD: Well . . . I . . . I don't, I guess . . .

JACKIE: What do you mean?

HOWARD: I don't go out that much.

JACKIE: What do you do?

HOWARD: Stay in.

JACKIE: You must be seeing someone.

HOWARD: No. I mean . . . you know . . . not really . . . no . . . just . . . dreaming about a boy like you.

JACKIE: I'd love to stay in sometimes.

HOWARD: Actually, I can't stray too far from my desk. I'm a writer.

JACKIE: A writer?

HOWARD: Yeah.

JACKIE: What do you write?

HOWARD: You name it, I write it. I should have little cards made up that say that.

JACKIE: Are you famous?

HOWARD: I have my plans.

JACKIE: Me too! Everyone I know does! *(Laughs.)* Did you write any of these?

HOWARD: Well . . . sort of . . . yeah . . .

JACKIE: Really? Which?

HOWARD: *(Finds a paperback and hands it to Jackie.)* Don't laugh.

JACKIE: You really wrote this?

HOWARD: It's not such a big—

JACKIE: Wait a minute. This says by Hillary Rose.

HOWARD: Howard Rosenberg. Hillary Rose.

JACKIE: Is it porno?

HOWARD: No! It's a romance.

JACKIE: *(Reading the cover.)* First Love, First Death. On a vacation to Mexico, a woman falls under the spell of two charming American expatriates. Are they friends? Guides? Or do they want her for purposes more evil than anything she could have dreamed of?" *(He opens the book.)* "She stood at the closed window, looking down the hill at the lake. Cerise boojan . . .

HOWARD: Bougainvillea.

JACKIE: " . . . bougainvillea spilled over the walls like a ser . . . "

HOWARD: Serape. It's like a cape.

JACKIE: "Serape. . . . serape carelessly tossed by a woman rushing to her lover. She opened the window. Gardenia moonlight flooded the room. I want to be in love, she thought." *(He looks up at Howard.)* God, I'd use my real name.

HOWARD: *First Love, First Death* is not exactly what I had planned for my literary debut. But the kind of stuff I write, well . . . I can't really sell the . . . I mean, nobody . . . everybody . . . You have to appeal to a wide audience, see, and . . . I mean, if you want to make any money. I mean, if you want anyone to read what . . . I mean, if . . . I don't know what I mean. I mean . . .

(Pause.)

JACKIE: Don't be so nervous.

HOWARD: I think I'll roll another joint.

JACKIE: Actually, I should really go.

HOWARD: Oh.

JACKIE: Yeah.

HOWARD: Back to the bar?

JACKIE: God no.

(Pause.)

HOWARD: Do you . . . ?

JACKIE: Huh?

HOWARD: Do you . . . want to stay here? *(Pause.)* You could stay here tonight if you want.

JACKIE: Mm. I don't know . . .

HOWARD: Oh I didn't mean . . . you know . . . We don't have to do anything.

JACKIE: Huh?

HOWARD: I mean . . . we don't have to do anything.

JACKIE: What do you mean?

HOWARD: I mean . . . you could just . . . just stay. Just . . . stay here.

JACKIE: Really?

HOWARD: Well now that you're finally here . . . I'd hate to see you go. *(Pause.)* Really. Just . . . just stay.

JACKIE: Well . . .

HOWARD: Come on. It'll be nice. Come on. *(Pause.)* I have a down comforter.

JACKIE: You're weird.

HOWARD: Does that mean yes?

JACKIE: Yeah.

HOWARD: Good.

> (Lights change to indicate that time is passing. Howard takes off his clothes
> and gets into bed. Jackie hangs up his jacket, takes off his clothes, and gets
> into bed. Howard picks up a pad and is writing.)

HOWARD: "He spread his arms for me that first time: a bird ascending from
water . . ." (Pause. He thinks.) " . . . like a bird ascending from waves . . ."
(He makes this correction.) I've been writing this story about him for weeks
but what I'm really doing is listening for the sound of him coming up
the stairs. And then he's here and I'm just so much . . . lighter! Even when
he's not here, he's here. I'll be looking for something in the closet and
one of his shirts'll brush across my face and . . . nobody else knows that
smell but me. Hmm. (He writes this down.) " . . . but me . . . "

JACKIE: (Quick toke on a joint.) O.K. I walk into the club. Howie, are you listening?

HOWARD: I'm listening.

JACKIE: O.K. I walk into the club. Everybody freezes. Everybody wants to see
me. Everybody wants to touch me. They're straining at the ropes but . . .
(Another toke.)

HOWARD: I like to count the little hairs on his fingers. I like to feel the bones
in his feet . . . ankles. (He writes this down.) "The bones in his ankles,
like . . . "

JACKIE: . . . but my, you know, bodyguards keep them back and make this
aisle for me to walk down. O.K. Past the coat check, past the bar. I don't
even look at anyone. I just walk past them. And there's all this whispering . . . Jackie. There's Jackie.
(Another toke.)

HOWARD: What is really amazing is that my actual vision has changed. I actually see things in a different way. The whole world is like a backdrop for us.

JACKIE: O.K. And then I'm on the stage and they're all out there, this whole
place, all these face floating out there, waiting for me. I'm in the spotlight. You can hear them gasp. Just a baby pin spot. Just on my face.

HOWARD: I'm really happy.

JACKIE: And I don't move. I don't even move my arms. No expression at all.
And my hair is bleached platinum blond and I'm all in white. And then
this drumbeat. And just this perfect pin spot.
(Sings.)

"Mm, mm
Baby love
My baby love
I need you
Yes I need your love . . . "

HOWARD: You know what would be great: two black girls singing backup.

JACKIE: But with shaved heads . . .

HOWARD: Jackie and the Baldettes!

JACKIE: It could be so great! *(Pause.)* It's still raining.

HOWARD: I'm glad we don't have anyplace to go.

JACKIE: Me too.

HOWARD: I may never go out again. *(Pause.)* Except to collect my Pulitzer Prize. *(Pause.)* They don't deliver.

(Jackie laughs. Howard snuggles up to him, touches Jackie's hair. Jackie squirms.)

JACKIE: Please. It's so hideous.

HOWARD: You can hardly even see it.

JACKIE: Really?

HOWARD: If you squint, I mean.

JACKIE: Oh thanks. I almost died, you know.

HOWARD: O.K. O.K.

JACKIE: I should have plastic surgery.

HOWARD: Actually, the scar makes the rest of your forehead even smoother.

JACKIE: You're sick. *(Howard kisses the scar.)* While I was being operated on, they filled the whole hospital room with white balloons. I thought I woke up in heaven. *(Howard continues to embrace Jackie.)* Howie . . .

HOWARD: Huh?

JACKIE: Could you just not . . .

HOWARD: What?

JACKIE: I just don't feel like it. It's . . . *(Howard moves away.)* Now you're hurt.

HOWARD: You just said you didn't want to.

JACKIE: I just wanted to lay my head down for a second. I didn't . . .

HOWARD: O.K! *(Picks up a magazine.)*

JACKIE: You're mad at me.

HOWARD: I'm not mad at you.

JACKIE: I just don't feel like it. O.K?

(Pause.)

HOWARD: What'd Gordon do when you didn't feel like it?

JACKIE: Oh please, don't remind me.

HOWARD: I'd like to know.

JACKIE: No you wouldn't.

HOWARD: No. Really. I would.

JACKIE: Listen, I mean . . . God, if it wasn't for Gordy I never would've made it in New York in the first place. He got me a job, I moved into his apartment, I met his friends. He gave me a whole life! But he just wanted to have sex all the time. It was horrible. He was always poking at me and kissing me. I couldn't stand it. So I just laid there and let him do whatever he wanted. I didn't even have my own apartment, what was I supposed to do? He's a good manager though. He's still a good manager . . . *(Pause.)* But I hated being out all the time. I'd rather stay in with you.

HOWARD: Would you? Really?

JACKIE: Don't you believe me?

HOWARD: Well . . .

JACKIE: Howie!

HOWARD: I just like hearing you say it.

JACKIE: You're paranoid.

HOWARD: Mm hm.

JACKIE: You're so nice to me. Why are you so nice to me?

HOWARD: You know what else I like? I like to say: "Howard and Jackie."

JACKIE: "Howard and Jackie."

HOWARD: You look just like my great high school crush. God. John McVie. He had these incredible eyes. Just like yours. Al Pacino eyes. *(Pause.)* You know what we should do this summer?

JACKIE: What?

HOWARD: Sail to Positano.

JACKIE: Where's that?

HOWARD: The coast of Italy.

(He goes to his pile of books and brings out a large photo book of Italy.)

JACKIE: Positano . . .

HOWARD: I want to show you . . . *(Opens book.)* This is Positano.

JACKIE: Wow!

HOWARD: *(Turns pages as he talks.)* And this. And this.

JACKIE: God.

HOWARD: You rent a house for . . . you know . . . like nothing. *(Turns another page.)* Look. You don't even need furniture. Just a couple of hammocks. You drink wine out of goatskins. Pick figs. Fish. On Fridays you rent a motorbike and drive into Naples.

JACKIE: Hey, I become a cult favorite in the cabarets, then they beg for me in New York.

HOWARD: Set up a portable Olivetti under the trees and write and nap and . . . Positano. We are definitely going to Positano.

JACKIE: *(At photo.)* Can you see the house where you stayed before?

HOWARD: Oh I've never been there.

JACKIE: What? Really?

HOWARD: I never had anyone to go with before.

JACKIE: Oh come on . . .

HOWARD: I mean it. Before I met you . . . Before I met you . . . I don't know . . . I just never thought I'd even love anybody. I mean . . . I didn't think that there was anybody in this world that would . . . that would . . . let me. Do you know what I mean?

JACKIE: You're crazy.

(Lights change to indicate time passing. Howard gets up from his bed and goes to his desk. Jackie dresses and exits.)

HOWARD: *(Writing.)* "He appears on a plain of loneliness and announces without warning that he is mine. Years without choice, time misspent and desperate nights made acceptance necessary. And now he has unlocked me from my past. And him. Him. Perfectly him. Why him? His eyes as clear as his cheeks are luminous, as his upper lip fans out like angel wings." Hmm.

(Lights change to indicate time passing. Jackie enters from outside.)

JACKIE: God it's miserable out there.

HOWARD: Nice and warm in here.

JACKIE: Hi.

HOWARD: I have an idea for this story about this kid . . . they find his body in a dumpster . . . and then we trace him back from the time he came to New York . . .

JACKIE: *(He goes to mirror.)* I can't stand the way Terry cut my hair.

HOWARD: How'd the rehearsal go?

JACKIE: Fine. Is there any grass left?

HOWARD: In the bathroom.

JACKIE: *(Going to the bathroom.)* His tongue was hanging out the whole time. I thought he was going to cut my ear off.

HOWARD: It looks fine.

JACKIE: It's shorter on one side. *(Re: can of grass.)* Great. It's empty. Just seeds.

HOWARD: Really? Oh guess who called.

JACKIE: Who?

HOWARD: The famous Gordon.

JACKIE: How'd he get this number?

HOWARD: Are you avoiding him?

JACKIE: Is that what he said?

HOWARD: No.

JACKIE: Did he . . . ?

HOWARD: What?

JACKIE: Did he . . . say anything?

HOWARD: What do you mean?

JACKIE: Never mind.

HOWARD: Oh you know what he did say?

JACKIE: It doesn't matter what he said. He's a total liar, Howie.

HOWARD: He said he wanted to meet me.

JACKIE: He'll say anything. Really.

HOWARD: He said he's friendly with a couple of editors I might want to know.

JACKIE: Oh shit.

HOWARD: We're going to have coffee.

JACKIE: Coffee.

HOWARD: How come you never told me he had publishing connections?

JACKIE: Howie!

HOWARD: What?

> *(Pause.)*

JACKIE: I have to tell you something. *(Pause.)* I'm afraid you're going to hate me.

HOWARD: What?

JACKIE: And that you're not going to want to be with me anymore and that you're going to kick me out like everyone else and . . . *(Pause.)* I'm afraid.

HOWARD: Jackie . . .

JACKIE: O.K. *(Pause.)* I didn't go to the rehearsal this afternoon. Gordon and I bumped into this guy I . . . used to know. He owns this Italian restaurant in Dallas. You'd like him. Really. He reads too . . . and . . . well . . . *(Pause.)* See . . . there's these guys I know . . . You know, older guys and . . . and I . . . I go out with them sometimes for . . . I mean it's nothing . . . but . . . Like if they're from out of town or something and they're staying at the Sherry Netherland or the Park Lane . . . and sometimes, usually, it's just for dinner . . . They're always really important, these guys, you know . . . and I never get hurt or anything. It's safe, so . . .

HOWARD: Is this why Gordon wanted to meet me?

JACKIE: You don't understand. *(Pause.)* I . . . lied about . . . a couple of other things.

HOWARD: Like what?

JACKIE: Well . . . *(Pause.)* Like . . . everything.

HOWARD: What do you mean, everything?

JACKIE: Everything. I mean everything.

HOWARD: Give me an example.

JACKIE: Uh . . . *(Pause.)* You know my . . . the . . . accident?

HOWARD: The train crash. Yeah. So?

JACKIE: It . . . didn't exactly happen that way.

HOWARD: What do you mean?

JACKIE: It didn't exactly . . . happen.

HOWARD: It didn't happen?

JACKIE: No.

HOWARD: But . . . what about the scar?

JACKIE: It's not from that. It didn't happen. My parents aren't even dead. I sort of . . . made it all up.

HOWARD: Jackie, come on . . .

JACKIE: Oh yeah, that's another one. It's Fred.

HOWARD: Who's Fred?

JACKIE: Fred. Fred is my real name.

HOWARD: Fred?

JACKIE: Yeah.

HOWARD: But . . . why?

JACKIE: And I'm not from Ohio. God. I'm from Trenton, New Jersey.

HOWARD: Why? I don't understand.

JACKIE: Oh Howie . . . My life was just such shit, O.K? Where I lived . . . everything . . . was just like . . . a big nothing. And I just would get stoned and think about . . . you know . . . getting out of there. I mean . . . you see all these people on TV and in magazines and they're all . . . you know . . . really . . . interesting . . . *(Pause.)* And then I came to New York and two weeks after I got here I saw Andy Warhol at Boy Bar and I accidentally set my hair on fire and everyone was screaming and Andy took a Polaroid of me and I thought: God, this is it. *(Pause.)* I'm sorry, Howie. I'm really really sorry. *(Pause.)* Don't hate me. *(Pause.)* I've tried to be a good boy. *(Pause.)* I'm fucked up. *(Pause.)* But I'll never do it again because . . . because that'd really be bad. I mean . . . you know . . . now that you know and . . . and I know you know and . . . Well, I mean . . . I just swear . . . I just really swear . . .

HOWARD: You don't have to swear.

JACKIE: No?

HOWARD: No.

JACKIE: No?

HOWARD: No.

JACKIE: You're fantastic, Howie. *(Laughs.)* You are so great. *(Pause.)* It's still raining. *(Pause.)* Howie?

HOWARD: Uh huh.

JACKIE: I don't want to go out, do you? *(Pause.)* Let's just stay in, O.K? *(Pause.)* Howie?

HOWARD: O.K.

JACKIE: At least until it stops. *(He lays down, picks up a travel book.)* God. Positano. Wouldn't it be great? Positano You have the best ideas, Howie. I mean it. You really do. You really really really do.

(Lights change to indicate time passing. Howard writes and as he does so he imagines Jackie as part of the story.)

HOWARD: "There was a little street vendor named . . . Johnny . . . who did his grinding out of the Old Mill, number one Bowery. You know the place. Johnny engaged many a dalliance with horse and snort and friendly feels, swapping sweets for meats on the even exchange system. Poor Johnny, a sweet kid. He dealt a line of smiles at discount rates, a promise of peace in the combat zone, and carried a pair of pliers in case any of his A.M. customers gave him the screws: tableau vivant of the neat street life."

(Jackie enters and continues the story.)

JACKIE: "So for example, a gentleman walks up to me and he makes his proposition. He wants me to impersonate his dead son in football cleats and mesh hose. He tells me it's an All-American success story. Then he tells me his name. A gent from Congress, yeah. I'm thinking that next I gotta see a guy in the Justice Department who wants me to . . . ah, I can't say. But we do it with canned peaches. The consensus of opinion is that I live out on the street so my info never leaks. Nothing bothers me but dirt. In my line of work a clean nose is Paramount Pictures incorp. You think I want to end up old? These four walls provoke me deadly. I got a reputation to consider. I got prospects lined up till Thursday. Ah, life looks the same no matter how you look at it. A john's just a john, you know. Just another guy with a midnight itch."

(The lights change. Later. Jackie starts pulling off his clothes and shoes as if he has just come in.)

HOWARD: It's noon.

JACKIE: Uh huh. *(He stumbles into the desk.)*

HOWARD: Hey be careful!

JACKIE: Sorry, sir.

HOWARD: You're stoned.

JACKIE: No I'm not. *(He gets into bed.)* Could you please close the shutters.

HOWARD: Where were you?

JACKIE: Nowhere.

HOWARD: Nowhere. Right.

JACKIE: I walked around, O.K?

HOWARD: Till noon?

JACKIE: So?

HOWARD: You know I'm trying to finish this thing . . .

JACKIE: The thing about me?

HOWARD: I need peace and quiet. I don't want to be all emotional. I do not need this kind of aggravation.

JACKIE: I went to a party. With Gordon. O.K? Now can I go to sleep?
(Pause.)

HOWARD: How come I never get asked to these parties?

JACKIE: You'd rather stay home and write, remember?

HOWARD: I can just see you there. "Oh this guy I live with. He never wants to go out. We never have any fun . . . "
(Jackie jumps out of bed and starts putting on his clothes.)
What are you doing?

JACKIE: Leaving.

HOWARD: Leaving . . .
(Jackie continues dressing.)
Jackie . . .

JACKIE: You always have to talk about everything and then everything gets all ruined . . .

HOWARD: Oh everything is always getting ruined! Sex ruins everything. Talk ruins everything.

JACKIE: You ruin everything! *(He sits, sighs, half dressed.)* We never do have any fun.

HOWARD: We have fun . . .

JACKIE: You never want to do anything, Howard. You just want to stay at your desk . . .

HOWARD: I'm a writer! I have to write!

JACKIE: I'm only twenty-three years old! I don't want to stay home all the time and be your inspiration!

HOWARD: You can go out. I'm not saying—

JACKIE: Oh God, I can't stand this.

HOWARD: What?

JACKIE: Haven't you had enough? Why do you even want me here?

HOWARD: Because I love you.

JACKIE: You're such a liar.

HOWARD: I'm a liar?

JACKIE: You want me to tell you everything but you keep everything to yourself. You don't tell me anything.

HOWARD: I tell you things . . .

JACKIE: Oh what am I even doing with someone like you? You can't do anything for me. You can't help me get anywhere. The sex is . . .

HOWARD: What? The sex is what?

JACKIE: I don't want to hurt your feelings, Howie . . .

HOWARD: About what?

JACKIE: You don't know anything about it! Sex is . . . it's not kissing . . . Oh Christ! It's not all this love stuff! Oh never mind. I don't care!

HOWARD: Well you can always just move back in with Gordon.

JACKIE: Shut up!

HOWARD: Isn't that where you usually wind up?

JACKIE: I'm sorry I ever told you the truth.

HOWARD: Do you still have sex with him?

JACKIE: Who told you that?

HOWARD: I'm guessing.

JACKIE: Oh God. It was a hundred years ago.

HOWARD: He's hung up on you. This whole management thing is bullshit.

JACKIE: It is not.

HOWARD: Jesus, Jackie. He doesn't book you anywhere. What does he do?

JACKIE: What does he do? What do you do?

HOWARD: All right. Forget it.

JACKIE: Well you know what Gordon says? Gordon says I'm wasting my time with you. He says that you've had me long enough and that you're holding me back. You have to know people in the business. You have to know how to get them to like you so they'll do things for you. Gordon knows a lot of really important people he can introduce me to, people who can help me get places, people who own clubs and record companies—

HOWARD: Well of course! He's your pimp!

JACKIE: Fuck you.

HOWARD: Right.

JACKIE: As if you're so . . .

HOWARD: What? As if I'm so what?

JACKIE: Never mind. It doesn't matter.

HOWARD: Come on. I want to know.

JACKIE: Why are you being like this?

HOWARD: Like what? *(Pause.)* Like what?

JACKIE: You never even go out of the house! How do you even know anything about anything? You stay in all the time with your books. It's sick. You don't know any real people. You don't do anything but sit there and make things up. At least I go out. At least I have a career!

HOWARD: Oh your career! Your career! You don't rehearse, you don't perform. What career?

JACKIE: I hate you.

HOWARD: Fine.

JACKIE: I'm leaving.

HOWARD: Do what you want.

(Jackie packs a few things in a bag.)

Jackie . . .

(Jackie stands at Howard's desk, then throws Howard's papers to the floor.)

Jackie.

(Jackie leaves.)

Jackie!

(Howard walks slowly around the room, picks up a scarf of Jackie's, a couple of his magazines, a cassette tape he's left behind, as if trying to figure out what they are, as if there is something about Jackie that will be revealed in these objects. Then he starts to put the apartment back in order, closes the sofa bed, cleans up the papers Jackie threw. He sits at his desk and takes up his pen.)

HOWARD: "He leaves in a whirl of . . . with a great whoosh of . . . with a slam of the . . . " *(Pause.)* "He's gone . . . he goes . . . he leaves . . . He leaves, he goes, he's gone. And . . . and in the void his leaving leaves . . . In the remains of his . . . in what remains . . . " *(Pause.)*

(The lights change to indicate time passing. Howard gets dressed. The telephone rings and is picked up by the answering machine.)

HOWARD'S VOICE: "This is 228-7532. I can't come to the phone right now. Please leave a message at the sound of the beep.

JACKIE'S VOICE: Hi Howie! It's me!

(Howard looks at the phone, doesn't pick up.)

Come on. Pick up. I know you're home. I can see your light on.

(Howard turns off the light.)

Oh fuck!

(Jackie hangs up. Howard sits in the dark. A moment later the door buzzer rings and keeps ringing. Howard finally gets up to answer through the intercom.)

HOWARD: Who is it?

JACKIE: Howie?

HOWARD: Hello?

JACKIE: Can I come up? Please?

HOWARD: Yeah. O.K. *(He buzzes him in, then goes to the door).* Hi Fred!
>   *(Jackie enters.)*

JACKIE: Huh?

HOWARD: Isn't that your name?

JACKIE: You can call me Fred if you want.

HOWARD: No, I don't care. Jackie's fine.
>   *(Jackie is wearing an expensive-looking overcoat and suit and dark glasses.)*
>   What's with the glasses?

JACKIE: Oh I'm on these antidepressants and they sometimes make my eyes
>   sensitive to the light.
>   *(He takes them off.)*

HOWARD: Well keep them on.

JACKIE: It's all right. It doesn't matter. I look horrible either way.

HOWARD: You have a tan.

JACKIE: Oh yeah. I was away . . . *(Looks around.)* When d'you get an answer-
>   ing machine?

HOWARD: About a year ago.
>   *(Pause.)*

JACKIE: Did you finish reading all your books yet?

HOWARD: Actually, I figured out that if I read two a week for the rest of my
>   life I would still not finish. It was a very humbling thought that has still
>   somehow not stopped me from buying . . .

JACKIE: Don't be nervous.

HOWARD: I'm not.
>   *(Pause.)*

JACKIE: Where's my mirror?

HOWARD: I threw it away.

JACKIE: Why?

HOWARD: It had a crack.

JACKIE: You're crazy. You just tape it from the back. Oh you never knew what
>   to do with anything. I loved that mirror.

HOWARD: You look fine.

JACKIE: I need a haircut. *(Pause.)* Do you have any grass?

HOWARD: I stopped.

JACKIE: You stopped smoking?

HOWARD: Yeah.

JACKIE: You didn't stop smoking.

HOWARD: I did. Almost a year. Mister Health.

JACKIE: I woke up once and this guy was putting out a joint on my shoulder . . .
I'm going to quit too.
(Pause.)

HOWARD: You singing anywhere?

JACKIE: What? Oh. Yeah. The Ballroom. Right. *(Pause.)* You seeing anyone?

HOWARD: Not really. You?

JACKIE: Me? Yeah. Sure. You know. *(Pause.)* Howie . . . Can I . . . can I stay
here? Just for tonight?

HOWARD: You want to stay here?

JACKIE: Please?

HOWARD: Why can't you stay with your friend Gordon?

JACKIE: Well . . . Yeah I . . . Oh God . . .

HOWARD: What's the matter?

JACKIE: Well I sort of freaked out. I mean, Gordon started bringing these really
young guys around and—

HOWARD: You don't have to explain anything to me.

JACKIE: Can I just lay down here for a second . . .
(Sits on sofa.)

HOWARD: Hey come on . . .
(Pause.)

JACKIE: You're still mad at me.

HOWARD: I'm not mad at you.

JACKIE: I guess I was sort of a shit. *(Pause.)* You still think about me, don't
you? No matter what I did? *(Pause.)* Oh come on. Not even a little? Be
honest.

HOWARD: So?

JACKIE: You never forget your first love, right? *(Pause.)* Hey, remember that
place we were going to go?

HOWARD: Positano?

JACKIE: Positano.

HOWARD: Yeah . . .

JACKIE: I was there.

HOWARD: What?

JACKIE: I went.

HOWARD: You went?

JACKIE: This . . . you know . . . guy I know has this factory in Naples and I went with him and we were driving along and I saw this road sign. This is my Positano tan, as a matter of fact.

HOWARD: You went to Positano . . .

JACKIE: It was no big deal.

HOWARD: What do you mean?

JACKIE: Hot and humid.

HOWARD: I don't think I want to hear this.

JACKIE: And the water tasted horrible. And our house had rats in the roof. *(He laughs.)* My friends said it was the stuff of tragedy. *(Pause.)* What've you been doing, Howie?

HOWARD: Nothing much. You know. The regular stuff. Writing. Nothing.

JACKIE: Are you famous yet?

HOWARD: Oh any second now.

JACKIE: Did you ever finish that book?

HOWARD: Actually, I just sold it.

JACKIE: Really?

HOWARD: No applause please.

JACKIE: Is it all about me? Come on.

HOWARD: You're in it.

JACKIE: O.K., so you're on the cover of *People* and then they interview me and I tell them I was your inspiration and then there's this big expose and then you sue me and then I countersue. Oh this is going to be so great. Are you rich?

HOWARD: Based on the time I put in, I guess I was paid about six cents an hour.

JACKIE: Oh.

HOWARD: No lawsuits. Sorry.

JACKIE: But when the movies buy it . . . *(Pause.)* I'm kidding! *(Pause.)* Would you read it to me? *(Pause.)* Please? *(Pause.)*
(Howard gets the manuscript. Jackie gets comfortable on the bed.)
What's it called?

HOWARD: Here. *(Shows Jackie the manuscript.)*

JACKIE: *Life in Positano* by Howard Rosenberg. You know what you should do, Howie? You should change it to Naples.

HOWARD: It doesn't matter where it is. The characters don't go anywhere. *(Leafs through the manuscript as Jackie leans back.)* The beginning is sort of . . . All right, all right. I'll just start from the beginning. *(He reads something to himself.)* O.K. *(Straightens the papers.)* You ready? *(Jackie doesn't answer.)*

Jackie? *(He looks at Jackie, who has fallen asleep. Howard closes the manu-script.)* Right.

END ACT TWO

ACT THREE

Howard and Martin's upper west side apartment. The bedroom. Howard is packing a small suitcase, mostly with manuscripts and papers.

HOWARD: Do I really want to go?

MARTIN: What do I win if I guess right?

HOWARD: No. I don't think I do.

MARTIN: Howie. For Godsake. It's all you've been talking about.

HOWARD: That was before they asked me. Now that they've asked me it seems like I've made my point. Actually going . . . I mean . . . actually going . . . you know . . . actually going . . . Seems sort of . . . I don't know . . . Slavish.

MARTIN: I think you are a complete wacko. And that is my professional opinion.

HOWARD: Thank you, doctor. *(Pause.)* I have to pack.

MARTIN: I thought you weren't going.

HOWARD: I just wanted to register my disapproval. And now that I have, I can go with a clear conscience.

MARTIN: I'm billing you for a full hour.

HOWARD: All right. So I go. They actually make the movie. The movie is a huge hit. I make an unconscionably enormous amount of money and reap critical acclaim as well. All my wants are met by people of extraordinary beauty who keep imploring me to enjoy life and asking if they can be of any assistance in helping me to do that. And here I am, there I am . . . I am just this book person, this pathetic little worm, this homonculus . . . is that the right word . . . this homo nucleus . . . is that the right word— this homo something . . .

MARTIN: Now you've got it: this homo something.

HOWARD: No but seriously. Don't you think people are going to be throwing themselves at my feet?

MARTIN: Is that why you're going?

HOWARD: Mmm . . . the groveling, the currying of favors. What do you think people'll offer me? What kind of degrading spectacles will they make of themselves in order to get in good with me? To what low levels will they sink so I'll think of them when I'm writing the screenplay? Oo, I have to write this down. You you and you but not you. Yes. You others will just have to commit suicide. What I can't figure is how people bear the shame once they don't succeed in getting the thing they've debased themselves to get.

MARTIN: But how do they bear it when they do succeed?

HOWARD: Success is its own reward.

MARTIN: I think it's a good deed that's its own reward. I know it's a fine ethical point but . . .

HOWARD: Marty.

MARTIN: What?

HOWARD: I love you.

MARTIN: Ah.

HOWARD: I mean . . . who in this world but you even thinks in terms of fine ethical points? *(Pause.)* Really. I do. I love you.

MARTIN: My patients keep saying that. What are they talking about? What does it mean?

HOWARD: I do. You're everything I'm not.

MARTIN: You don't love me for that, you resent me for it.

HOWARD: I resent having such a good opinion of you when you don't have the same of me. You think my concerns are trivial. You think my pain is shallow. You hate the fact that I'm a Jew.

MARTIN: And that you're gay. You left that out.

HOWARD: When I look back to that year with Jackie. The basement year. God, if I'd been with him when my book came out . . . Well, the money would be gone, that's for sure. We would've smoked half of it away and the other half would've gone to buying dance tapes. Just my luck to be rescued by Dr. Right.

MARTIN: I hate it when you say that.

HOWARD: Which part do you hate? That I'm lucky? That you rescued me? That you're right? I mean. I mean. Come on. We are a pretty neat couple, aren't we? I'm serious. Look at everyone else around us. Joined at the hip. Or trying to be . . . And then miserable because the other one is so . . . something that they don't like and want to change but anyway they don't and there they are . . . stuck in the myth they've created about themselves. *(Pause.)* We, on the other hand, are the perfect American couple. Independent. Ambitious. And we have dinner home three nights a week. He's shaking his head. I mean it, honey. We have what everyone wants. We're what couples aspire to be. And when Gavin does the movie . . . Ah . . . *(Pause.)* What?

MARTIN: What?

HOWARD: You're looking at me.

MARTIN: You really think Gavin will play a homosexual?

HOWARD: Well he should. He is a homosexual.

MARTIN: You don't know that.

HOWARD: He is totally queer!

MARTIN: Mister Macho Action Hero?

HOWARD: I rest my case.

MARTIN: All right, for the sake of argument, let's say he is.

HOWARD: Oh is this an argument?

MARTIN: If he is, isn't that even more reason for him not to do it?

HOWARD: You never think I can get anything done!

MARTIN: That's not true. I'm just trying to inject a little—

HOWARD: I'm serious! Cut it out! *(Pause.)* Look. He requested the meeting. He read my book and requested the meeting. Why would he request a meeting and pay for my airfare if he wasn't interested?

MARTIN: Oh Howie . . . Your airfare?

HOWARD: Yes. My airfare.

MARTIN: O.K. Fine.

HOWARD: And I am going to be so well prepared, so brilliantly persuasive, so lucid in my arguments, that whatever lingering doubts he has will simply turn to mist.

MARTIN: This is sounding more like a seduction every minute.

HOWARD: Oh right.

   (Pause.)

MARTIN: *(Pause.)* When are you coming back? *(Pause.)* You haven't answered me.

HOWARD: What did you ask? Oh. About coming back?

MARTIN: Yeah.

HOWARD: You think I won't?

MARTIN: As any schoolboy knows, the correct answer is: I'm coming back on "fill in the blank."

HOWARD: No, really. Why do you think I won't?

MARTIN: Because I know you.

HOWARD: You know my habits, doctor. And that's not the same thing.

MARTIN: All right, Howard.

   (Pause.)

HOWARD: Why don't you tell me why you think I won't come back?

MARTIN: Why don't you just say what's on your mind?

HOWARD: Oh. Yes of course. Yes, doctor. I'm "avoiding the painful truth." That's it. I'm avoiding the painful truth. No, no. No, no. I'm "in denial." That's it. Yes. I'm in denial. *(Pause.)* Cut it out! I'm going and I'm coming back. *(Pause.)* I am going. And I am coming back.

MARTIN: O.K.

(Pause.)

HOWARD: You're not convinced

MARTIN: Then convince me.

HOWARD: You really think I might not come back.

MARTIN: It's been known to happen.

HOWARD: Why so insecure, doctor?

MARTIN: Because you make the rules and you change the rules.

HOWARD: Is that what you think I do?

MARTIN: That is what you do. And then you get battered by the world and I'm supposed to be the shore you get washed up on. Well, you know, you're not the only one in this family who gets to entertain second thoughts. *(Pause.)* Christ, Howard, you won't even tell me when you're coming back.

HOWARD: But look, all I'm taking is my writing . . .

MARTIN: Just don't do anything on my account. Don't—

HOWARD: No, I want to know why you—

MARTIN: Wait. Don't. Don't make me a part of it. I don't want to be the reason you think you don't do things.

HOWARD: What things?

MARTIN: Come back because you did what you went out there to do, not because you think you owe it to me, not because you think I expect it.

HOWARD: What's wrong with someone doing something because of someone else?

MARTIN: What's wrong is that someone is usually fooling and someone is usually being fooled.

HOWARD: We have a life together, don't we?

MARTIN: So far.

HOWARD: Don't you think we're going to be together forever?

MARTIN: I don't know. Do you?

HOWARD: I don't know.

(Pause.)

MARTIN: What time is your plane?

HOWARD: I don't have to go.

MARTIN: You're scared, aren't you?

(Pause.)

HOWARD: You're very strict, Marty.

MARTIN: I thought you liked it.

HOWARD: Well I do. Sometimes. And sometimes . . .

MARTIN: *(Pause.)* Honey. Be honest. *(Pause.)* Come on. This relationship . . . these years with me . . . This hasn't ever really been what you've wanted, has it? *(Pause.)* Come on. You've got a plane ticket in your hand and your bag is packed. What better time for the truth?

HOWARD: Well . . . but . . . *(Pause.)* I thought we had everything.

> *(Pause.)*
>
> *(Howard takes his bag and walks to the next scene with it, puts on a black leather jacket, deposits the bag outside the door of Gavin's house on the beach at Malibu. A living room that opens onto a deck overlooking the ocean. Howard sits down on the sofa, where Angel is holding forth.)*

ANGEL: I can't stand to have people I don't know touching me. I'm a very sensitive person. I mean, my actual literal actual skin is extremely sensitive to anyone's touch. You should see me after I've had sex. I'm bruised all over even if it's been a totally like normal scene. Sometimes I bleed. Oo. Scary. My dermatologist says it has something to do with my blood vessels being close to the surface. The House of Windsor has a history of the same problem and my ancestors are English so . . . you may bow down and kiss my ring. *(Pause.)* I read your book. Oh right! Like that's a big deal. Like hundreds of other people haven't read it too.

HOWARD: Hundreds?

ANGEL: Oh . . . Well . . . you know . . . thousands. Millions, I don't know. Millions?

HOWARD: Let's stay with thousands.

ANGEL: But . . . hundreds of thousands.

HOWARD: Hundreds of thousands.

ANGEL: Yeah. *(Pause.)* The boy. Johnny, right? The singer?

HOWARD: Johnny, yeah.

ANGEL: I understand this boy.

HOWARD: You do.

ANGEL: I'm reading, I'm thinking: How does this writer know about me?

HOWARD: No. Really?

ANGEL: I love that scene where Johnny's singing. I mean, the way you described the spotlight. Makes me want to howl.

> *(Gavin enters, unobserved, and watches for a moment.)*

ANGEL: I would love to play that part

HOWARD: Oh you're an actor.

ANGEL: It wouldn't be acting. Just turn on the camera and follow me around.

GAVIN: Angel.

ANGEL: Yeah?

GAVIN: You're bothering Mr. Rosenberg.

ANGEL: I'm not bothering anyone. *(To Howard.)* Am I bothering you?

GAVIN: What're you doing?

ANGEL: Nothing.

GAVIN: Well go do something.

ANGEL: I am doing something.

GAVIN: What're you doing?

ANGEL: I'm talking.

GAVIN: Go do something else.

ANGEL: Yeah. Yeah. O.K. I'm going to bed. *(To Howard.)* Nice . . . uh . . . nice shirt

HOWARD: Uh huh.

> *(Angel exits)*

GAVIN: My sister's son. She wanted him off the streets. So he's out here with me for a year. Looking for a purpose. *(Pause.)* You've written some little book here.

HOWARD: You read the whole thing?

GAVIN: I've got whole passages committed to memory, you nut.

HOWARD: Oh. Right. Right. You requested my presence.

GAVIN: Do you think I invite unknown writers to my home that I don't know if I haven't read their book?

HOWARD: I guess not.

GAVIN: I don't like most of the writers out here. Or let me put it another way: I am suspicious of them as a breed. I don't have that feeling about you. *(Pause.)* Don't you want to know why?

HOWARD: Tell me.

GAVIN: I'll tell you later. *(Laughs.)* I'm in recovery from several different substances so I won't offer you what a host usually does. I don't know if Angel offered you anything. Speed is his drug of choice but he's clean while he's here.

HOWARD: You promised his mother.

GAVIN: That's right. *(Pause. With Howard's book.) Life in Positano.* A romance for our times: yearning . . . fruitless pursuit . . . doom.

HOWARD: So. You requested my presence.

GAVIN: You're an articulate guy. What do you see as your purpose as a writer?

HOWARD: To speak the truth.

GAVIN: Ah.

HOWARD: And to have it reach people.

GAVIN: Of course.

HOWARD: And to have people respond.

GAVIN: That's fascinating. But . . . People? People in general?

HOWARD: I don't want to limit myself by defining my audience.

GAVIN: Smart.

HOWARD: Just because I have gay characters in my novel, for example, doesn't mean that I should be thought of as a gay writer.

GAVIN: But you can see how people might draw that conclusion.

HOWARD: Oh it's very convenient to categorize me that way. It's also a way to marginalize me, to put me on the fringe, to make it easy not to take me seriously, not to consider me at all, to reduce me, to view me as a silly little queer whose concerns are no concerns of quote regular people, unquote.

GAVIN: Very interesting. But do you think straight people can identify with gay characters?

HOWARD: Two of the people in my book happen to be gay. There's nothing in their relationship that's strange or unknown to straight people.

GAVIN: Right. Good point. Except all that cock-to-cock stuff.

HOWARD: In terms of the emotions involved.

GAVIN: Are you one of these gay men who believe gay people are the same as straight people?

HOWARD: In most ways they are.

GAVIN: Hm. But now I'm wondering. Why make the characters gay at all?

HOWARD: But that is an implicitly homophobic question. Not that I'm saying you're homophobic but—

GAVIN: No, it's a good point.

HOWARD: But it's like asking what Hamlet would be if the main character wasn't a prince.

GAVIN: Very perceptive comment. Very interesting. But isn't it well . . . naïve to think that writing about gay people is something that is necessarily going to interest straight people? Isn't it enough to reach your own kind? Or are you one of those gay men that hates gay men?

HOWARD: I want people to take their heads out of the sand.

GAVIN: So you can rub their faces in it?

HOWARD: I do not see any glory in being part of the great and horrible tradition of gay writers who write about men and women when they really mean to write about men and men or women and women. And I don't see any glory either in writing about two men just so two other men can read it. All right. I admit it. I want everyone to love me.

GAVIN: Howard, you have come to the right place.

(They laugh.)

My agent thinks I ought to do your book. He thinks the public is tired of seeing me dodge bullets. He thinks the public wants to see me in a love story.

HOWARD: It sounds like you don't agree.

GAVIN: I'm suspicious of them.

HOWARD: Agents or love stories?

GAVIN: Both, wise guy.

HOWARD: And the question is: Can you afford to be suspicious of either?

GAVIN: My agent doesn't think so.

HOWARD: No, he wouldn't.

GAVIN: *(Laughs.)* No he wouldn't.

HOWARD: I agree with you. Does that surprise you?

GAVIN: Most people agree with me.

HOWARD: I mean about romance. It's a dead end.

GAVIN: That's not what your book says.

HOWARD: Read it again. That's exactly what it says.

GAVIN: An anti-romance?

HOWARD: A warning.

GAVIN: Are you trying to talk me out of doing your book?

HOWARD: Oh no. I think you should do it.

GAVIN: I'm teasing you. The problem is . . . Look. O.K. So I play the tormented drunk with the beautiful wife but—

HOWARD: No. You play Bobby.

GAVIN: The queer?

HOWARD: It's the star part. Of course you should play it.

GAVIN: Now why would I want to take a chance like that?

HOWARD: To earn your place in history.

GAVIN: I've already got that.

HOWARD: But as a real hero, not a screen hero. Brave, unafraid to face danger, risking all for what you believe in.

GAVIN: Oh do I believe in something?

HOWARD: Do it so maybe men like you won't have to have "nephews" like Angel.

GAVIN: What if I took the gamble and lost? What if I went down in flames?

HOWARD: You honestly think the public wouldn't come out to see you do this?

GAVIN: If they did, it would be the last time. *(Pause.)* Because, you see, the public believes in men in drag. The public believes in men with AIDS. The public believes there shouldn't be job discrimination and maybe some of them even believe in equal rights, maybe. The public does not believe in men in love.

HOWARD: But—

GAVIN: Ah ah ah ah. But. Yes. You're right to object. But . . . isn't it the emotions that you're really writing about? Hear me out. Isn't your real point this "anti-romance" as you call it? This story is universal. And the beauty of it is, almost nothing would have to be changed to make it work. Oh and by the way . . . that they don't go to Positano. That is a great touch. O.K., so let's say Johnny is a girl . . . Humor me for a minute. She's a waitress and not a waiter. She can still be called Johnny. You see what I'm getting at. It's a retyping job. They can rewrite your script at Studio Duplicating! *(Pause.)* At least think about it.

HOWARD: I don't think so.

GAVIN: Will you think about it?

HOWARD: It doesn't seem . . .

GAVIN: Will you promise me at least to think about it?

HOWARD: Well . . .

GAVIN: I'm only asking you to think about it. *(Pause.)* Let me get you a glass of wine. *(He pours Howard some wine.)*

HOWARD: Those seagulls certainly make a racket. *(Pause.)* This is really not at all what I was expecting.

GAVIN: The course of true love never did run smooth. *(Pause.)* Are you yourself a romantic? I mean, as a person.

HOWARD: Not very. What about you?

GAVIN: Me?

HOWARD: Does the mood have to be just so . . . or do you take it where you find it?

GAVIN: I don't usually take anything. People usually make me offers.

HOWARD: That's right. You're a movie star. I forgot.

GAVIN: You want material? I could give you material.

HOWARD: Are you currently attached?

GAVIN: I get my needs met on a daily basis, if that's what you mean.

HOWARD: Is that how you live in this town as a homosexual?

GAVIN: There aren't many people who would ask that question.

HOWARD: But that's why you asked me here. So we could have this conversation.

GAVIN: Interesting.

HOWARD: What have you had to give up to live this way?

GAVIN: Nothing I wanted very badly.

HOWARD: But what about who you really are?

GAVIN: Who I really am is nobody's business but my own.

HOWARD: Aren't you lonely?

GAVIN: Yes, of course. Aren't you?

HOWARD: Well . . . yes but—

GAVIN: Well then, you know.

> *(Pause.)*

HOWARD: Can you be in love?

GAVIN: Who says I'm not in love?

HOWARD: Are you?

GAVIN: Ah. Writer digs for secrets of the stars. *(Pause.)* I just refuse to be defined by other people.

HOWARD: But everybody thinks you're straight. You define straightness.

GAVIN: You've got to admit . . . there's a lot more mileage in it. *(Pause.)* Look, I simply do not consider a hard cock in my mouth as the defining experience of my life. *(Pause.)* Come on, no more business . . . *(Pause.)*

HOWARD: Doesn't your air-conditioning work?

GAVIN: Christ, I know. This fucking palace cost six point five and I still have to sleep with the windows open.

HOWARD: I thought maybe I was running a fever.

GAVIN: Some people have a higher body temperature. I read it. In a book. By some writer.

HOWARD: The breed that breeds suspicion.

GAVIN: You mind a personal question?

HOWARD: Try me.

GAVIN: How come if you're so hot you're still wearing that jacket?

HOWARD: Because it looks so great.

GAVIN: Yeah. I had my eye on it the second you walked in.

HOWARD: It was a birthday present.

GAVIN: You have a generous friend.

HOWARD: From me to myself.

GAVIN: Yeah. I had my eye on it right away.

HOWARD: I didn't mean to buy it. I always thought a jacket like this was . . . obvious.

GAVIN: Uh huh.

HOWARD: But as soon as I tried it on . . .

GAVIN: Something changed your mind.

HOWARD: I got a hard-on.

> *(Gavin laughs.)*

GAVIN: So now you're a new man, huh?

    (Pause.)

HOWARD: It is hot, isn't it?

GAVIN: It's cooler upstairs. *(Pause.)* I sleep with the windows open.

    (Pause.)

HOWARD: Well . . . Hmm . . . I don't want to lead you on.

GAVIN: Oh I like being lead on.

HOWARD: No, no, no. I wouldn't want you to think that I was . . . *(Pause.)* Available.

GAVIN: You breaking my heart so soon?

HOWARD: I just don't want to be responsible for . . . *(Pause.)* I mean . . . I am available. In a certain way . . . but . . . *(Pause.)* Look, you seem like a decent guy. *(Pause.)* Am I right? Are you a decent guy?

    (Gavin takes out a little cocaine.)

GAVIN: For not leading me on.

HOWARD: You see . . . *(He snorts a line.)* I live with someone. *(Long pause.)* So . . .

GAVIN: So you're a wife.

HOWARD: What?

GAVIN: You're telling me you're a wife.

HOWARD: Why do you put it like that?

GAVIN: Just trying it out. *(He looks Howard up and down.)* That jacket gives you a hard-on, huh? *(He laughs.)*

HOWARD: I'll probably be sorry I said that.

GAVIN: You won't be sorry. *(Pause.)* You trust me?

HOWARD: Well . . .

GAVIN: Yeah. You do. I can tell.

HOWARD: You seem . . . like a . . .

GAVIN: I like how your ass looks in those pants.

HOWARD: Uh huh.

GAVIN: You don't have to be afraid of me. I have something you're going to like.

HOWARD: You don't know what I like.

GAVIN: Sure I do.

HOWARD: You don't know anything about me. *(Pause.)* You think you know who I am?

GAVIN: I read your book.

    (Pause.)

HOWARD: Tell me.

    (Pause.)

GAVIN: Pussy.

HOWARD: What?

GAVIN: I said: pussy.

HOWARD: Come on.

GAVIN: Pussy. *(Pause.)* Puss puss.

HOWARD: Hey.

GAVIN: Pss pss pss. *(Pause.)* C'mere.

HOWARD: A starstruck faggot. Is that who you think you're talking to?

GAVIN: Puss puss.

HOWARD: Don't call me that.

GAVIN: Aren't you a pussy?

HOWARD: Fuck you.

GAVIN: I thought you were gonna be my pussy.

HOWARD: Cut it out.

GAVIN: C'mere. C'mon. *(Pause.)* C'mon. *(Pause.)* I wanna tell you something.

HOWARD: What?

GAVIN: *(Gavin pulls him closer, puts his hands on Howard's waist.)* Mmm. You know . . . this jacket . . . It sort of gives me a hard-on too.

HOWARD: *(Laughs.)* Meow.

GAVIN: *(Gavin keeps his hands on Howard.)* Honey. I know how you feel. You want to be loyal to the cause. Hey, what's the cause done for you lately? You know what I'm saying? You don't have to be gay. Why limit yourself? Why cut your career off at the knees? A story is a story. Emotions are universal. People are the same inside. Love has no gender. People do what they have to do. *(Pause.)* Think about it. *(Pause.)* Will you think about it?

HOWARD: Fuck you, O.K?

GAVIN: Oh, sweetheart. I can barely remember what it's like to be as hungry as you are. *(Pause.)* I'll be waiting for your answer.

(Gavin exits. Howard stands there for a moment, then picks up a copy of his book and, furious, tries to tear it in two. He walks out onto the terrace overlooking the beach. He stands looking at the sea for a long moment. Angel comes out. Howard sits down. Angel looks at the beach.)

ANGEL: Sometimes he likes it if I come and sometimes he likes it if I don't come. I'm undecided myself which I like better. If you don't come you can go with a lot of different guys and the financial rewards increase exponentially. *(Pause.)* Not that I do, I'm not crazy. *(Pause.)* AIDS. Aa! *(Pause.)* The other way—personal orgasms, I mean—you could get something out of it, you know, pleasure, release, a good night's sleep. *(Pause.)* I personally don't place a high pleasure thing on coming. Actually, in my experience, it hurts. I don't mean Gavin. He don't hurt me. He don't mean to, I mean. Oh he don't know what he does to me. I mean, he don't know cause I don't let him know. *(Pause.)* A boy's got to have secrets because if they know everything you are yesterday's news and you cease to be of interest . . . your level of intrigue plummets . . . they don't want to touch. *(Pause.)* I'm nothing to him, anyway. He just wants me to be here for when he's in the mood. *(Laughs.)* So I'm sitting on his face one time . . . I tell him: You like it so much, put me on a retainer, man. He laughed at me. *(Pause.)* He's loaded, the lousy fuck. He is too. A lousy fuck, I mean. I mean . . . I mean . . . I go to see his movies, you know, and he's like fantastic, he's so hot . . . those eyes . . . But in the actual flesh . . . I mean . . . in the actual bedroom and in the actual bed and in the actual, actual flesh . . . He is out of it. He starts like it's gonna be the Fuck of Life and then it's over and I'm left there in a state of high anticipation. *(Pause.)* I wish Gavin kept drugs here. He's scared of getting caught with a fucking gram or something. Like anyone cares. Like anyone would even arrest him. Like it fucking matters when he blows. Me they'd lock up. Me they'd throw in with a bunch of AIDS-related cheap street shit and then I'm worth nothing to Gavin. I got a reputation to protect. I got the appropriate face on the appropriate body. I'm an important commodity. *(Pause.)* I put in a lot of time perfecting my instincts seeing as how there's no particular training for my line of work. The School of Temptations, maybe. The Seven Temptations of Saint Anthony. Something . . . *(He laughs. Pause.)* I dig guys that do men. It's hot, you know. Cocks and stuff. It's fun. Gays is a whole other story. It's creepy. It's like disgusting. Gavin is an actual one hundred per cent homo. Like he sometimes takes me in his arms and kisses me. I let him, you know, yeah, I mean it's his dime but I'm thinking: Fuck, is he putting me down or what? The thing is: How can I make this clear to him? Because I have to establish my boundaries, even if he is who he is. *(He rolls his pants at the waist until they are tight in the crotch.)* When you hustle on Santa Monica Boulevard you like hitch your pants up and show what you got. It's advertising. That's how I met Gavin. He picked me out. He said he liked my display efforts. He said he wanted to get to know me better. *(Pause.)* I did him in the hallway before we even got upstairs. He liked my style, he said. He said let's do it again. So I'm sitting on his face and I say: Put me on a retainer basis. He got a kick out of that. *(Pause.)* I like the beach. *(Pause.)* But Gavin don't wanna go steady. Gavin wants to fuck 'em and then . . . you know . . . *(Pause.)* He's pretty cool. In the movies. In bed . . . he tastes funny . . . like . . . you know when you suck a penny? *(Pause.)* He says he's putting me to work soon. Says he's gonna make me honest. Give me a job in the movies. I said: You ever seen *The Studs of Santa Monica?* You can rent it. I'm in the hot-tub scene. Gavin says: Join a union. Be something. Stand on your own two feet. *(Pause.)* Where's he think I been all my life anyway? Pisses me off. Working to fulfill my dreams, you know. Like anyone. Jesus. He's fulfilled his so what the fuck? Right? Guy's got no compassion. *(Pause.)* He's got problems. I mean, it's mental, you know. Like I think he hates being homo. I know what he means. It's like, what's it get you, being homo? Or gay, you know? I don't even say I'm gay. I do men, yeah, but that's not the same thing. Like I would never love a man. That's what separates me from the hard core. *(Pause.)* Hey I got a great idea. You're a writer. Write me a way out of this. Write . . . how I get home from here. Write about me living with my romantic double. Give me great sex that feels good too. Give me a lover that fucks to Metallica. And a big contract. And reserved seats everywhere. And . . . you know . . . everything else. *(Pause.)* Look at those birds. The shit they have to go through to get a lousy fucking fish. *(Takes something out of his pocket.)* You do crack? Come on. We'll go on the beach. Gavin is such a fucking old lady. You're gonna like this, man. Makes you feel so good. You're high on this . . . you don't want nothing. *(He lights it and inhales.)* You only want more.

END OF PLAY

Carry the Tiger to the Mountain

Cherylene Lee

INTRODUCTION

by David Dower, Artistic Director, The Z Space Studio

Over the past seven years as the Artistic Director of The Z Space Studio in San Francisco, I have been fortunate to work in the presence of many gifted and committed artists of the contemporary American theater. The Studio nurtures new voices, new works, and new audiences for Bay Area theater. For much of that time, much of the best of what has emerged from The Z Space can be traced back to Cherylene Lee.

Carry the Tiger to the Mountain is just one of the many gifts she's given us, but it is the one that has touched me most deeply. I will never forget the complicated emotional paces I went through as the final blackout faded on the Contemporary American Theater Festival's 1998 production. In the very unlikely setting of Shepherdstown, West Virginia, this play raised a whole host of questions for each of us and we turned to our neighbors immediately to discuss them. Improbably, given the location, the audience was as culturally diverse as any audience you'll find in an urban setting. The lobby was buzzing with discussions of race, of justice, of the presence and influence of cultural heritage in daily lives, of community activism and how it backfired in the story we just saw, of the differences between the actual events and the story told on the stage. The feeling was electric; passions had been stoked, the issues engaged, and the drama continued well past the standing ovation that greeted the performance. This is the kind of response to theater that makes us devote our lives to it.

But Cherylene also sets a stirring example of the many ways an artist can contribute to the quality of life in our communities. Inside The Z Space Studio, Cherylene has been a leader in our artistic and programmatic growth. With other members of our Residency program, Cherylene launched The New Music Theater Project, a home for the exploration and development of contemporary music theater. She leads the TheatreWorks Playwrights' Project, inspiring high school students to find their own voices and tell their own stories. Cherylene is one of those rare people in the theater who seem always to be moving forward — artistically, professionally, and personally. Trailing along behind her is an astonishing collection of new plays, new programs, and new collaborations between artists and between organizations that she believes in. The Z Space Studio is a vastly better place for her involvement here. The same can be said of the American theater itself.

Cherylene Lee is a former child performer, dancer/actress, paleontologist/geologist, and waste-water (yes, sewage) treatment consultant. Her writing includes poetry, short fiction, and a novel. As a fourth-generation Chinese-American, her writing examines the broad spectrum of Asian-American experience. Her poetry and fiction have been widely published and her short stories anthologized in *American Dragons* (Harper Collins, 1993) and *Charlie Chan Is Dead* (Viking/Penguin, 1993). Recipient of a San Francisco Arts Council Grant in Literature, she has also received a Fund for New American Plays Grant and a Rockefeller MAP Grant. She has been co-winner of the Mixed Blood Theater's Playwrights Competition, and she has been chosen for the O'Neill National Playwrights Conference, the Sundance Playwrights Lab, and an Asian Theatre Workshop Fellowship with the Mark Taper Forum. *Carry the Tiger to the Mountain* was commissioned by the Contemporary American Theatre Festival, Shepherdstown, West Virginia. World Premiere, July 10 to 26, 1998, Contemporary American Theatre Festival, Shepherdstown, West Virginia; New York Premiere, November 12 to December 5, 1998, Pan Asian Repertory Theatre, New York; West Coast Premiere, East West Players, Los Angeles, February 24 to March 14, 1999. *Knock Off Balance* won the 2000 Rela Lossy Playwriting Award and was produced by San Francisco State University, March, 2000.

ACKNOWLEDGEMENTS

The playwright wishes to thank the following people for their support in bringing *Carry the Tiger to the Mountain* to the theater: Helen Zia, Dale Minami, Beulah Quo, Xie Yang, and Bruce Ostler for their collective faith in me to tell this important story; Ed Herendeen of the Contemporary American Theater Festival who first commissioned this play and produced its world premier in West Virginia; Tisa Chang of Pan Asian Repertory Theater, who brought this play to New York; Tim Dang of East West Players who brought this play to Los Angeles; and all the talented actors, directors, designers, and crew members who, through their contributions at every performance, made sure that Vincent Chin would not be forgotten. Finally, the playwright wishes to thank Mrs. Lily Chin for her courage in fighting for justice and for allowing her story to be told on stage.

ORIGINAL PRODUCTION

Carry the Tiger to the Mountain had its world premiere by The Contemporary American Theater Festival in Shepherdstown, West Virginia, in July, 1998. It was directed by Ed Herendeen and choreographed by Jamie H.J. Guan. The set design was by Michael J. Dempsey, lighting by Michael Angelo Tortora, costume design by Anne Kennedy, sound design by Kevin Lloyd, casting by Beverly D. Marable, and the stage manager was Sarah M. Delia and percussionist was Todd Campbell. The cast, in alphabetical order, was as follows:

Bonnie Akimoto	Hannah Hsu
Mary Fortuna	Edsel girl/Showgirl/Nurse
Michael Goodwin	Katz/Customer #1/Policeman/Doctor
Steven Michael Harper	Tommy/Customer #2/Clerk
Marcus Ho	Vincent Chin
Jim Ishida	David Chin/Fortune Teller Wong/Sifu
J.P. Linton	Donald Evans
Beulah Quo	Lily Chin
Paul Sparks	Mark Stetz
Mia Tagano	Patti Lin/Eva Louie/Fa Mu Lan
Rudolph Willrich	Car Salesman/Bouncer/Judges

CHARACTERS

CAR SALESMAN/BOUNCER/JUDGES: white male, 40ish.

DAVID CHIN/FORTUNE TELLER WONG/SIFU: Asian-American male, 70s does Tai Chi.

HANNAH HSU: Asian-American female, 27.

LILY CHIN: Asian-American female, 60s, does Tai Chi.

VINCENT CHIN: Asian-American male, early-mid 20s, does Tai Chi.

PATTI LIN/EVA LOUIE/FA MU LAN: Asian-American Female, mid-20s, does Chinese sword play.

DONALD EVANS: white male, 45ish.

MARK STETZ: Evans's stepson, white male, 20ish.

KATZ/CUSTOMER #1/POLICEMAN/DOCTOR: lawyer, white male, mid 30s.

TOMMY/CUSTOMER#2/CLERK: Vincent's best man, male of color, mid 20s.

EDSEL GIRL/SHOWGIRL/NURSE: white female, 30ish

NOTE

Once the play begins, it should be in continuous motion, just as the movements in Tai Chi never come to a complete stop until the set is finished. This play is based on a true incident that took place in Detroit, 1982, though some names have been changed to protect both the innocent and the guilty.

CARRY THE TIGER
TO THE MOUNTAIN

PROLOGUE

In the dark

JUDGE: *(Voice-over.)* I hereby sentence you to three years probation, and to pay fines and court costs totaling $3,780. Case closed. Next?
(Sound of gavel. A screen lights up with a slide of a new 1982 American car. A white car salesman in a pool of light near the screen, a white showgirl beside him.)

CAR SALESMAN: Three thousand seven hundred and eighty dollars. That's all? Well, you can't get a new car for that, forget it. Payments over three years, hell, that's only *(He calculates.)* $125 a month, hardly pays for the paperwork. *(The slide disappears.)* But how about a used car, two years old, low mileage, mint condition, original owners—we only sell cars from original owners, you know. *(Slides of cars appear as they're mentioned.)* A 1980 Oldsmobile air conditioned, power steering, power brakes, all new upholstery. A 1980 Ford Pinto, very frisky, drives like wildfire. A 1980 Citation, gets great gas mileage, excellent condition. And here's something else you can get . . . *(A slide of Vincent Chin, brain dead, head in bandages.)* Uh, that was a mistake. *(Slide disappears quickly. A pause.)* No, absolutely not. We don't sell any imports. This is an American dealership. American. Got it? This is Detroit. Motor City, US of A. You want one of those unsafe, ugly, boxy, poorly made pieces of Jap shit which are putting us all outta work? Hey, you can take your lousy three thousand bucks and shove it up your . . .
(Fade out on car salesman. Fade up on Lily Chin, mid 60s, a Chinese-American woman in a pool of light. She is dressed in black. She is doing Tai Chi to calm herself, to meditate, to take her mind off her problems. She does the first few moves slowly, trying to breathe deeply, until she gets to the Lady Looking at the Mirror movement. She freezes, staring at her outstretched palm.)

LILY: Lady looking at Mirror. What does she see?
(Hannah, a young Chinese-American woman enters the pool of light also dressed in black. She is gentle, respectful. Lily stays frozen in her position.)

HANNAH: Mrs. Chin. It's time.

LILY: I didn't teach him. If he knew. Must keep both feet planted, keep horse even, shift weight, this hand goes for throat, keep tongue to roof of mouth, let life force move to fingernail, sharp like ax to wood . . . I didn't teach him, Hannah.

HANNAH: The limousine is outside.

LILY: Mama coming, Vincent, mama coming.

(Lights fade down on Lily Chin as she and Hannah exit. Music of "Dancing in the Streets" or an identifiable Motown sound. In another pool of light, two white men, one holding a baseball bat, and Vincent Chin, a young Chinese man, stand together. They start facing the audience, doing in unison the same opening movement Lily used in Tai Chi. Then in slow motion they turn to confront each other. They struggle in slow motion. Vincent is grabbed by one white man, he is held with his arms behind him. The other white man approaches with baseball bat swinging it like a sword in Chinese Opera fashion. Lights fade.)

END PROLOGUE

ACT ONE

A white car salesman dressed in 1940s clothes with a hat, stands in front of a slide of a 1947 Packard, a showgirl in 1940s garb beside him.

CAR SALESMAN: Looking for a reliable car to fit the whole family? One that goes zero to fifty miles per hour in less time than it takes to say, *(Slowly.)* "We not only won the war, we're on the road of the American Dream." This is the car for taking Gramps, little Martha, and your favorite nephew for a spin. Gotta a job in the next town over? Arrive in comfort. The family automobile built for the future in . . .

(Lights come up on a scrim behind which stands a young Lily Chin in China, 1946, reading a letter from David, her husband-to-be, in America. We cannot see Lily's face, but we see her dressed in a Chinese Wedding outfit. We hear David's words from the letter overlapping with the Car Salesman.)

CAR SALESMAN/DAVID: This land of opportunity, promise, and hope . . .

(Light fades on Car Salesman, but remains on Lily behind the scrim as she continues preparing her wedding dress. Lights up on David as a young man.)

DAVID: I know you will like it here. After so many years of waiting, I am finally able to honor our families' arrangement and bring you to America, my bride. I will be there to welcome you when the ship docks in San Francisco. From there, I have booked passage on the Silver Comet to Detroit where I have started my own business, the Chin Family Laundry, a thriving enterprise to support many future sons. I enclose a photograph of myself. Will you send me one of you? I imagine you to be a patient, everlasting flower waiting to bloom in these United States.

(Lights fade on Lily. David Chin is now an infirm Chinese-American man in his late 70s. It is 1975, the Chin home. He is dressed in a bathrobe, barefoot, walking slowly with a cane, carrying a single sock, he has recently had kidney-stone surgery, and is somewhat delusional and cranky from his medication, mixing up people and times. He is searching for his sock, after a few cursory glances around.)

DAVID: *(Calling out.)* Lily, I can't find my sock. *(To himself.)* What good is one sock without its mate? LILY. LILY.

(Hannah enters carrying a pair of socks, David doesn't see her.)

HANNAH: Will these do?

DAVID: You can't be Lily. You're, you're . . . young.

HANNAH: I'm Hannah Hsu, community center volunteer, remember? Your wife asked me to stay with you until she or Vincent returned.

(She helps him to sit, she hands him socks, he hands them back.)

DAVID: I don't take socks from strangers.

HANNAH: *(Handing socks back.)* But you owned a laundry once, Mrs. Chin told me. Here, let me.

(She begins to put socks on his feet, he refuses to let her, always doing the opposite of what she asks.)

DAVID: I don't like strangers playing with my feet.

(He looks at Hannah.)

DAVID: You're nothing like the photograph at all.

HANNAH: Photograph?

DAVID: Right on the dock, in front of everyone. *(Mimicking a woman's voice.)* "But you look so . . . different." That meant old. I sent a picture of me at my best. Young, handsome, I was young and handsome at 21.

HANNAH: I'm sure. Left foot?

DAVID: Disappointed. Again.

HANNAH: Right foot?

DAVID: Was it my fault? Hard work, lots of sweat, and there was the war. *(He looks closely at Hannah.)* Did you think I was a big shot? United States citizen, a high class mucky-muck?

HANNAH: I'm not your wife, Mr. Chin, I'm just trying to help you—

DAVID: Were you more disappointed in me or my laundry? Or because I was not rich?

HANNAH: Maybe you should lie down some more.

DAVID: It wasn't my fault. I kept my promises as best I could. And Lily, it could have been your fault too, the doctor said . . . but we got Vincent anyway, eh? A fine boy, but I wish he wouldn't be so car crazy. All the time, car this, car that, you have to tell him, *(Loudly.)* "Son, life is not a car."

HANNAH: Don't get all worked up, Mr. Chin. It can't be good for your stitches. Try to stay—

DAVID: I don't want stitches, woman, I want socks. Two socks. Mates. A sock needs a mate. *(Calling out.)* LILY? LILY—

HANNAH: She's not back, yet, Mr. Chin. Why don't you lie down and relax, I'll get you some jook, Mrs. Chin made you some rice broth. Hungry?

(Lily enters, she is now in her early 60s.)

LILY: Vincent not home yet, Hannah? Baba, what you doing out of bed?

DAVID: Still disappointed, huh, Lily? At least you didn't wait 20 years this time.

LILY: You talk crazy.

HANNAH: I think he's a little confused from his medication.

DAVID: Where is my mate? *(He stands too quickly, a throbbing pain hits him.)* Oh. *(He moans, collapses onto the chair, he moans throughout the following.)*

LILY: You should be in bed. Do Tai Chi breathing. *(She demonstrates.)* In, out. Slow, in, out. It ease the pain.

(David moans, exhaling loudly. Vincent, at age nineteen enters, carrying baseball bat.)

VINCENT: Sorry, I'm, late, Ma, you should have seen practice—*(Seeing Lily bent over David.)* What's happened? Dad? Are you okay?

LILY: Vincent, help your father back into bed. He thinks he's young man. Doctor say to stay in bed. He never listen. I say do tai-chi breathing, in and out. He only want out.

VINCENT: *(Helping David up.)* Come on, Dad. Up we go, take it easy, I got you. *(As soon as Vincent touches David, David stops moaning. David leans heavily on Vincent as they exit.)*

DAVID: *(To Lily.)* Disappointed . . . again.

HANNAH: Vincent's very good with his father.

LILY: He a good boy.

HANNAH: Looks like his Dad.

LILY: *(Quickly, firmly.)* No, he doesn't.

HANNAH: *(Realizing she said a faux pas.)* No . . . maybe not. He looks like you.

LILY: You think so? Vincent always happy.

HANNAH: Like you, Mrs. Chin.

LILY: Umm. You have husband yet, Hannah?

HANNAH: No.

LILY: Boyfriend?

HANNAH: No.

LILY: How old?

HANNAH: I'm twenty-seven.

LILY: Not good to wait so long, Hannah. When I your age I already married, working in Chin Family Laundry, waiting to have children. You should at least have boyfriend by now.

HANNAH: I'm not interested in getting married Mrs. Chin. I want a career.

LILY: Career. Life is not career. Children, that is the future. You want me to find you boyfriend? Vincent know some *(Pointed.)* older Chinese boys, have steady jobs, engineers—

HANNAH: Thank you, but I'm still finding out what kind of work interests me.

LILY: In China, everyone thought I was old maid because husband didn't send for me for twenty-four years. Neighbors call us family of old maids, family of aunties. All my sisters had to wait for me. My father thought he never see grandchildren. Whole family wait on me to marry first.

HANNAH: And I thought I was under pressure.

LILY: Promised at three, not married until twenty-seven. *(Pointed.)* Your age. Take longer than you think.

HANNAH: Yours was an arranged marriage? I can't imagine what that feels like.

LILY: Leave family, leave home, leave my friends to come to strange country to marry man I don't know except for one picture? What do you think? *(She looks around to see if Vincent is listening.)* Scary. Husband say in letters "Land of Opportunity, American Dream" He send me picture, very handsome, young man, so I do my duty, I come. I leave my home, arrive in San Francisco, but no handsome young man like picture to greet me, only older man, one with teapot belly and hair sprouting in his ears. Same smile, kind smile, but . . .

HANNAH: False advertising.

LILY: He was so . . . different . . . Laundry business not too good . . . Detroit not so happy . . . we don't have children for long time . . .

HANNAH: Until you got pregnant with Vincent. You're very lucky. *(Lily remains silent.)* I could never marry someone I'd never seen, let alone move to a strange country to do it.

LILY: Better than being all alone. Old maid with career.

HANNAH: I'm not worried about that.

LILY: No? *(She takes Hannah's hand, looks at her palm.)* You have a good life line. Strong like me. See? *(Lily shows Hannah her palm.)* You live long time. But when you my age, you see, your hands cannot work so fast, work not enough. Career can go away. Disappear, like that *(She squeezes the career line out when the palm is bent.)* But see there? *(She points to offspring line.)* Those lines are for children, those do not disappear, no matter what. *(Hannah looks at her palm and compares it with Lily's.)*

HANNAH: Then according to your palm reading, I'm to have three children in the future and you won't have any, but you already have Vincent. You don't really believe in this do you? It's just superstition, Mrs. Chin.

LILY: You should find boyfriend anyway.

HANNAH: I'll pass. Call me if you need any more help with your husband, Mrs. Chin. I'll be glad to come over.
(Hannah exits. Lily waves, then stares at her palm, looking at her children line as lights fade.)
(The Car Salesman is in front of a slide of a 1958 Edsel. He is a joined by a female model dressed in a 1958 evening gown as if the two were in the

1958 Motorama in Detroit. As the car salesman speaks, the woman poses to show off both car and her figure.)

CAR SALESMAN: This slippery-skinned sleek finned missile is powered by a dual quad V-8 rear mounted transmission and De Dion rear suspension. Upholstered in crushed grain vermilion leather, it's the smoothest ride on the road, the one you've all been waiting for. When you hold the key to this car *(Woman holds up car key.)* you are holding your future —

CAR SALESMAN/LILY: This is your dream come true.

(Lily as a young woman in 1956 from behind the scrim. She is in western clothes writing calligraphy to her mother in China.)

LILY: — except nothing works, mother. I do not know what is wrong. Perhaps it is the steam of the laundry presses, perhaps the heat. I use the herbs you sent. Mei mei says they worked for her, she has three boys now. Perhaps I am too old. My husband is a good man, but he . . . I am sorry I cannot come visit. Money is scarce . . . our savings are invested in making Edsel key chains, a sign of good luck. I hope so. I will write if I feel any change . . . we are still trying . . .

(Lights fade on Lily. Lights up on Vincent, 20, sitting with his dad, showing him pictures of different cars. David is in bathrobe, Vincent is dressed for his job. It is the Chin household, 1976. David has declined further, he pays scant attention to Vincent, he lives almost totally in the past.)

VINCENT: I'm getting it with $2000 down, brand-new, manual trans, fuel injection, catalytic converter, gas mileage isn't great, but with two jobs, I can make the payments easy, I've got insurance, Ma won't even—

DAVID: NOT MY FAULT.

(David grabs the brochures from Vincent and throws them on the floor.)

VINCENT: Dad—

DAVID: That Harry Teng said join the Edsel bandwagon. Get an exclusive contract. Be one of a kind. SO WHAT?

VINCENT: Dad. I didn't mean to upset you. I just wanted you to see the car I —

DAVID: Make the key chains of the future, he said. For the dream car, he said. You can't go wrong with Ford, he said. Harry always made money, so I put in . . . everything. EVERYTHING. Disappointed, again. *(Calling.)* Lily, LILY.

(David moans as if in pain, he holds his head, Lily enters.)

VINCENT: Sorry, Ma, not one of his good days.

LILY: *(To David.)* Close eyes, breathe slow, in, out. In, out.

(Lily uses finger acupressure on David's head.)

VINCENT: I shouldn't have shown him the brochure, I just wanted him to see what I've been saving up for —

LILY: *(To Vincent.)* Not your fault. *(To David.)* Not your fault. You try. That's all. *(Soothingly, doing Tai Chi breathing.)* In, out, slowly, in, out. *(David quiets, his breathing becomes regular, he falls asleep.)*

LILY: *(To Vincent.)* He say no to your car?

VINCENT: I don't think he knew what I was talking about.

LILY: Don't worry. Go ahead, you buy car. I help you. I get overtime at brush factory. I get you special brush for car, I get it free.

VINCENT: Ma, you don't have to, I can pay for this. I got a second job.

LILY: Second job?

VINCENT: Frank Wong said I could wait tables at his restaurant on weekends.

LILY: Frank's father give your father restaurant job after Edsel car go downhill. After Baba lose everything. *(Worried.)* What happen to first job?

VINCENT: Don't worry Ma, I'm still there. Apprentice draftsman, I'm not quitting. *(Beat.)* Wait till you see her, she rides like a dream. You and Dad will be my first passengers.

LILY: Don't go too fast, now, too dangerous. I never like cars go too fast. Make me scared. That's why I never drive.

VINCENT: Well, no more buses anymore, Ma. I will take you anywhere you want to go. Hey, I could take you and Dad on a vacation, see some sights. Wanna go to New York? What do you think?

LILY: "See the USA, in your Chevrolet" *(Blows kiss.)* MOOAH.

VINCENT: What?

LILY: You too young. You don't need take me anywhere special, Vincent. I happy when you happy. When you pick up car?

VINCENT: Tonight after work. Last time on the bus for me.

LILY: Never say last. Bad luck.

VINCENT: Okay then, my first time driving home in my own car. Finally. I can't believe it.

LILY: Like dream come true?

VINCENT: What a pest I was when Dad drove the delivery van for the restaurant, constantly begging him to let me sit in the driver's seat, always putting my hands on that big steering wheel. And he told me I had to choose. I was so little, I could either put my hands on the wheel, or I could slide down the seat to work the pedals. Either I could make something go, or I could steer something straight, one or the other, I couldn't do both. And it was a tough decision, I wanted to do everything. I couldn't wait until I was old enough, not just to reach the pedals and the steering wheel, but for the time when I'd have my own car. Rolling down my window, putting one hand on the steering wheel, one hand on the stick shift, one foot flooring the gas. Knowing I could do whatever I wanted do, to finally feel . . . feel . . . I've waited for so long, I can't explain it, Ma.

LILY: Your feeling for car? You're like that for me. Drive safe, okay? You promise?

VINCENT: Promise.

(Lights fade.)

(Lights up on the Car Salesman and showgirl in front of a slide of a 1965 Ford Mustang.)

CAR SALESMAN: Affordable. Sporty. Fun to drive. Everything you've wanted in a car and it looks fast just standing still. "Ford has a better idea." You asked for it . . .

(From behind a scrim, Vincent sits alone. In his head, he is going through his life with his father.)

VINCENT: *(As a child of ten in 1965.)* At ten, I asked, "Baba can I join Boy Scouts?"

(From Vincent's disappointment, we know the answer was no.)

VINCENT: *(As child of ten.)* Dad, how 'bout Little League, if I promise to do my homework first?

(The answer: I'll think about it.)

VINCENT: *(At sixteen.)* I asked about getting my driver's license so I could help drive Ma to work. *(Answer: yes.)* ALL RIGHT!

(A female doctor hands the adult Vincent a report, makes a conciliatory gesture, and exits. Vincent tries to digest the news.)

VINCENT: *(In present.)* I asked if I could be his donor since I had two healthy kidneys. I felt so stupid finding out from the doctor, I guess I should have realized . . . but I was always treated like a son—

(Lily downstage, terribly distraught, Vincent steps out from behind the scrim to face Lily.)

LILY: YOU ARE MY SON. I don't care what doctor say. You just like flesh and blood. Everyone say so. Everyone think you my son.

VINCENT: But I'm not, I'm adopted. Why didn't you tell me? Why did I have to find out from a doctor?

LILY: Why should young boy know? Make more friends in school? Make you feel better? Already so few Chinese here. I think maybe people tease you, say mean things, say you are different, they stare at you like women stare at me in China before I get married. Always whispering, gossiping, pointing, they . . . they pity me. I HATE IT. Old maid, no children. I pretend I don't hear. I don't want you to feel that, feel that shame. I don't lie to you, Vincent. I think no reason to bring it up. Does not do you any good to hear all the bad things that happen before you come. All the doctors, tests. How long I wait. How long I search for you, go agency after agency, I look for young Chinese boy, not Japanese, not Korean, young Chinese boy. I wait six years, month after month, sometimes I think you only dream in my head. I cannot believe you really come. My life start when you come. I try very hard to be good mother. I'm not bad, not bad person. Please do not be mad at me.

VINCENT: I'm not mad exactly, but Dad . . . *(Catching himself.)* David—

LILY: *(Correcting.)* Your baba, your father—

VINCENT: The man I've called Dad for the last sixteen years needs a kidney. If I were his son, his real son, I could help him.

LILY: You help him already. You everything to us, make us happy. You make us family, real family. You have his name, just like flesh-and-blood son.

VINCENT: But my flesh and my blood don't match, Ma—*(He catches himself.)* It's just so . . . so . . . *(He's overwhelmed.)* I've got to think, I'm going for a drive.

(Vincent starts to leave, Lily tries to stop him.)

LILY: Vincent don't drive crazy, please. I sorry I not tell you, VINCENT—

VINCENT: Don't worry, I'll be back . . . Ma—

(Vincent exits, Lily stares after him.)

LILY: Promise?

(Lights fade on Lily alone.)

(Lights up on Car Salesman. A slide of a 1979 Pontiac Firebird on the screen. This time the Car Salesman seems, nervous, his tie is askew, he sweats, and has to repeatedly wipe his brow. The showgirl is equally nervous. Sales of American cars are way down with the 1979 gas shortage and rationing. Two white customers come up to the salesman.)

CAR SALESMAN: Look at this beauty. Is she gorgeous or what? The 1979 Pontiac Firebird, bucket seats, AM-FM stereo radio and cassette, power every-thing, and, and—

CUSTOMER #1: And what's the miles per gallon?

CAR SALESMAN: You can not find a more fuel-efficient car on the market with this kind of—

CUSTOMER #1: The mileage?

CAR SALESMAN: Miles per gallon isn't everything, I can offer—

CUSTOMER #2: It is when you're in line at the pump.

CAR SALESMAN: The Firebird has class, comfort. It's safe. It's real steel, not one of those flimsy fiberglass—

CUSTOMER #1: Less than fifteen?

CAR SALESMAN: We have lots of options, a dealer warranty for only—

CUSTOMER #2: Less than twelve?

CAR SALESMAN: Look at the styling—

CUSTOMER #2: I wait every other day to get gas, you think I care about styling?

CUSTOMER #1: How come Datsuns can do twenty-three miles per gallon around town when American cars can't break twelve?

(The two customers walk away, leaving the salesman staring after them. Vincent Chin enters, looks over the car.)

VINCENT: Great car. I have the 1976 model. Engine still purrs.

CAR SALESMAN: You willing to testify, kid?

VINCENT: What?

CAR SALESMAN: I could really use a Japanese guy saying my car is better than any import.

VINCENT: But I'm not.

CAR SALESMAN: You just said so, you taking it back?

VINCENT: I'm not Japanese. I'm Chinese. I just want to know what the dealer trade in is for a mint-condition, pampered, waxed twice monthly, 1976 Firebird.

CAR SALESMAN: Are you a wiseass or what? I can't get rid of the new models, what the hell would I do with an old one?

VINCENT: Sell it?

CAR SALESMAN: Hey, like Iaccocca says, "If you can find a better car, buy it." My motto, "If I can't sell a better car, dump it."

VINCENT: But I don't want to dump my car, I'd just like to trade my Firebird in for something a little less expensive—

(As soon as he hears "less expensive" the car salesman turns away from Vincent in disgust.)

CAR SALESMAN: You Japs make me sick.

(The salesman snaps his fingers and the slide of the Firebird disappears. Vincent stands alone getting madder and madder at his dismissal by the salesman.)

VINCENT: —a little less expensive to maintain. You think I want to turn it in? You think I like trading down? I gotta save money, my dad's really sick, I've got a new girlfriend and . . . and . . . AND I'M NOT JAPANESE.

LILY: *(Offstage.)* VINCENT, VINCENT, who is this Patti girl who call you all the time?

(Vincent steps into scene of Chin home, 1981. David is now in a wheelchair, almost always unconscious. Lily pushes the wheelchair into a pool of light. A

young, pretty Chinese-American girl, Patti Lin, Vincent's soon-to-be fiancée stands next to Vincent.)

VINCENT: Dad, Ma, I'd like you to meet Patti Lin.

LILY: How you do, Patti. Please excuse Vincent father, he not feeling well. *(She touches David's shoulder.)* David, this is one of Vincent friends, Patti.

PATTI LIN: *(Holding out hand.)* A pleasure to meet you Mrs. Chin, Mr. Chin. Vincent's told me so much about you.

LILY: *(Shaking her hand.)* Really? He not say too much about you.

VINCENT: Ma—

LILY: But Vincent hardly home these days. He work two jobs you know, always so busy making money to take care of his father.

VINCENT: Ma, Dad. I wanted you to meet Patti because, well, because she's more than a friend to me. She's much more.

LILY: You work with Vincent? You have . . . career?

VINCENT: Ma, I've asked Patti to marry me.

(A split second of silence.)

LILY: Congratulations, children. You make me very happy. You make grand-children. Baba, you hear good news? Vincent marry Patti.

(She shakes David gently. She whispers in his ear, he seems to rouse himself and looks directly at Patti without recognition.)

DAVID: You're not Lily. You're . . . you're young.

(David returns to his stupor.)

LILY: Don't listen to words, Patti, he confused, but he mean well. He very, very happy for you both. I know. See how his eyes smile even when closed?

PATTI LIN: I'm honored to become part of your family, Mr. Chin, Mrs. Chin.

VINCENT: Don't be so formal, Patti, you can call them Ma and Dad now.

PATTI LIN: Thank you for your good wishes . . . Ma.

LILY: Maybe you call me grandma instead, eh? Let me see your palm, Patti.

(Patti gives her hand to Lily.)

LILY: Very good. Yes, very good. You have good health, strong lifeline, and see here? At least three grandchildren. I help you pick names.

PATTI LIN: Mrs. Chin . . . Ma, we have to get married first.

LILY: You have to get married?

VINCENT: Patti means you're rushing the grandchildren a bit. We haven't even set a date for the wedding. We'd like to have it next summer.

LILY: We go to fortune-teller. He give us auspicious day for wedding. I take care of it, don't worry.

PATTI LIN: I'd like a June wedding, if that's all right.

LILY: June good month. Lots of people like June. We have big guest list. Four hundred people.

PATTI LIN: Four . . . hundred?

(Patti looks at Vincent in controlled panic.)

VINCENT: Ma, maybe we should go easy on this, even with my raise, I'm still going to—

LILY: Don't worry, I work overtime at brush factory, I help you pay for this. Can't be cheap on wedding. You have big Chinese banquet like one your father and I couldn't have.

VINCENT/PATTI LIN: You don't have to —

LILY: When we get married, no one to celebrate, no money for banquet. But for you, Vincent, I order all your favorite dish, steamed bass with black bean sauce, whole roast suckling pig, dried oysters braised with fa choy, anything you and Patti want.

PATTI LIN: That's very generous of you, Mrs. Chin . . . Ma . . . Mom.

LILY: We have special dress made for you, Patti. Show off all your gum hay, wedding jewelry. And father have special Chinese locket for Vincent. He get from his father to give to son for wedding day to lock out all bad fortune. *(To David.)* Time to give him brass locket, eh?

(Lily leans over David to whisper in his ear. David is slumped in his wheelchair and doesn't respond.)

LILY: Time for locket, Baba. Your son getting married. *(She nudges him gently.)* Baba? You hear? Pretty soon you be grandfather? Goon goon, eh? *(No answer.)* It's Lily, wake up, it's Lily, it's time—

VINCENT: Dad . . . DAD? *(To Patti.)* Call an ambulance, quick.

(Patti rushes out. Lily stands over David stroking his head, Vincent kneels in front of his father. Their dialog overlaps.)

LILY: Do Tai Chi breathing, In, out. Slowly. In, out. Ease pain. In, out. In, out.

VINCENT: Dad, it's Vincent, your son, Dad. Wait, please, not yet, please, not yet. Dad?

(The sound of a Buddhist bell is heard. Vincent and Lily freeze. The bell is rung long and repeatedly as it would be at a funeral. During the ringing of the bell, two men dressed as emergency ambulance workers enter and wheel away David and the wheelchair. As the bell continues, Patti enters with a black jacket for Vincent and a black coat for Lily. Patti helps Vincent up from his kneeling position and helps him put on his black jacket. They embrace. Patti and Vincent help Lily put on her black coat. Patti embraces Lily, then Vincent embraces Lily. Lily gives Vincent the Chinese brass locket, which David

would have given to Vincent. She puts it around his neck. Patti and Vincent exit, leaving Lily alone facing audience. The bell ringing ends.)
(A moment of still silence, then in a pool of light Lily begins a set of Tai Chi, we hear her inhaling and exhaling as she slowly goes through the opening moves. A light comes up on Vincent speaking to Patti.)

VINCENT: I'm worried about her, I took her for a long drive . . . she seems sort of lost without Dad to take care of . . . Yeah, she says after forty years, she misses hearing him shout out her name whenever he was looking for something. Nights are the worst for her, too much empty space . . . I know, but she still wants us to have the wedding next summer, says it will give her something to look forward to . . . Uh, Patti, there is one thing, Ma wants to go to a geomancer to choose an auspicious date . . . I don't believe in fortune-tellers either, but for her sake, I think we should go. Is that okay with you?

(Lily should finish the first Tai Chi set as light fades down on Vincent. Lily holds her arms in the opening stance.)

LILY: Not disappointed again.

(Lily steps into a scene with Vincent, Patti, and the geomancer Wong in a fortune-teller's shop represented by hanging scrolls, mirrors, incense, and a chaotic mixture of Chinese and American knickknacks. Somewhere in the shop a Detroit Tigers baseball cap should be visible.)

LILY: Vincent, this Fortune-Teller Wong.

WONG: It's been many years since I saw you, Vincent, but you've grown up to be the fine young man, I knew you would become. Do you remember me?

VINCENT: Uh . . . Not exactly, Mr. Woo.

WONG: Wong.

LILY: Vincent only six when I first brought him to you.

WONG: Of course, of course. You wouldn't remember that. I see you wear a brass lock for protection, Vincent, to lock out bad fortune.

VINCENT: A gift from my father.

WONG: Perhaps you want one for your lovely bride-to-be? A wedding present? *(Wong starts rummaging amid his clutter looking for a locket, blowing dust from some objects.)*

PATTI LIN: Uh, no. Brass makes my skin turn green. *(Sotto to Vincent.)* This is too weird.

VINCENT: *(Sotto to Patti.)* It's for Ma. Humor her, okay?

WONG: Then allow me to offer my warmest congratulations to you both.

LILY: Thank you, Mr. Wong. My husband not live to see his son and Patti marry.

Carry the Tiger to the Mountain 137

WONG: I was sorry to hear of his passing Mrs. Chin. He was a respected man. My condolences.

LILY: No more sorrow. We move ahead. Vincent start own family soon. I like to have special fortune read for them, Mr. Wong. For their wedding.

(She pays the fortune-teller.)

WONG: With pleasure. Where do you want to start, skull physiognomy? Do you have any questions?

(Wong starts to feel the lumps on Patti's head. Patti is uncomfortable and embarrassed. She doesn't want her fortune told.)

PATTI LIN: *(To Lily.)* Mom, maybe we could just ask for a good date for the wedding?

LILY: Ask whatever you want. I pay him already.

VINCENT: We're looking to get married next June, Mr. Wong. What would be the best time?

(Wong looks up the dates in his book.)

PATTI LIN: Say around the middle of the month, like June nineteenth?

(Wong checks, then shakes his head, no, vigorously.)

WONG: Not good. Not good date. June nineteenth is very, very bad.

(Wong is emphatic, Vincent and Patti are amused. Lily is concerned.)

LILY: Pick new date, quick, don't want bad luck.

VINCENT: How about the twenty-seventh? June twenty-seventh?

(Wong checks in his book. He speaks quietly.)

WONG: Day of momentous change. Especially between one and three in the afternoon.

VINCENT: Then it's settled. We'll get married on June twenty-seventh, 1982. At one o'clock in the afternoon, Patti, you'll become Mrs. Vincent Chin.

(Vincent gives Patti a kiss. Lily looks on and smiles. Lights fade.)

(The slide of a brand new 1982 Japanese car appears)

CAR SALESMAN: *(Offstage.)* Before . . .

(The slide changes to a Japanese car completely trashed.)

CAR SALESMAN: *(Offstage.)* After . . .

(The slide of another new 1982 Japanese car appears.)

CAR SALESMAN: *(Offstage.)* Before . . .

(The slide changes to another completely trashed Japanese car.)

CAR SALESMAN: *(Offstage.)* After.

(The Car Salesman enters with a baseball bat, swinging it as if taking batting practice, the showgirl shows attitude.)

CAR SALESMAN: See that? *(Referring to slide.)* Well listen, Honda, Toyota, Datsun, Nissan, or whatever the hell you're calling yourselves these days, Americans

are mad and we're not going to take it anymore. You think you can take over American roads, you think you can take over American jobs, you think you can take over America by selling cars at ridiculously cheap prices without the American auto industry fighting back? Let me tell you, when we play ball, we want a level playing field. Some things are sacred to us— baseball, free enterprise, apple pie. And when my mom heard that Jap imports were responsible for closing two Chrysler dealerships right here in Detroit, *(Using baseball bat to point to the slide of battered car.)* well, she took this here bat, and that is what she did to that poorly made piece of shit. My mom, bless her heart, knows how to swing a bat. But if a sixty-two-year-old, gray-haired grandmother could put that much damage on a two-door, subcompact, tinny, roller skate of a car, how safe would you feel driving in one? American cars are built to last, *(Slide comes up of a 1982 Monte Carlo.)* "Nobody sweats the details like GM."
(Crossfade.)

(Lights up on Lily and Vincent in Chin home, 1982. Lily does Tai Chi throughout, Vincent must constantly move to stay in front of Lily's face.)

VINCENT: Patti doesn't want to live here in Oak Park, Ma. It's got nothing to do with you, she just doesn't think it's the best area to raise kids.

LILY: I raise you here. You turn out good.

VINCENT: Times have changed, it's not as safe as it was before.

LILY: You and Patti move far away, how will I visit grandchildren?

VINCENT: We're not moving far away, we're just looking at houses in another part of Detroit.

LILY: I don't drive, too old to take bus. Grandmother forgotten. Unwanted stranger. That what you think of me?

VINCENT: Of course not. I'll pick you up, we'll bring the grandchildren to visit often. *(Beat.)* What am I saying? Patti and I aren't even married yet. Ma, you're just thinking too far ahead —

LILY: You want house far away. Fancy neighborhood. Where you raised not good enough?

VINCENT: We're just starting to look, we haven't made any decision.

LILY: What's wrong with look near me? I take care of your children, built-in baby-sitter, very safe. No charge. Don't you trust own mother? Patti not trust me?

VINCENT: Of course she trusts you. Ma, it has nothing to do with you. It has to do with where Patti and I want to live.

LILY: Far away from me.

VINCENT: Ma —

LILY: You think your life have nothing to do with me? Your life have every-thing to do with me. I raise you in this house. When you gone, I'm all alone. I say you and Patti marry, move in with me, save lots of money.

VINCENT: Ma —

LILY: You can't even afford wedding without my help.

VINCENT: If you weren't inviting 400 hundred people maybe Patti and I could afford the wedding.

(Lily freezes.)

LILY: What you say? You think it my fault?

VINCENT: No, it's not your fault, it's just I —

LILY: You think it bad to have only son have big wedding celebration, bad to have friends see you marry? Bad to make me happy when you happy?

VINCENT: No it isn't bad. It's just . . . I'm . . . Ma, I have lived with you and Dad since you . . . adopted me.

LILY: Forget adoption. You just like flesh-and-blood son, we do everything for you, father work hard in restaurant, I work hard in factory, try to give you everything you want, give you good home, this your house—

VINCENT: I know you've done everything for me, I'm grateful, but . . . Don't you see? It's . . . it's . . . it's like my first car. You wanted to help me buy it then, but I wouldn't let you, remember? The car was my dream, and I made it happen. Me. I could play the radio real loud if I wanted, I could drive too fast on highways —

LILY: You promised me not drive fast —

VINCENT: — if I wanted. I could go wherever I wanted to go. Because that car was my own.

LILY: Silly American idea.

VINCENT: But I didn't buy it because I wanted to get away from you, or because I thought you and Dad couldn't afford it, I bought it because I wanted to. *I wanted to.*

LILY: Life is not a car, Vincent —

VINCENT: Ma, I'm twenty-seven. I'm getting married, I've got a new life ahead of me. It's my time. It's my life.

(Lily turns away from Vincent.)

VINCENT: But just because I bought that car on my own didn't mean I wouldn't drive you anyplace you wanted to go. I always took you with me, didn't I, Ma? When you asked me to?

(A long pause. Lily turns back to her son, this is the first time she's had to ask Vincent for something important.)

LILY: Take me with you again, Vincent.

(Lights dim.)

(Lights up as Lily moves to join Patti who has come to take Lily on a walk-through of their new house.)

PATTI LIN: I told Vincent it was okay, he's with his buddies . . . It's a guy thing, they've been planning June 19th as his last Saturday night of freedom.

LILY: Don't say last, bad luck. I don't like Vincent going to bar, drinking. Everybody act too crazy. What kind of place best man take him to?

PATTI LIN: Different places, sort of show places.

LILY: For cars?

PATTI LIN: Uh, not exactly, it's a bachelor party, Mrs. Chin . . . Mom.

LILY: I tell him come home early, too many bad drivers at night. What kind of place show cars at night?

PATTI LIN: You don't want to know.

(Lights fade on the two women. Disco, driving bass and drum music blares, headlights of cars light a themed girlie/car bar called "The Body Shop." The car salesman is now a strip joint bouncer with a scantily clad showgirl beside him. A slide of a red Corvette comes up, the showgirl gyrates around it. A bar with two white men, Evans and Stetz, drinking beers, obviously getting plastered. Evans tries to dance with the showgirl in a very clumsy fashion, constantly pawing her, until the Car Salesman separates them. Music continues, but low.)

CAR SALESMAN: Use the brakes till you find a green light, man.

(Salesman rubs his fingers as if asking for money.)

EVANS: Fuck you.

(Tommy, Vincent's best man, enters pulling a reluctant Vincent.)

TOMMY: Come on, just one more, my treat.

VINCENT: It's late, Tommy, all the other guys —

TOMMY: They're party poopers, it's my job as best man to take care of you, come on one last drink.

(The Showgirl approaches them.)

SHOWGIRL: Hey cuties, haven't I seen you before?

VINCENT: Don't think so. My first time.

TOMMY: And his last. He gets married next week.

SHOWGIRL: Then you better floor it, honey.

(She starts to dance with Vincent, pulling him toward the slide of the Corvette, which seems to take a lot of Vincent's attention. Tommy goes to the bar.)

SHOWGIRL: *(Shimmying at Vincent.)* Like my headlights.

VINCENT: Uh . . . Blinding.

(He keeps his attention on the slide of the Corvette, the dancer insisting he

pay her attention, pulling him closer to her. Evans is watching and doesn't like what he sees.)

EVANS: Keep your hands off, Nip.

VINCENT: What?

EVANS: *(Slanting his eyes.)* No touchee the merchandise.

(Evans cuts in to dance and is pushed aside by the showgirl. Evans is pissed.)

EVANS: He's a mama's boy, he don't even have a stick shift.

(Vincent tries to ignore him, but Evans gets in Vincent's face.)

EVANS: You little motherfucker don't know nothing about good pussy.

VINCENT: Don't call me a motherfucker.

EVANS: Because of motherfuckers like you, we're out of work.

VINCENT: I'm not a motherfucker.

TOMMY: *(Pulling Vincent away.)* Hey, let it go. It's not worth it.

EVANS: *(Following Vincent.)* I don't know if you're a little fucker or a big fucker.

(Vincent strikes Evans and Stetz gets up to help his stepfather. Tommy tries to intervene. Stetz raises a chair, Tommy goes down. Sound of screeching brakes. Everyone in the bar freezes. A Chinese wood block picks up pulse of disco beat. Light change. Patti and Lily walk through the tableaux as if looking at the new house.)

PATTI LIN: It's okay, Mrs. Chin . . . Mom. We want you to live with us. You do like the house, don't you?

LILY: I don't want to be in way. Keep big room for nursery.

PATTI LIN: *(Laughing.)* We still have a week till the wedding, don't you think planning a nursery is a little premature?

LILY: Baby need big room. I don't need much space. Just enough to do Tai Chi.

PATTI LIN: You can do that in our garden outside.

(Patti and Lily move off stage left. Light change, bar scene unfreezes. Driving disco beat continues. Car Salesman/Strip Joint Bouncer breaks up fight between guys.)

CAR SALESMAN: Outside. If you're gonna fight. Take it outside.

(He takes the chair away from Stetz and moves Tommy off with Tommy holding his head. The showgirl backs away, taking the bar with her. The car salesman snaps his fingers, the slide of the red corvette disappears, the driving beat continues under the sound of honking and traffic. Only the headlights remain on stage. Stetz and Evans face off with Vincent in what is now the parking lot.)

STETZ: We're outside now, gook. Ready?

(Evans goes off, returns with a baseball bat. The two men close in on Vincent.)

VINCENT: You want to fight? I'll fight, but not with a baseball bat.

EVANS: Wanna Jap sword, motherfucker?

> *(The men freeze. Light change. Chinese wood block takes over. Patti and Lily walk through the tableaux continuing the tour of the house.)*

LILY: I teach you Tai Chi, very good for pregnant woman. Move life force to new baby.

PATTI LIN: Does Vincent know Tai Chi?

LILY: He think Tai Chi too slow. I tell him not only help breathing, but good for balance. Oldest of all Chinese Martial arts. I never teach him before.

> *(Patti and Lily move off to stage right. Lights change. The driving beat of Chinese wood blocks becomes the Motown sound of the Prologue. The three men unfreeze. The confrontation is in slow motion, the bat swung around the head as in Chinese Opera movement. The positions are stylized in the way of Chinese sword play. Stetz pins Vincent's arms, as Evans wields the bat, thrusting and swinging it at Vincent's head. A wood block sound emphasizes each blow which become faster and louder until the Motown sound is gone and only the Chinese wood block is heard. Red silk ribbons representing blood are thrown around Vincent's head as if spurting blood. When Vincent is finally beaten to the ground, Evans continues to bludgeon him until the stage is almost covered in red ribbons. After the final blow, the final wood block sound, a moment of silence.)*
>
> *(Lights up on Lily and Patti stage right.)*

LILY: After wedding, Patti, I teach Vincent, after.

> *(The lights fade on Lily, then slowly fade on Vincent.)*

END ACT I

ACT II

In place of the car salesman and the slides of American cars in ACT I, we now see a Chinese man, the Sifu (Tai Chi teacher) and a female student/warrior doing the Tai Chi movement of "Carry the Tiger to the Mountain."

SIFU: Tai Chi Chuan, the ancient Chinese art of exercise and self-defense. "Tai Chi" refers to the whole circle, with its two complementary parts Yin and Yang, light and dark, softness and strength. "Chuan" is combat, an integration to harmonize antagonistic movements within oneself and with an opponent. Here *(The Sifu refers to the warrior.)* at the beginning of the second set, we see the move "Carry the Tiger to the Mountain." The weight of the horse shifts, the right foot takes a step to the southeast, the left foot turns its sole to face east . . .
(Light fades down on Sifu. Sound of telephone ringing. Lights up on scrim of Lily in her bathrobe, sleepily answering the telephone.)

LILY: Vincent, you forget key again? *(A pause as Lily gets news.)* NO.
(Lily quickly leaves the scrim, lights fade down. In another pool of light Vincent is wheeled in on a hospital bed by a nurse. His head is in bandages, we hear the sound of a ventilator, the sound of a heart monitor. He is on IV. The nurse exits. Lily enters the pool of light in a rush, but stops dead in her tracks when she sees Vincent. For a moment, she is too horrified to move, then she goes to his bedside, stroking his hand, his head.)

LILY: Vincent, Vincent, what happen? What they do to you?
(Lily freezes. From the darkness outside the pool of the hospital light, a cascade of voices, each person coming into a light, the voices should almost overlap. The voices include Tommy, the showgirl, the car salesman/bouncer, Evans, Stetz, and a policeman.)

TOMMY: Started in the bar—

SHOWGIRL: Called him a motherfucker—

CAR SALESMAN: Told them to take it outside—

EVANS: I had a few drinks—

STETZ: Just a bar room fight—

POLICEMAN: Last assault took place in a McDonald's parking lot—

TOMMY: Chased him for twenty minutes—

SHOWGIRL: Said his kind put them outta work—

CAR SALESMAN: I am not responsible—

EVANS: It was just in my hands, I don't know how—

STETZ: Wanted to teach him a lesson is all—

POLICEMAN: At least four blows to the skull with a baseball bat, Louisville slug-
ger—

TOMMY: Called an ambulance right away—

SHOWGIRL: Called him a nip—

CAR SALESMAN: I had nothing to do with it—

EVANS: I was drunk—

STETZ: He started it—

POLICEMAN: Arrested the two immediately as an off-duty officer at the scene—

TOMMY: Before he lost consciousness he said, "It isn't fair"—

SHOWGIRL: A shame, a real shame—

CAR SALESMAN: Keep me out of it—

EVANS: Arrested? But it was an accident—

STETZ: Arrested? What's the big deal here?

(The police officer is replaced by a doctor, who steps into the hospital scene
with Lily.)

DOCTOR: I'm very sorry, Mrs. Chin, we tried, we worked on him for eight
hours, but the brain sustained too much trauma. Your son is brain-dead.

LILY: Dead?

DOCTOR: All the scans show no activity in either lobe. He's being kept alive
entirely through artificial means.

LILY: Alive?

DOCTOR: There is nothing we can do.

LILY: Nothing?

DOCTOR: In cases like this, the hospital lets the next of kin decide when to
remove the life support. I'm sorry. There is no hope of recovery.

LILY: No hope?

DOCTOR: As his surgeon, I will respect your wishes.

LILY: If mother can not give son hope, what else can she give?

DOCTOR: Mrs. Chin, I know this is hard to accept right now—

LILY: Mother always have hope. You know better than mother? *(Beat.)* GET
OUT.

DOCTOR: This is a very difficult time—

LILY: GET OUT.

DOCTOR: The hospital will respect your decision.

(Doctor exits. Lily bends over Vincent.)

LILY: I teach you Tai Chi breathing. In, out, slow like this. *(She demonstrates.)*
Make you better, make you well. Doctor don't know how. Mama know.

I teach you, Vincent, mama here. I stay with you. Mama always with you, always here.

(She holds on to Vincent's hand, she touches her forehead to his hands, lights change, as Lily freezes. A healthy Vincent appears, he does the Tai Chi movement he describes.)

VINCENT: I'm getting it down. That move, what is it called? Clouds? Yeah, clouds. Keep the arms in motion, hold your hands like you've got a basketball in them, and at the end you do a single whip, which is sort of like shifting gears in a car, transferring into fifth after cruising in fourth without changing speed. What do you think? Am I doing it right? Ma . . . Ma?

(Patti enters hospital light, overlapping on Vincent's "Ma.")

VINCENT/PATTI LIN: Ma?

(Lily raises her head.)

PATTI LIN: Ma . . . Mom . . . Mom? It's me, Patti.

LILY: I want you to squeeze Vincent hand, Patti. Doctor say no hope, but you squeeze his hand. Say hello. Vincent your bride-to-be here. Vincent open eyes. Say hi to Patti.

PATTI LIN: Vincent? Vincent?

(In silence, Patti embraces Vincent lying in the bed, she is saying good-bye. Lily still does not accept that Vincent is brain-dead. The healthy Vincent continues to practice his Tai Chi throughout.)

VINCENT: One of my favorite moves is "Snake creeps down" and then "Golden cock stands on one leg." And what comes next? Oh yeah, "Repulse the monkey" Have I got the order right? Is that what comes next?

(Tommy, enters the hospital light to say good-bye to the Vincent in the bed.)

TOMMY: Mrs. Chin?

LILY: *(To Vincent in bed.)* Vincent, best man here. Vincent say hello to Tommy. Vincent open eyes, Tommy here for you. Vincent?

TOMMY: *(To Vincent in bed.)* Buddy, I'm sorry, man. I'm so, so sorry.

(Tommy gives the Vincent in the bed a farewell handshake. He gives his condolences to Patti, the two exit the hospital pool of light. The healthy Vincent continues to do Tai Chi.)

VINCENT: I think I missed something. "Step up to form Seven Stars?" Did I do that already? Did I miss something? What have I missed?

(Fortune-teller Wong enters the hospital light.)

WONG: It's time, Mrs. Chin.

LILY: Not yet. He too young. Whole life ahead. He and Patti marry, have children, I live with them. You say June 27th, wedding day.

WONG: A day of momentous change, when the funeral takes place. The day his spirit must leave, three days after death. It's time, Mrs. Chin.

LILY: No, no, NO.

(A nurse enters the pool of light.)

NURSE: I'll be outside, Mrs. Chin. Ring when you're ready.

(The nurse exits. Fortune-teller Wong gives Lily another brass locket. The healthy Vincent should be finishing his last set of moves, freezing with his hands crossed in front of him in the closing position. Light on him fades.)

LILY: Vincent, you hear Mama? You always good boy . . . Never talk back. Always happy, laugh, make joke. Make me smile, make me so proud. You hear Mama? Doctor say no hear, no see, no feeling. Doctor say no hope, If Mama can't give you hope what else I give? I not protect you, Vincent. I fail. Mama fail. Vincent . . . my Vincent . . . Mama protect you now. Mama, keep you safe.

(She takes the brass locket fortune-teller Wong gave her, and places it on Vincent's inert body. Wong exits to get the nurse. The nurse enters, Lily stands aside, as the nurse disconnects the ventilator, the IV. The sound of the ventilator should cease, the beep of the heart monitor getting slower.)

NURSE: He's going fast, Mrs. Chin.

LILY: *(Rushing to bedside.)* Mama here, Vincent, Mama here.

(The flatline sound of the heart monitor signaling death should drone on merging with the sound of a Buddhist bell heard before that signaled David's death. The monitor sound ceases as the bell continues to ring. The nurse wheels away Vincent's body leaving Lily standing alone. The ringing of the bell stops. In silence, in her separate pool of light, Lily tries to do her Tai Chi exercise as in the prologue. She cannot get through it, freezing at the Lady Looks at the Mirror move.)

LILY: Lady looking at Mirror. What does she see?

(Hannah enters as in the prologue.)

HANNAH: Mrs. Chin. It's time.

LILY: I didn't teach him. If he knew. Must keep both feet planted, keep horse even, shift weight, this hand goes for throat, keep tongue to roof of mouth, let life force move to fingernail, sharp like ax to wood . . . I didn't teach him, Hannah

HANNAH: The limousine is outside.

LILY: Mama coming, Vincent, mama coming.

(The lights fade down as Lily and Hannah exit.)

(Lights up on the Sifu giving another demonstration of Tai Chi with the female warrior. This time the move is, "White stork cools its wings.")

Carry the Tiger to the Mountain 147

SIFU: When opportunity and conditions of strength are not grasped, the body is scattered and in disorder. Then the fault must be sought in the center and at the extremes. Up or down, forward or backward, offense or defense, in all movements, this fault is to be guarded against. White stork cools its wings.

(Lights fade down on Sifu. Lights up on Evans and Stetz talking to their attorney, Katz.)

KATZ: You're lucky I got you out on bail. The boy died, you know. That makes this murder two.

EVANS: Look, I admit I was drunk, but I didn't mean no harm—

KATZ: Mr. Evans, you were arrested in the McDonald's parking lot standing over the victim whose head you just bashed in with a baseball bat. There were witnesses.

STETZ: Hey, the gook started it, he sucker punched him, got us all thrown out of that bar —

EVANS: Son, let me tell this my way—

KATZ: Son? You two are related?

EVANS: Mark is my stepson. But I raised him like my flesh and blood. And he's an eye witness, that kid hit me first.

KATZ: So it was an unprovoked attack on you which started it?

EVANS: Hell, I don't know, it was a bar fight, one thing led to another, right, Mark?

KATZ: Did you feel your life was in danger, is this a case of self-defense?

STETZ: Damn right, it was self-defense. Don works at Chrysler. Me too, but only part-time. Those stinkin' Japanese think they can kick butt, take away our livelihood—

KATZ: Mr. Stetz, Mr. Evans, Vincent Chin was Chinese-American, he was not Japanese.

(Pause.)

EVANS: You know how it goes after a few beers, who can tell the difference. All I know is the kid hit me first, so naturally I had to stand up for myself, way I was raised. Nothing wrong with that, right Mark?

KATZ: So you're saying in the heat of the battle, things got out of hand.

STETZ: Yeah, and driving around looking for that chickenshit didn't make it no better.

KATZ: You drove around looking for Chin after he left the bar?

STETZ: Yellow-skinned gook took off, scared as hell once he saw a piece of good ol American lumber—

KATZ: How long did you drive around looking for him?

STETZ: 'Bout twenty minutes or so.

KATZ: Twenty minutes before you confronted Chin again?

STETZ: Maybe it was thirty minutes, hell, what difference—

KATZ: *(Overlapping.)* That's not exactly the heat of battle—

STETZ: *(Overlapping.)* So what, that chink had it coming—

EVANS: *(To Stetz.)* SHUT THE FUCK UP. KEEP YOUR DAMN MOUTH SHUT OR I'LL BUST YOU ONE GOOD. *(Silence, then to Katz.)* Like I said, we'd had a few drinks, the kid punched me, next thing I remember was some cop reading me my rights and me holding a baseball bat. I don't remember nothing else. Now, can you do something for us or not?

KATZ: *(Sighing.)* I'll try for a plea bargain, but I don't know if the DA will go for it. I'll try knocking the charge down to manslaughter in exchange for a clear admission of guilt.

STETZ: Hey, I'm not admitting to nothing. I didn't even hit him with the bat, *(Pointing to Evans.)* he's the one who took the cuts.

EVANS: SHUT UP, SON. *(Beat.)* Will I have to do time?

KATZ: The boy is dead.

EVANS: But I've got a wife, a family, house payments, it was an accident—

KATZ: You drove around searching for him for twenty minutes by accident.

EVANS: Well, we was driving . . . we was driving around . . . looking for a hospital . . . yeah, a hospital.

KATZ: A hospital?

EVANS: Yeah, Mark's eye was messed up bad by that kid in the bar fight, right, son?

STETZ: What?

EVANS: YOUR EYE—

STETZ: Uh, right. Skin above my eye was bleedin' so bad I couldn't hardly tell Japanese from Chinese.

EVANS: Naturally when I saw my stepson hurt, we had to find a hospital. So we was driving around and I saw that kid, and I was so mad . . . no, so scared about my stepsons' eye, that I . . . I . . . and that's why it all happened in the McDonald's parking lot. Does that explain it?
(Long pause.)

KATZ: Okay. *(To Evans.)* You'll plead guilty to manslaughter. *(To Stetz.)* And you'll plead—

STETZ: I don't plead nothin.

EVANS: DO AS YOU'RE TOLD—

KATZ: *(To Stetz.)* You'll plead: Nolo contendre.

STETZ: What's that mean, huh? No to what?

KATZ: It means: No contest.

(Crossfade. Lights up in Chin home. Lily sits behind a scrim, zombie-like. Hannah is helping to clear out wedding presents. Patti, also in dark clothes, enters, carrying a carton of Chinese food.)

PATTI LIN: I brought over some noodles, Hannah, I thought I could help out.

HANNAH: Mrs. Chin, Patti's here. Mrs. Chin? *(No answer. To Patti.)* She's been like this since . . . how are you doing?

PATTI LIN: Trying to stay busy. I thought maybe I'd come by and do something . . . Ma, have you eaten? Ma, can I come in?

LILY: No say Ma. Vincent say Ma. I'm not your Ma.

PATTI LIN: I thought I could help you sort things out, maybe together we could clean Vincent's room—

LILY: I don't touch Vincent's room. It make me cry. I don't go into garden, it make me cry, I don't go out—

PATTI LIN: Then let me do something for you—

LILY: I don't want your help. You make me cry. You make me see him, see future he never get, house he never buy, children he never have. Go away.

PATTI LIN: Mom . . . Ma *(She stops herself.)* please. I lost Vincent too. I want to do something. Let me.

LILY: You lose Vincent, you lose a flame. I lose Vincent, I lose my whole life. Nothing you can do. GO AWAY.

(Patti doesn't know what to say, she looks at Hannah, at Lily, not knowing what to do, Patti hesitates, then gives the carton to Hannah. Patti is about to leave when Lily steps out from behind the scrim to face her.)

LILY: Patti, you young beautiful, sweet girl. Still have whole life ahead. You marry someday, have family, have good life. Vincent . . . Vincent love you very much. Good-bye.

(Lily goes back behind the scrim, back to sitting in her old position leaving Patti staring at her.)

PATTI LIN: Good-bye, Mom. Mrs. Chin.

(Patti rushes out. Hannah looks at the food.)

HANNAH: *(To Lily.)* You can't go on like this, you've got to eat something.

LILY: I didn't help him. I fail, Hannah. I fail Vincent, I fail my only son,

HANNAH: No you didn't. Don't punish yourself. The two men who killed Vincent are the ones to be punished. Mrs. Chin . . . Mrs. Chin? *(Beat.)* Wouldn't Vincent want you to eat something?

(A beat. Then Lily comes out from behind the scrim,)

LILY: He always worry over me. Even when little, when he first come into family. He hold my hand crossing street, always say, watch out, car coming, look both ways. *(She looks both ways.)* I give him live pet rabbit for eighth birthday, but rabbit freeze outside, not move. Little Vincent say, quick, put him in oven, thaw him out, ma, make him well again. He . . . he . . . so . . . gentle. Can't even kill fish for supper. He go fishing, with me and Baba, he catch fish and let it go. Baba say, "Just hit fish over head with stick, Vincent, make good dinner." Not Vincent. He can't. He say, "You do it, Ma." So I hit fish. I do it with eyes closed to make Vincent his favorite dish. Steam bass with black bean sauce. Vincent serve me fish cheek, sweetest part. Always give me sweetest part. I hit fish on head with stick . . . I hit . . . I hit . . . the way they kill . . . they kill Vincent like animal . . . like animal, Hannah.

HANNAH: They'll be punished. They'll be in jail for a long, long time. Don't worry, they'll be punished.

(Lights fade.)

(Lights up on Sifu, with a demonstration of Tai Chi with a healthy Vincent and the female opponent. The move is "Needle at the bottom of the sea" a defensive move to ward off an opponent with a stick.)

SIFU: This move is called, "Needle at the bottom of the sea." Notice only the toe touches the floor, the torso bends forward from the waist, the body is lowered as much by the bending of the legs as by tipping forward. The head is held upright, not bent down, and the eyes are looking straight ahead. A mistake of inches, but an error of a thousand leagues, therefore the student should pay careful heed to what is said.

(Light on Sifu fades, but the two Tai Chi students continue their movement behind a scrim, their movements should bear some similarity to the beating of Vincent Chin. Lights up on a Judge who sits before defense attorney Katz, Stetz, and Evans. The prosecution side of the court is noticeably absent.)

JUDGE: Before the sentencing, does the prosecution for the state have anything to add? *(Silence.)* As no one from the prosecution is present, this court will proceed. Will the defendants please rise.

(Evans, Stetz, and their attorney rise for the sentencing.)

JUDGE: You have pleaded guilty to the charge of manslaughter in the beating death of Vincent Chin. Donald Evans you are a responsible man who has worked at Chrysler for eighteen years with no previous criminal record. Your stepson, Mark Stetz, has also worked for Chrysler and also has no criminal record. Mark, I understand you are a part-time student as well. I do not think putting either one of you in prison would do you or society any good. In my court, you don't make the punishment fit the crime: You make the punishment fit the criminal. I believe you two men are still responsible citizens who would not go out and harm anyone else. Therefore, I hereby order each of you to serve three years probation, and to pay fines and court costs totaling $3780. You are ordered to repay this debt to society at a rate of $125 dollars a month. Case closed.

(Katz, Evans, Stetz shake hands, congratulate each other as they exit. The Tai Chi demonstration ends, the light on them goes out as the Judge pounds the gavel. At the sound of the gavel, as in the prologue, a slide of a new 1982 American car appears. The Judge throws off his judicial robes and reveals himself to be the car salesman seen in the prologue.)

CAR SALESMAN: Three thousand seven hundred and eighty dollars? That's all? Well, you can't get a new car for that, forget it. No, we don't sell any imports. This is an American dealership, American got it? This is Detroit, Motor City, US of A. Hey, you can take your lousy three thousand bucks and shove it up your—

(Lights up on an outraged circle of Asian citizens and Lily, again a cascade of voices that almost overlap.)

TOMMY: Three thousand dollars? You're joking.

WONG: Three years probation? Outrageous.

TOMMY: There's a bigger punishment for dog killing—

HANNAH: They killed a Chinese man like an animal—

TOMMY: It's open season on Asians—

HANNAH: It's all right to kill so long as you work for Chrysler?

WONG: What do I teach my grandchildren about American Justice?

TOMMY: Just like Vincent's last words, "It isn't fair."

LILY: No punishment? NOTHING? Vincent not worthless, my son, not animal, my son good, my son, my son . . .

(Lily collapses, she is tended to by Hannah, who helps Lily to sit in a chair in the Chin house. A very business-like Asian lawyer carrying a briefcase, Eva Louie, steps into Chin home pool of light. Lily sits utterly desolate.)

HANNAH: Mrs. Chin, Mrs. Chin, there's a lawyer here to see you, her name is Eva Louie.

EVA: Mrs. Chin, I'm sorry to intrude on your grief, but I want you to know, the Asian community of Detroit is outraged by the sentence given to your son's murderers.

LILY: My son good, Vincent not animal . . .

EVA: Many of us want to take action against this travesty of justice.

HANNAH: Can you get the men re-tried?

EVA: That would be double jeopardy, that's against the law.

LILY: Law. What kind of law let killers go free?

EVA: What we can do, Mrs. Chin, is to circulate petitions against the decision, get as many people as we know to sign them, we can call up our elected officials and let them know this sentence stinks.

HANNAH: What will that do?

EVA: Our hope is to put public pressure on the judge, bring in the media, let him know that Asian Americans are united against this injustice and force him to rescind his decision. We have to make waves, hold demonstrations, petition people on the streets, and . . . and Mrs. Chin, we'd like your support.

LILY: You want me to talk to strangers on street? Stranger not care, strangers kill Vincent.

EVA: There are many, many people who want justice for Vincent. We have to take action or we'll be condoning this kind of discrimination. Do you understand what I'm getting at?

(Eva puts her left hand on Lily's hand. Lily notices Eva doesn't wear a wedding band.)

LILY: Not married. You have boyfriend Miss Louie?

EVA: Please call me, Eva. We'd like you to stand with us at rallies, press conferences . . . maybe say a few words. I know how painful—

LILY: How can you know? Only a mother know. You not even married, yet.

EVA: You would help people to understand what happened, be a symbol—

LILY: I'm the mama, I only have son. One son. Now no more. No more dream.

HANNAH: Mrs. Chin has suffered enough grief, she doesn't need to take it public.

EVA: She would put a face and voice to anti-Asian discrimination—

LILY: You want me to talk about Vincent. How much my heart ache for him, how every day feel empty? You not know what it feels like to have child, watch him grow, watch him die. When I think of my Vincent, such a good son, his hair always combed so nice, all gone . . . all gone . . .

(Lily breaks down.)

HANNAH: Perhaps you should go, Eva.

(She starts to show Eva out.)

EVA: Thank you for seeing me, Mrs. Chin. We'll respect your privacy. My deepest sympathy.

(The women freeze. A healthy Vincent appears. He is doing Tai Chi. He is practicing the end of the second set, getting ready for the third, he does the movements as he says them. Lily is the only one aware of him.)

VINCENT: Watch this. Step up, parry and punch. Pretty good, huh? So I'm ready for the third set, now. After the carry the tiger to the mountain move, after the single whip, part the wild horses' mane, and grasp the bird's tail, then comes . . . then comes what? . . . then comes, fair lady works at shuttles. Have I got it?

LILY: Very good, Vincent. But I didn't teach you. How did you learn?

VINCENT: Fair lady works the shuttles. Yeah, it's a good one, real defense. Gotta show the bastards. Sifu says, "When you yield to a hard force, it is called moving away, when you take on a hard force, this is called, sticking with it."

LILY: Vincent, who taught you?

VINCENT: Fair lady works at the shuttle. "When you take on a hard force, this is called, sticking with it." Got it.

(The healthy Vincent disappears. The other two women unfreeze. Lily calls Eva back.)

LILY: Miss Louie? Eva? You want me talk to stranger, I talk. I want justice for Vincent. I stick with it.

(Crossfade, lights up on five white auto workers facing audience protesting Japanese imports. They carry protest posters "Park it in Tokyo" "U.S. cars for U.S. roads" "Buy American" "Jap Cars = No Jobs." They chant.)

AUTOWORKERS: HEY, HEY, HO, HO,
JAPANESE CARS ARE PRICED TOO LOW

(The auto workers continue to chant, but are replaced by Asian faces who takeover the posters and turn them around. The posters now read "Justice for Vincent" "It's not fair" "Jail Racist Killers" "$3000 ≠ human life." The Asian demonstrators chant:)

DEMONSTRATORS: HEY, HEY, HO, HO
RACIST KILLERS HAVE GOT TO GO

(Eva and Hannah are among the protesters. Eva holds a bullhorn, she addresses the audience.)

EVA: We, the United Citizens for Justice seek a reversal of the lenient sentence given to the murderers of Vincent Chin. There were two crimes committed in Detroit, the first one killed Vincent, the second one let his killers go free. Today, we stand united behind the person who has suffered the most terrible loss imaginable, but who has chosen to speak out against these Anti-Asian crimes, Vincent's mother, Lily Chin.

(Lily comes out and faces the crowd, the bullhorn is passed to her, she is shy, uncertain how to use it, but she speaks.)

LILY: I want justice for Vincent. I want justice for my son.

(The chant "We want justice, we want justice," starts and is continued as flashbulbs go off. The protesters and Lily move to one side of the stage. On the other side of the stage, we see Attorney Katz, Evans, and Stetz.)

EVANS: What's to sweat over? The judge refused to reverse his decision, even with all those demonstrations. He even said if he had it to do all over again, he'd do the same thing.

KATZ: Don't you get it? The publicity has brought in the F.B.I., they're reinvestigating the way the entire case was handled. The Justice Department is getting involved.

STETZ: So? The judge let us go.

KATZ: Because you pleaded guilty. You weren't acquitted, you cut a deal.

EVANS: You think it could backfire?

STETZ: Shit, I knew it, you said it was no contest, I knew we shouldn't have pleaded nothing—

EVANS: *(To Stetz.)* SHUT UP. *(To Katz.)* So what's the worst that could happen?

KATZ: You could both be tried in a Federal criminal court for violation of Chin's civil rights. They're making this a racial thing.

EVANS: Oh for crying out loud—We ain't racists, it was an accident.

STETZ: I thought you said we'd be done with this shit, I'm still a part-time student—

KATZ: It's not certain things will go that far. But with all this hoopla over the Chin woman . . . she's been going to so many support rallies, you'd think she was running for office.

EVANS: What are our chances?

KATZ: I don't know, the Feds have never tried a case like this before. Blacks, yes, but not Asians. We might still get by if the media focused on some other issue besides that . . . that . . . that mother.

(Crossfade to Lily standing at a podium, her supporters behind her. She addresses the audience. This time Lily is much more assured, much more forceful in the way she speaks.)

LILY: I speak to you as Vincent's Mama, so no other mama have to go through what I go through. If two Chinese kill white person, they go to jail, maybe for whole life. My son, Chinese. Two white men kill him, beat him like animal *(Her voice breaks, but she continues.)* . . . they don't go to jail, only get three-year probation, pay fine, three thousand dollar. This not justice. This not fair. Skin is different, but heart the same. A mother always want to protect children, give children hope. No hope without justice. I want justice for Vincent. I want justice for my son. Thank you.

(Sound of applause. Lily steps away from the podium, she is totally exhausted. The podium is wheeled away, Hannah helps Lily to sit.)

HANNAH: You did great. Tired?

(Eva enters very excited.)

EVA: We've got letters of support from the Mayor of Highland Park, the Attorney

General of the State of Michigan, the archdiocese of Detroit, the Roundtable of Christians and Jews, the Latino-Americans for Social and Economic Development, the Anti-Defamation League, and the NAACP. And here's the topper, Mrs. Chin, I just got word that the Justice Department has granted us an interview with Asst. Attorney General William Bradford Reynolds. We fly to Washington next week. We're finally going to get a federal court to put those killers away. Isn't that great?

(Eva and Hannah high-five each other. Lily stays seated, lost in her own thoughts.)

LILY: *(To herself.)* Vincent twenty-nine year old today. If he live.

(This cuts short the celebration of the two younger women. Lights fade.)

(Lights up on the Sifu. He is demonstrating "repulse the monkey" to a healthy Vincent who continues the movement as Sifu speaks.)

SIFU: Step back and repulse monkey. Often one encounters someone who even with many years of study is still subdued by others. To avoid this one must know to stick is also to move away, to move away is also to stick. Understanding of this is necessary in order to understand force.

(Lights fade on Sifu and Vincent, Cross fade up on Eva Louie with Tommy, the showgirl, the car salesman. Eva starts a tape recorder.)

EVA: In filing our brief with the Justice Department, it's important to discover exactly what was said that night leading up to the beating. If Vincent was interfered with because of his race while enjoying the services of a public place.

TOMMY: Like I said, I heard Vincent saying, "I'm not a motherfucker."

EVA: In response to Evans saying to him: It's because of motherfuckers like you, we're out of work?

TOMMY: I remember that white guy saying something like: I don't know if you're a big fucker or a little fucker.

EVA: And the thing about jobs referring to being Asian?

TOMMY: Ms. Louie, the music was real loud—

SHOWGIRL: I remember hearing it, that white guy cut in and shoved Vincent out of the way, and that's when he said motherfuckers like him took away jobs.

CAR SALESMAN: Yeah, right, like you remember everything you hear from johns.

SHOWGIRL: I am an exotic dancer in a public place and he wasn't a john.

CAR SALESMAN: And I have a car that gets a 1000 miles to the gallon.

(Eva turns to the Car Salesman.)

EVA: What did you hear that night?

CAR SALESMAN: What's the matter? Afraid no one will believe little miss exotic dancer here?

EVA: I'm trying to make sure of the facts. There was a terrible miscarriage of justice, and I want to help make it right.

CAR SALESMAN: You have a lot riding on this case, don't you? Helping the Justice Department, helping the Asian community, helping that poor mother whose face has been in every single newspaper in Detroit for the last two years. You're just really helpful. I bet you think you can right all the wrongs of the world, all the little slights, anytime anyone ever looked at you the wrong way. I bet you think you're ready for the big leagues now, law school education, standing on high ground, breathing clean air, not like some of us in Detroit who have to sell cars for a living.

EVA: What do you remember Donald Evans saying to Vincent Chin on the night in question?

CAR SALESMAN: Me? *(He thinks, then pointedly into the tape recorder.)* I didn't hear anything, I just stopped a fight.

(Loud sound of a gavel, representing the first federal court decision. Crossfade. Lights up on Katz, Stetz, and Evans.)

EVANS: NO WAY. On top of all this mess, she thinks I'm going to pay her? How am I supposed to pay her when a Federal court sentenced me to twenty-five years?

KATZ: Take it easy. We filed an appeal, you're still out on bail.

EVANS: I don't care how many wrongful death suits she brings against me, no way I'm going to pay that Chin woman nothing.

KATZ: The civil suit can't go forward until after the appeal. You don't have to pay her anything yet.

STETZ: I hear Chrysler's rehiring. Maybe you could get your old job back—

EVANS: Shut your mouth. You go to work and support this family. You're the only one found *(Mimicking woman Judge's voice.)* "Not Guilty."

STETZ: Hey, I wasn't the guy who swung the bat, I wasn't the guy who said it was motherfuckers like him who took away our jobs, I'm only part-time—

EVANS: *(Pointing to Stetz's brain.)* Part-time up there.

STETZ: You could still make a few bucks before—

EVANS: Are you kidding? Every cent I make will end up going to that Chin woman. After what she's put this family through? I'll starve first. It's been four fucking years, and I'm still in fucking court. When does this thing end?

KATZ: Don't worry. The conviction will be declared a mistrial. We've got copies of the tapes.

EVANS: The judge didn't let you use them.

KATZ: That's why it's a mistrial. The tapes should have been admitted. To me they sound suspiciously like a certain over-achieving Chinese lawyer was interfering with justice by attempting to coach witnesses. I mean what the hell was she doing interviewing people, she's not the prosecuting attorney? *(Crossfade. Eva steps into the Chin home, Hannah is with Lily who is seated. Eva is exasperated.)*

EVA: I'm sorry Mrs. Chin. The federal conviction was declared a mistrial.

HANNAH: A mistrial? What happened?

EVA: The district court ruled that the tapes I made should have been admitted as evidence. The defense claims they show I coached witnesses. I wasn't coaching witnesses, I was checking the facts to file our brief.

HANNAH: So the case will have to be retried?

EVA: And there's more bad news. The new trial will be held in Cincinnati, not Detroit.

HANNAH: Cincinnati? Why?

EVA: The court ruled there was "intolerable prejudice" created against Evans by all the publicity surrounding Mrs. Chin, that Evans couldn't get a fair trial in Detroit.

LILY: What "intolerable prejudice" mean?

EVA: Virulent and inflammatory in intensity and duration—

HANNAH: Like beating someone to death with a baseball bat?

EVA: I'm really, really sorry Mrs. Chin. I was sure the conviction would stick, but . . . we can still win.

HANNAH: Everything we've done is being used against us. We've got to organize demonstrations in Cincinnati.

EVA: I don't think there will be time. They're going to re-try very quickly so we can't prejudice the jury pool.

LILY: "Intolerable prejudice?" I don't understand. I have to speak out or Vincent forgotten, killers go free. They say I speak out too much?

EVA: Once this second jury hears all the facts, they will bring a conviction. We just have to . . . to go through a whole new trial in Cincinnati. I'm sorry.

HANNAH: *(To Lily.)* You'll have to listen to the evidence about what happened to Vincent again, Mrs. Chin. You don't have to go, if that would be too painful—

LILY: No hear, no see, no feeling. The way killers leave Vincent. Brain-dead. They don't want to hear us. Don't want to see us, don't want us to feel.

They want us invisible. Brain-dead. Don't be heard, don't be seen. *(Beat.)*
White snake put out tongue.

HANNAH: What?

LILY: Like this.

(Lily does the Tai Chi move "White snake puts out tongue.")

LILY: This hand go for throat. Move life force to fingernail, sharp like ax to
wood. I go to Cincinnati trial. I *make* them see me again.

(Lights down.)

*(Lights up on Tai Chi demonstration. This time Vincent is acting as the teacher,
the Sifu is the pupil, doing "wave hands like clouds.")*

VINCENT: The hand which is above descends, and the hand which is down
comes up. The leg which bears the weight becomes empty as the weight
shifts to the empty leg which in turn becomes full. The arms continually
describe circles, large or small, the hands continually move through the
globe-holding positions of Yin and Yang. No movement is complete in
itself: it is always becoming something else, moving toward its opposite.
And the end is not an end, but the beginning of another movement.

*(Lights up on split scene. On one side of the stage are Katz, Evans, and Stetz,
on the other side, Hannah, Eva, and Lily. The two sides do not interact, though
they may address someone on their side.)*

EVANS: I know I never called him a motherfucking Nip. I told you I'm no racist.

LILY: What mean mother Fukien? I not from Fukien, I from Guangzhou.

EVANS: I was just drunk, I didn't single him out because of race.

STETZ: He calls lots of white guys motherfuckers, too—

EVANS: SHUT UP MARK—

EVA: The defense is going to make it sound like race had nothing to do with it.

EVANS: He never said he wasn't Japanese cause race never came up. He said he
wasn't a motherfucker.

HANNAH: But the worst thing Evans could have said to Vincent was to call
him a motherfucker. That's a terrible insult to a Chinese son.

EVA: Vincent reacted to racial slurs.

KATZ: Chin simply over-reacted to nonracial name-calling and threw the first
punch.

HANNAH: Of course he would react. Vincent was extremely dutiful and respectful to his mother. He was a filial son.

STETZ: Could have called him an asshole instead—

EVANS: SHUT UP, MARK—

EVA: A witness heard the baiting. She said it was racial—

HANNAH: It was cultural—

EVANS: It wasn't nothing personal—

STETZ: It was an accident—

KATZ: Not everything is about race.

EVA: He practically called him a Jap—

STETZ: Gook—

EVANS: Nip—

HANNAH: Chink—

LILY: What difference what word he use? HE KILL MY SON.

(*Change in lighting. Eva, Hannah, and Lily are seated on one side of a court-room, Evans and Stetz, sit on the other. Katz stands, delivering his closing address to the jury, the audience.*)

KATZ: And in conclusion, the jury must see that this was a tragic event that had nothing to do with racial hatred, but everything to do with two men who had way too much to drink. You have seen the evidence, you have heard the tapes. The prosecution has not delivered on its promise, to prove beyond a reasonable doubt, that Donald Evans willfully singled out Vincent Chin because of his race, color, or national origin. And that is all you are being asked to decide. My client has never denied what happened on June 19th, 1982. He has never attempted to jump bail, break his probation, or tried to run away from his responsibility in the four long years it's taken to process this case through the justice system. He is extremely remorseful over what happened and will continue to live with that fateful night for the rest of his days. I ask you to judge Donald Evans as you would judge yourselves. Look at the man before you, a man who has never had a criminal record, who has a family to support, who like all of you, has worked all his life, tried to be a good father, tried to make amends for his past mistakes. He has already been sentenced for the crime he committed, he has paid his debt to society and continues to pay every day of his life. Enough is enough. I ask you to find Donald Evans: Not Guilty. (*The lights go back to the split scene lighting, with the two sides separate as before.*)

HANNAH: What do you think the jury will do?

EVA: I don't know, they're inscrutable. There's not one Asian face on it.

EVANS: So what do you think?

KATZ: I think I hit a home run.

LILY: Nobody look me in eye. Look through me like invisible. They not see me, not see Vincent.

STETZ: The white guy on the end looked right at you, Don.

HANNAH: Is there anything more we can do?

EVANS: What if I'm found guilty?

LILY: What if he go free?

EVA: This is it.

STETZ: Will this be it?

KATZ: This is it, as far as I'm concerned.

HANNAH: The jury's back.

EVANS: Then this is it.

(*Lights change back to courtroom. Lily, Eva, Hannah seated on one side, Evans, Stetz, and Katz on the other. A judge's bench is wheeled with the Judge behind it.*)

JUDGE: Will the defendant please rise?

(*Evans and Katz rise, Stetz remains seated.*)

JUDGE: Will the clerk please read the verdict?

(*The clerk enters.*)

CLERK: The Southern District Circuit Court of Ohio, in the case of the United States vs. Donald Evans in violation of section 18 United States Code 245(b)paragraph (2)(F), on the charge of willfully injuring, intimidating, and interfering with Vincent Chin on account of his race or national origin, we the jury, find the defendant, Donald Evans: Not Guilty.

(*An audible gasp of disbelief from Mrs. Chin, Hannah, and Eva.*)

JUDGE: The defendant is hereby acquitted of all charges. Mr. Evans you are free to go.

(*The judge pounds his gavel. The clerk and judge exit with the judges bench. Stetz jumps up and high-fives Evans, Katz congratulates him, the three celebrate. The three women on the other side of the aisle are stunned. Lily in particular cannot move, she simply stares straight ahead. The three men finish their celebration and start to exit, passing by where the three women sit. For the first time there is actual face-to-face confrontation. There is a tense silent moment, then the men continue on their way.*)

HANNAH: There's got to be something we can do.

EVA: I don't know what to say, Mrs. Chin. I'm sorry. I'm really sorry.

(*Eva rushes out overcome with the failure, Hannah runs after her, leaving Lily alone. During the following voice over, Lily wants to find her center through Tai Chi movement, but cannot, she is almost in a trance, listening to a litany in her head.*)

LILY: (*Voice-over.*) How can I live in America with that kind of law? My heart is dim. How can I live in America? My heart is dim. How can I live? My heart is . . .

(*Light change. Sifu enters carrying a Tai Chi sword.*)

SIFU: (*Voice over.*)Tai Chi refers to the whole circle, yin and yang, light and dark, offense and defense, mercy and vengeance.

(*Sound of Chinese wood block. From Sifu, Lily picks up a sword to do Tai Chi sword play. Now her moves are strong, sure, punctuated by the Chinese wood block, and though she starts off slowly, the sword play gathers momentum. Vincent Chin enters the light leading Stetz and Evans with their hands tied behind their backs and placards around their necks, in the way Chinese criminals in the 1940s were paraded publicly before their execution. Vincent leads the two in a circle stopping before Lily and forcing them to kneel. Vincent exits. Lily stares at the two killers sword in hand. A Chinese woman warrior enters the light, she is the other student of martial arts in Sifu's Tai Chi demonstrations. She is the legendary Fa Mu Lan who takes revenge on the killing of family. Fa Mu Lan takes the Tai Chi sword from Lily. After circling the two men and demonstrating her prowess with the sword using many of Lily's sword moves, she finally takes batting practice, taking a few practice swings, knocking the dirt from her slippers, spitting on her hands, then Fa Mu Lan steps up to homeplate and with one slow motion swing, beheads Evans and Stetz. The wood block sound stops. The lights flood red, then a rousing chorus of "Take me out to the ball game," is heard as Fa Mu Lan raises her sword in triumph. The lights slowly fade to black.*)

END ACT TWO

EPILOGUE

Lights fade up on Hannah and Lily in the Chin home, 1987. Lily has a suitcase at her feet an airline ticket in hand.

HANNAH: *(Referring to suitcase.)* Is this the last one?

LILY: Never say last, bad luck, Hannah.

HANNAH: Are you sure about this? After living here for forty years?

LILY: I cannot live where my son life have no value. Nothing left for me here.

HANNAH: What are you going to do in China?

LILY: I think of something. What you going to do, Hannah? Find husband? Or career?

HANNAH: Actually, I found a career. I want to work in civil rights, continue what we started. Vincent united Asian Americans all across the country against discrimination. He showed us that we aren't treated equally. I want to continue to speak out, be seen, the way you said, stick with it.

LILY: Umm, I write to you, Hannah. I tell you if I find nice, Chinese boy.
(Hannah embraces Lily.)

HANNAH: I'm going to miss you.

LILY: You good girl, very helpful all the time. Thank you, *taw jeh.*

HANNAH: Thank you. We'd better get started, you have a long journey ahead.
(Lily and Hannah exit as the lights dim. In the dim light, one by one, the entire cast assembles. They are seen in silhouette. We hear wind chimes, an erhu or a peipa. The ensemble stands taking the position of the opening stance in Tai Chi. A light comes up on Hannah as she reads a letter from Lily. Lily enters and stands in front of the ensemble, she leads them in the first set of Tai Chi.)

HANNAH: Dear Hannah. Vincent Chin Recreation Center in my old village doing very good. Many young people come.

LILY: *(Voice-over.)* They call me Grandmother Chin, make me smile. You find husband yet? Remember, don't wait too long. I teach young people Tai Chi, teach them to breathe in and out, teach them balance, respect, I teach them to use chi, the life force. I teach them, "Carry the Tiger to the Mountain."
(The cast continues to do Tai Chi. We can hear them inhaling and exhaling. They continue the movement as the lights slowly fade to black.)

END OF PLAY

Acapulco

Jacquelyn Reingold

This play is for Sylvia

INTRODUCTION
by Warren Leight

Acapulco, the second you hear it, you think of Sinatra on the *Come Fly With Me* technicolor record cover. Acapulco Bay, "perfect for a flying honeymoon," in the stylish, glamorous 1950s. Unfortunately for Doris, it's February, 1966. The Rat Pack is gone, the honeymoon is long over, and the only rat is her husband Dick. Who has left her for Candy . . . the Whore of Brooklyn. Desperate, she finds herself on a plane to Acapulco, about to have her first affair . . . with a guy named Stew who dyes his chest hair, and runs a factory that makes hollow plastic cigarettes that never helped anyone quit smoking.

Welcome to Jackie Reingold's *Acapulco,* a terrific play about the end of an era and the end of a marriage. Her characters are real and funny and almost congenitally unable to see things as they really are. It's the mid-60s and life in the middle-class Jewish neighborhoods of Brooklyn is changing. At the center of the play is Doris, who came to New York when she was eighteen, to be a dancer: "But I had these terrible teeth from a baton-twirling accident and I couldn't afford to fix them and when I went to auditions I didn't smile. Who's gonna hire a girl without a smile?" Now she's a thirty-five-year-old woman who has been dumped in the middle of a major crossroad. Her husband has left her and her two kids and neither he, nor his mother, nor his girlfriend want him to pay alimony. Doris is justifiably petrified about starting out on her own and providing for them. The only option she can see is to remarry. Fast.

The play is structured brilliantly. As Doris flies south, and begins her affair, the story of Dick's betrayal unfolds in flashback scenes. These scenes are inter-cut with real time as all the players — the mother-in-law, the floozie, the lover, and the friend — make their way to Acapulco. There the past literally catches up with them, in a cheesy hotel room where we and Doris piece together the truth.

Even though her characters are flawed, and very funny, Jackie never makes fun of them. She tells their stories with insight and compassion. Doris is a hero in Loehmann's clothing. Dick and Stew and Ben and Candy and Nettie exist as fully realized characters, not just comic or dramatic foils. They all grope in the dark, and squint in the sunlight, desperate to find a shortcut to happiness or security. It's a bumpy flight, and Jackie's a great pilot.

Jacquelyn Reingold's play *Acapulco* received New Dramatists' 1999–2000 Whitfield Cook Award for best unproduced play. It was developed at various theaters: Bay Street Theatre, Manhattan Class Club, the Atlantic Theatre Company, Ensemble Studio Theatre, Naked Angels and HB Playwrights Theatre in New York; and in Los Angeles at EST/LA and the A.S.K. Theatre Projects. Jacquelyn's other plays, which include *Girl Gone, Dear Kenneth Blake, Dottie and Richie, Tunnel of Love, Lost and Found, A.M.L., Joe and Stew,* and *Freeze Tag* have been produced in New York at MCC, EST, Naked Angels, HB Playwrights, All Seasons, Working Theatre; in Los Angeles at Theatre of Note, TheatreGeo, the City Garage; and at theaters across the country and in London.

Jacquelyn received New Dramatists' 2000 Joe Callaway Award, a commission from EST/Sloan Foundation for her new play *String Fever,* the Kennedy Center's Fund for New American Plays' Roger Stevens Award, two Drama-Logue Awards, and she was a finalist for the Susan Smith Blackburn Prize. Her work has been published by Dramatist Play Service, Samuel French, in *Best American Short Plays 1997–98, 1996–97,* and *1994–95,* and Smith and Kraus's *Women Playwrights: The Best Plays of 1994.* Her screenplay adaptation of *Girl Gone* has been optioned by Beech Hill Films, and she has written for MTV's *Daria.*

Special thanks to the generous actors and directors who worked in the countless readings of *Acapulco.* They are too numerous to name, but my heartfelt gratitude to all of them. And most of all, thank you, Todd London, and the brilliant, amazing writers and staff at New Dramatists.

This play was developed in part with the support of A.S.K. Theater Projects.

CHARACTERS

DORIS: 35. Quirky, vulnerable, sexy, on edge. Upbeat on the outside, desperate on the inside. A survivor.

DICK: 40. Doris's soon to be ex. A liar. Handsome, successful, no morals.

BETTY AND BEN (A man): 40. African-American. A good-looking good guy.

NETTIE: 60s. Dick's mother. Strong but easily rattled. Came from Russian in her teens.

STEWART: 40–50. Gregarious. Too much but not bad. In lust with Doris.

CANDY: 35. Brooklyn babe. Knows what she wants.

SETTING

Various locations in Brooklyn, Queens, and Acapulco.

TIME

Early 1966.

ACAPULCO

ACT ONE
SCENE ONE

February 7, 1966. An airplane in flight. Doris, a bleached blonde, wears a bright, tight-fitting outfit. Next to her is Betty, a black man dressed as a woman, wearing a conservative suit. Their half-eaten meals are in front of them. Doris is crying.

DORIS: Oh, I'm sorry, I don't usually — I don't know what happened.

BETTY: It's O.K., look, here, um.
(Betty gives her a man's handkerchief.)

DORIS: Thank you — I just — I'm sorry. I guess it's all the talking. I haven't actually talked about it much, I guess.

BETTY: Can I get you some water?

DORIS: Thanks, but what I really want is a drink. *(Doris takes two miniature scotch bottles out of her purse.)* You want one?

BETTY: Please.

DORIS: I took these while the stewardess wasn't looking. I mean they charge a dollar fifty. I can't afford that.

BETTY: Oh, who can. *(Betty pours, then toasts.)* To Mexico.

DORIS: *(With a bad accent.)* México. *(They drink.)* I'm very glad to meet you. I don't usually tell a stranger all about my life. You're a very nice person, Susan.

BETTY: Betty.

DORIS: Right. Betty. I guess I'm a little nervous. *(Doris gets out a cigarette, Betty quickly lights it.)* Thanks. You want one?

BETTY: No.

DORIS: This is the smoking section, right? *(Betty nods.)* You don't smoke?

BETTY: No.

DORIS: You're right. I should quit. *(Doris puts it out, takes out a plastic cigarette, cleans off the lint, inhales.)* Menthol. It's supposed to work. It doesn't.
(Doris lights a real cigarette, inhales with pleasure, puts it out.)

BETTY: So. Tell me more: about this trip.

DORIS: *(Picks up the silverware from her meal, wipes it off, puts it in her purse.)* I think I'll keep these. My girls, Tracy and Robyn are five and nine, if I collect these by the time they're eighteen I'll have two full sets for them. They won't have to worry.

BETTY: Oh, that's a good idea, very resourceful.

DORIS: Thank you. *(Picks up the little salt and pepper shakers, empties them, puts them in her purse.)* These would be wonderful for large dinner parties, you could spread them around the dining room table, not that I have a dining room table anymore, or even a dining room, but maybe soon I will.

BETTY: Stewart. The man you're meeting in Mexico.

DORIS: Yes, Stewart. He's quite successful, did I tell you that?

BETTY: I think you did.

DORIS: He sells those plastic cigarettes. Very popular, since the Surgeon General's report. The factory's in Mexico. So, he's already down there. We met at the Concord — over Christmas. It's over six weeks now.

BETTY: Do you feel a little better?

DORIS: Yes. So. My cheating husband can have his divorce and his bimbo girl-friend.

BETTY: Candy.

DORIS: Yes, Candy, what a name. Did I tell you that story?

BETTY: I don't know, which one?

(Doris puts on lipstick, Betty watches, imitates.)

DORIS: Well, I met this man.

BETTY: Stewart.

DORIS: No, Harry, this is before Stewart. Oh, did I tell you my cheating husband's name?

BETTY: Uh, no, I don't think so, did you?

DORIS: Well, my cheating soon-to-be-EX-husband, I mean. Did I tell you how he left?

BETTY: No.

(Lights up on husband.)

DICK: Doris, since the heart attack.

DORIS: *(To Betty.)* He had a heart attack, thirty-nine years old.

DICK: Doris, since the heart attack, my doctor feels, well, it would be better for my health Baby, the family, the girls, the house. We need to, I have to, it would be better for my heart if we —

DORIS: *(To Dick.)* What?

DICK: Separated.

DORIS: What??

DICK: Separated. For my heart, my health, I talked to the doctor.

DORIS: You mean if we don't you'll —

DICK: My heart.

DORIS: — You might, you mean —

DICK: My life.

DORIS: Oh, God, well then, yes, of course. Whatever's best for you, of course.
(Lights out on husband.)

DORIS: And then he left. Took his shoes out of the closet. Drove the Cadillac
out the garage. Gone. And months later, the day I was moving with the
kids out of the house in Brooklyn, my neighbor, Mary, who looks like a
witch, came over and said, "Oh, it must've been so hard for you with that
woman here all the time." And I said, "What woman, Mary?" And she
said *(Mimes big breasts.)* "That woman." So I found out about Candy.
Dick and Candy. Candy and Dick.

BETTY: That's his name, Dick.

DORIS: Well, his mother named him Hyman.
(Lights up on mother-in-law.)

NETTIE: He had a heart attack, at that age, go easy on him, Doris.

DORIS: Of course, Nettie.

NETTIE: Do what he wants.

DORIS: I am, Nettie.

NETTIE: He's not well, don't ask for much. It'll kill him. Oh, and by the way,
I want my samovar back.
(Lights out on mother-in-law.)

DORIS: Hyman. When he turned eighteen he changed it to Dick. Then he spent
the next twenty years trying to put the two together.

BETTY: That's very funny. You're very funny. So, I'm curious, about you and
Stewart.

DORIS: Oh, wait, about Candy. You'll love this. I went to a singles party, you
know Jewish singles in Brooklyn, after Dick left, but before I moved with
the kids into the city, and I met this man, Harry, who said, "Oh, Doris
Goldman, were you married to Dick Goldman?" And I said yes, and he
said, "Oh, I know your husband's girlfriend, everyone knows her, she's
the Whore of Brooklyn."

BETTY: No.

DORIS: Yes.

BETTY: No.

DORIS: Yes. I told Stewart that story, he laughed.

BETTY: Horrible.

DORIS: That's just the tip of the iceberg.

BETTY: So he was with her.

DORIS: Oh God, for years. Every night he'd go out for a drive, if only I'd known who he was riding. Why, he had me sign fake income tax returns so I wouldn't know how much money he had.

BETTY: Maybe you married the wrong man.

DORIS: Oh, I don't think so.

BETTY: But now you met this other man and —

DORIS: Can you believe I didn't notice? It's like I can't see what's right in front of me, Susan. I don't know how that could be. I'm a grown woman, a smart person, awake, aware, with it. It's like I can't see past my own blue eyes — or his. I loved him.

BETTY: Oh.

DORIS: Like I'm looking at you and seeing someone else.

BETTY: *(Clears his throat.)* Well, um, I'm sure things are different now that you've met this other man, I mean, I'm sure you've met lots of men. Haven't you?

DORIS: What?

BETTY: I mean, you must meet plenty of men. You're very attractive.

DORIS: Oh?

BETTY: Well you're very —

DORIS: What?

BETTY: Well, you're quite, you know —

DORIS: What?

BETTY: You have a certain quality.

DORIS: Oh?

BETTY: You can see that, can't you?

DORIS: Um.

(*Doris fixes her hair by looking at her reflection in Betty's eyeglasses.*)

BETTY: What is it?

DORIS: Oh, I just saw myself in your glasses.

BETTY: Oh. So.

DORIS: So.

BETTY: Mexico.

DORIS: *(With bad accent.)* México.

BETTY: Acapulco.

DORIS: Did I say that?

BETTY: Why, yes, didn't you? I mean that's where the plane is going. I figured, Acapulco, Stewart; Stewart, Acapulco.

DORIS: Sí.

BETTY: For a week, right? To get to know each other.

DORIS: To see if we should get married.

BETTY: Ah.

DORIS: Depending how it goes, he'll propose.

BETTY: So you're in love.

DORIS: He's very nice. Well off. Plastic cigarettes. I work for a travel agent. I feed the fish. The red one, the blue one. No one comes in.

BETTY: Oh.

DORIS: So, it's good I get this all out. Nothing chases away a man like a crying woman. We all know that. I mean, I'm thirty-five, and I can't pay my rent. I look in the mirror, I see what's coming. A face like a waffle, a neck like a turkey. Are you married?

BETTY: No.

DORIS: Really. What do you do?

BETTY: I'm a school teacher. We get a week off beginning of February.

DORIS: Huh. My kids don't get a week off beginning of February.

BETTY: Private school.

DORIS: Oh. That's nice. I never went to college. I've had eight jobs in the last seven months. My daughters cry at night. The older one cause she misses her father, the younger one cause she misses me.

BETTY: Oh.

DORIS: They see their father on Sunday. He takes them out to restaurants. So I took them out one night. They ordered lobster, like they would with him. I didn't have the heart to tell them I couldn't afford it, so instead I ate nothing. I dipped bread into the melted butter. My girls. The older one blames me, the younger one worries about me. So yes, Stewart. I mean, Acapulco. Olé.

(They toast. They drink.)

BETTY: Where are you staying? I mean, maybe we can have a drink? I'm by myself, you could tell me how it's going.

DORIS: Oh, I'd like that.

BETTY: So you're at the —

DORIS: The Gold Sombrero. Have you been there?

BETTY: *(Shakes her head no.)* And are you, I don't want to pry, but if I want to find you, you're in the room — with Stewart, right?

DORIS: I don't know, I think so.

BETTY: For the week.

DORIS: Right.

BETTY: When are you coming back? Maybe we could sit together.

DORIS: Uh, February 14th.

BETTY: And his last name, Stewart's last name?

DORIS: Rubin.

BETTY: Right. Stewart Rubin. Gold Sombrero. For the week. Excuse me, I have to use the men's room.

(Betty exits. Doris, after a beat, takes the silverware and salt and pepper shakers from Betty's tray and puts them in her purse.)

SCENE TWO

A month ago. January, 1966. Dick's apartment in Brooklyn. Dick is counting stacks of money. Candy is reading a magazine, licking her finger each time she turns a page. She has big boobs and big beehive hair.

CANDY: Dick?

DICK: What, Candy?

CANDY: Dick?

DICK: What?

CANDY: I was thinking about the new apartment. Dick?

DICK: What?

CANDY: I think the carpet should be an olive green, ok?

DICK: Sure, honey.

CANDY: Wall-to-wall. Thick.

DICK: Whatever you say.

CANDY: And a yellow couch. Not from your uncle's store.

DICK: What's wrong with Seaman's?

CANDY: It's cheap.

DICK: All right.

CANDY: And I'd really like to have on the living room wall, a mural.

DICK: Sure.

CANDY: I was thinking — of Venice. With, you know, gondolas, and bridges, and uh water.

DICK: Uh huh.

CANDY: And then custom build some arches in front of it, green ones. To match the carpet.

DICK: Fine.

CANDY: And have light bulbs put in behind the arches, so when you turn the switch they light up the painting, the mural.

DICK: Sounds nice.

CANDY: It might be expensive to have someone paint your own Venice.

DICK: Uh huh.

CANDY: Wouldn't that be great? Our very own Venice — right in Brooklyn? And we could have people over like my sister, Honey, my other sister, Bunny, her husband, Sonny, my mother, and . . . Dick, when're you gonna tell your mother about me?

DICK: Not yet.

CANDY: But you gotta soon, you know. I'm tired of being a secret.

DICK: When the time is right.

CANDY: When is that?

DICK: Not yet.

CANDY: Oh, Dick, can you write me a check? I saw this thing in the Sunday News magazine, in the back where the ads are? Dick?

DICK: Yeah?

CANDY: It's a bra. Dick?

DICK: Uh huh.

CANDY: A minimizer.

DICK: A what?

CANDY: A minimizer, cause my breasts are so well, big, you know? I thought sometimes I should minimize them.

DICK: What?

CANDY: You know, minimize, it says it can reduce up to two cups.

(Dick stops counting.)

DICK: No.

CANDY: What?

DICK: No, I won't pay for that.

CANDY: Why not?

DICK: To make your tits small? You want me to pay for something to make your tits look small?

CANDY: Yeah, cause it can be very cumbersome, they get in the way, they make buying clothes difficult. And the new style is very slim, very boyish.

DICK: The answer is still no.

(Candy unzips her dress.)

CANDY: I mean, look at them, don't you think they're just too, well, big?

DICK: Candy.

CANDY: What?

DICK: I'm —

CANDY: What?

DICK: I was trying to —

CANDY: What?

DICK: Baby, I told you — there's only two things in life that matter.

CANDY: Oh?

DICK: What I'm doing here, *(He points to his money.)* and what I'm doing here. *(He points to his crotch.)*

CANDY: Oh?

DICK: I'll show you.

CANDY: Why don't you?

(The phone rings. Dick answers.)

DICK: Hello? Oh, Tracy, hi. Uh huh. How's school? That's good. Your sister's good, uh huh. Happy 1966 to you, too. How was your New Year's? Mommy let you stay up and watch Alan King at the Concord til midnight? Wow. Mommy met a new friend up there? Yeah? What's her friend's name, sweetie? Stewart, Stewart Boobin, you think? They're going somewhere? Where are they going? You don't know? Oh… Yeah, I'll see you Sunday, sweetie. Me, too. *(He hangs up.)*

CANDY: Come here.

(Dick puts all his money away.)

CANDY: Dick? Come here… Dick. What's the matter? Who's Stewart Boobin?

SCENE THREE

Back to the present.

A room in the Gold Sombrero Hotel in Acapulco. A large sombrero hangs over the bed that Stewart and Doris have just had sex in. Stew is bare chested, hairy, with a pendant. Doris wears a negligee that is covered with black streaks.

STEWART: Wow.

DORIS: What?

STEWART: Wow.

DORIS: Yeah?

STEWART: Yeah.

DORIS: Really?

STEWART: Really wow.

DORIS: Yeah? You're not disappointed?

STEWART: No. Baby. You're something else.

DORIS: You, too.

(He takes out a plastic cigarette.)

STEWART: You want one?

DORIS: Thanks.

STEWART: This one's a Kool, this one's like a Winston.

DORIS: I'll take the Kool.

(They inhale deeply.)

DORIS: You want a real cigarette?

STEWART: No, do you?

DORIS: Oh no, just asking.

STEWART: What I want is you. Again.

DORIS: You do?

STEWART: Yeah, I want you all week.

DORIS: Yeah?

STEWART: Over and over.

DORIS: Really?

STEWART: I can't get enough of you.

DORIS: Wow.

STEWART: *(He starts to growl.)* Grrrr. *(He moves toward her, sees the black streaks on her negligee, then stops.)*

DORIS: What?

STEWART: Nothing.

DORIS: What? *(She looks at her negligee.)* Oh God, what is that?

STEWART: I don't know.

DORIS: God. *(She gets up.)*

STEWART: Um.

DORIS: Look at me.

STEWART: Uh oh.

DORIS: What?

STEWART: Well —

DORIS: What??

STEWART: Well, it could be…

DORIS: Stewart.

STEWART: Um, I have to tell you something. . . I'm grey, on my chest. I'm really grey. And I used this — this new formula and, well, it's supposed to be permanent.

DORIS: Oh. You mean — ?

STEWART: I guess it isn't. Damn. I'm sorry. I'm really sorry. I just. I thought if I was grey — you might not, you know. It's too much, huh? O.K., some-

times, I'm too much. So if I'm ever too much, you can just say, "Stew —
too much."

DORIS: Stew?

STEWART: Yeah.

DORIS: It's fine.

STEWART: It is?

DORIS: Sure.

STEWART: Oh. Great.

DORIS: Good.

STEWART: *(After a beat.)* It's on your hands.

(Doris goes to the bathroom.)

STEWART: It might not come off too easy.

(She re-enters, hands still black.)

DORIS: Well, that's O.K.

STEWART: You are really just — wow. . . This is great, isn't it?

DORIS: Yeah.

STEWART: Us, Acapulco. Alone.

DORIS: Yeah.

STEWART: Alone, Acapulco.

DORIS: Yeah. . . So far so good?

STEWART: So far so good.

DORIS: I mean with us.

STEWART: Yeah. Wow. Yeah. You're a helluva girl.

DORIS: Yeah?

STEWART: Yeah. I mean, I haven't. I mean, for years. I mean, a whole week,
yeah!

(A beat. They inhale their plastic cigarettes.)

STEWART: So. What do you wanna do tonight?

DORIS: Well, we could go have dinner, and we could go to the nightclub or —

STEWART: Hey, let's just stay right here.

DORIS: O.K.

STEWART: We'll order room service!

DORIS: Great. Stew, you mind if I call my kids?

STEWART: No, Baby, whatever you want.

DORIS: *(Doris dials.)* Hi Honey, it's Mommy. Put Robyn on the other line. . .
Hi, Sweetie, how are you girls? Oh, yeah. Well I just want to tell you I
love you, I can't talk much, it's long distance, O.K? So be good, and listen to Aunt Lily. . . O.K., I'll try to bring back a souvenir. For both of

you. O.K. sweeties, bye bye Mommy loves you. *(She hangs up. She hides her tears.)*

You're a nice man.

STEWART: You're a nice girl. *(He growls.)* Grrrrr.

(He grabs her, he rubs his chest hairs up against her. She lets out a shriek, which turns into a laugh.)

SCENE FOUR

Three weeks ago. The Queens laundromat run by Nettie. A large calendar reads January 15. Nettie folds and sorts a pile of socks. Dick sits with his feet up, an unlit cigar in his mouth.

NETTIE: Please don't light that.

DICK: Why not?

NETTIE: You think people want to get their socks back smelling like cigars?

DICK: Their socks won't smell.

NETTIE: I don't like it. I don't like you smoking. The doctor said.

DICK: The doctor said no cigarettes.

NETTIE: A cigar is just a cigarette that smells worse.

DICK: The doctor said I could smoke a cigar.

NETTIE: Well, not here. Bad for business. So, how are you feeling?

DICK: O.K.

NETTIE: You look pale. You should make it up with Doris.

DICK: Listen Mom —

NETTIE: She wasn't the best cook, but she was learning.

DICK: She's a terrible cook. Remember that meat loaf?

NETTIE: She forgot to turn on the oven.

DICK: Or the steaks she aged until they were green?

NETTIE: She was learning. I taught her how to make a brisket, that was good.

DICK: Mom —

NETTIE: How's business?

DICK: Fine.

NETTIE: What are you tearing down?

DICK: Buildings, Mom, that's what we do, tear down buildings. Look —

NETTIE: You making money?

DICK: Yeah.

NETTIE: Good.

DICK: Look, Mom, there's something. . .

NETTIE: What?

DICK: About Doris.

NETTIE: What?

DICK: I didn't want to tell you but. I. I have this friend.

NETTIE: What kind of a friend?

DICK: A friend, a person, a friend.

NETTIE: Uh huh.

DICK: Candy.

NETTIE: What kind of a name is that?

DICK: That's her name.

NETTIE: Is she Jewish?

DICK: Yeah, she's Jewish.

NETTIE: Married?

DICK: Divorced.

NETTIE: Why can't you people stay married? I was married to your father til he died, and now I'm married to Sam til he dies. Everything has to change, huh? Look at this neighborhood. It used to be nice, now they're moving in. Every day there's more of them.

DICK: Who's "them" Mom?

NETTIE: You know who. The shvartzes. Soon it'll be like Harlem here, and this is Jamaica, this is Queens.

DICK: O.K., Mom.

NETTIE: In the building, in my building, there's one on every floor, and now the elevator has scratches and drawings like it never had before.

DICK: Yeah, it did.

NETTIE: No, not like this. The whole borough's changing. Soon we're gonna go to Florida.

DICK: Look, I'm trying to tell you something. This woman, Candy —

NETTIE: What kind of a mother names her daughter Candy?

DICK: I don't know Mom, I don't know her mother.

NETTIE: What's her last name?

DICK: Cane.

NETTIE: That doesn't sound Jewish.

DICK: It's a joke.

NETTIE: Does she have kids?

DICK: Three.

NETTIE: What are you telling me?

DICK: I'm trying to tell you that Candy, this person, this friend of mine, found out through someone else, a man named Lenny, that Doris has been, uh, with someone else.

NETTIE: What?

DICK: She's been with another man.

NETTIE: Is that another joke? You're telling me a joke.

DICK: It's not a joke, Mom.

NETTIE: But you're still married, right? I mean, legally you're still married.

DICK: Right. See, Candy knows this man. And, apparently, Doris has been with him. For a long time.

NETTIE: I don't believe it.

DICK: For years.

NETTIE: Doris? Little Doris?

DICK: Why do you think I wanted the divorce?

NETTIE: For your health, for your heart. You lied about that?

DICK: No no, that was true. But this is also true. I didn't want to upset you, but now I have firsthand information, and it seems this man's a gold digger, you know, a gigolo.

NETTIE: *(Gasps.)* What?

DICK: So she thinks he might be —

NETTIE: What?

DICK: Trying to get her money.

NETTIE: What money? She has no money.

DICK: Exactly. The only money she has is my money. And, you know, in six weeks we go to court.

(Nettie drops the socks.)

NETTIE: I I I don't believe this. Not Doris.

DICK: His name is Stewart, Stewart something — Boobin, O.K? And what I just found out is that she's going away with him.

NETTIE: What? Where? When?

DICK: I don't know yet. But don't you worry, my friend Candy's a smart cookie, she'll find out.

NETTIE: Who, Cookie?

DICK: No, Candy.

NETTIE: *(She stands.)* I I I. If this is true Hymie, she's — she's not getting a penny, you understand? She's not entitled to a damn penny. If she's a cheater and a liar and she'll take you for everything you're worth. If if it's true.

DICK: Believe me. It's true.

NETTIE: You know what I say: There's only one thing in life that matters to me, and that's you. And Sam. And my grandchildren. And money.

SCENE FIVE

The present. Acapulco. By the pool at The Gold Sombrero. Doris, in a lounge chair wearing a bathing suit, her face covered by an oversized sombrero. The slurping sound of her finishing a drink through a straw. Ben, a handsome black man, enters carrying two drinks.

BEN: Hola. Senora. Miss? Do you speak English?
(She turns, her eyes are covered by little plastic eye shields. She takes them off, and can't see a thing in the bright sun.)
DORIS: What?
BEN: Forgive me for interrupting.
DORIS: Sorry, I didn't realize —
BEN: Would you like a Margarita?
DORIS: I didn't order another drink.
BEN: I'm not a waiter.
DORIS: Oh, I am sorry. It's the sun, I can't see your face.
BEN: See, I ordered one drink, but with my Spanish I ended up with two. I just thought I'd offer someone the other one.
DORIS: Sure.
(He holds it out to her, she reaches and misses.)
DORIS: Oh.
(She tries, misses again.)
BEN: I'll just put it in your hand.
DORIS: Oh.
(He does. She puts on her sunglasses, looks at him. He is handsome.)
DORIS: Oh.
(They drink. She removes the plastic stirrer from the drink and puts it in her bag.)
BEN: Do you happen to have a cigarette?
DORIS: No. Trying to quit.
BEN: Me, too.
DORIS: I could give you one of those plastic ones.
BEN: They don't work.
DORIS: No, you're right, they don't.
BEN: Some things — you just have to grin and bear it.
DORIS: True.
BEN: Or not grin and bear it.
DORIS: Even more true.

BEN: Beautiful day.

DORIS: Isn't it? I'm delighted to be outside.

BEN: Oh?

DORIS: I mean, in the sun — beautiful day.

BEN: You on vacation?

DORIS: Yes with my friend, Stewart. He's um well he went to the barber. You?

BEN: Just down here, relaxing.

DORIS: Alone?

BEN: Recently divorced.

DORIS: Really? I'm almost divorced.

BEN: Really.

DORIS: It's tough, isn't it?

BEN: I know this is none of my business, but are you wearing suntan lotion?

DORIS: Oh.

BEN: I was just noticing, well, your color and my color they're very different, and you wouldn't want to get a burn.

DORIS: Oh. *(She starts to put on lotion with her blackened hands.)*

BEN: You staying here at the hotel?

DORIS: Oh, yes.

BEN: You like it?

DORIS: Oh, yes. I mean. This is where Richard Burton and Liz Taylor got married. I mean, not right here, but. And Johnny Weismuller lives here somewhere. I mean, Acapulco, playground of the world. Where anything can happen. *(She continues to put on lotion with her blackened hands.)*

BEN: Did you, uh, take the finger-painting workshop?

DORIS: What? Oh. You wouldn't believe it if I told you.

BEN: Try me.

(Doris looks around, then leans over and whispers into Ben's ear. He laughs, she laughs. They look at each other.)

BEN: I'm Ben Adams.

DORIS: Doris Goldman.

BEN: Nice to meet you.

(They shake hands.)

DORIS: Um, I know this is none of my business, I mean, absolutely none of my business, but I met a woman on the plane and she was very nice and and alone, and a Negro, I hope it's all right if I say that — maybe you'd like to meet her.

BEN: Well —

DORIS: Damn, I don't know where she is. I was so busy going on about myself

I didn't even get her number. But I'll ask around. I know she's here somewhere.

BEN: That's O.K.

DORIS: I'm sure it's better to stay within your own group.

BEN: Sure.

DORIS: I mean it should be. I mean, more in common.

BEN: That makes sense.

DORIS: Except look at my husband. He was my group.

BEN: Uh huh.

DORIS: And he left me for the Whore of Brooklyn

BEN: Oh, I think I know her. *(Doris looks at him.)* It was a joke.
(She laughs, he laughs.)

DORIS: Anyway, I'm sure she'll show up.

BEN: Might not.
(He offers her the stirrer from his drink. She takes it.)

DORIS: For my kids.
(She tries to put the lotion on her back.)

DORIS: Would you?

BEN: Oh. I.

DORIS: Please.
*(Ben looks around, then tentatively spreads lotion on her back. It feels good.
To both of them. He stops. A beat.)*

DORIS: Um, have we met before?

BEN: No.

DORIS: Can I ask you a question? Is that — is that your real hair?

BEN: Yes.

DORIS: Oh.

BEN: Doris, you should be careful, this is Mexico, you don't want to get burned.
That would be very painful.

SCENE SIX

*Ten days ago. A Chinese restaurant in Brooklyn. Nettie slurps soup, Candy,
in a low-cut blouse, eats a large plate of spare ribs with her pinkies raised,
while Dick eats a bowl of corn flakes, the box on the table. No one speaks,
then:*

NETTIE: You want some soup?

(Dick shakes his head no.)

NETTIE: Just the broth.

DICK: The doctor said corn flakes.

NETTIE: Why corn flakes?

(Dick shrugs.)

NETTIE: I don't know why we had to go out. I have corn flakes.

DICK: It's an occasion.

CANDY: It's nice to finally meet you, Nettie. I've heard so much about you.

NETTIE: You have?

DICK: How are the ribs?

CANDY: Fine. We love this place. One night we had a banquet, we said, bring us a banquet, and one of the dishes was pigeon, that's what they said — a pigeon.

DICK: I'm sorry Sam couldn't make it.

NETTIE: Someone has to work. You don't *work*, you don't *earn*.

CANDY: So, this week the groundhog looks for his shadow. I can never remember if that means six weeks of cold or six weeks of hot.

NETTIE: Did you eat it?

CANDY: What, the groundhog?

NETTIE: No, the pigeon.

CANDY: Oh, yeah, it was delicious, a Chinese pigeon, not a New York one.

(Candy eats her ribs, Dick shovels in his corn flakes, Nettie examines her soup.)

NETTIE: So what's the news?

DICK: About what?

NETTIE: You know about what.

DICK: We said we'd talk about it later. Dinner was for you and Candy to meet.

NETTIE: So we met. Candy and I met.

DICK: Lemme have a spare rib.

NETTIE: Don't give him a spare rib.

CANDY: But he wants one.

NETTIE: He wants a lot of things. What are those — pork? Spiced up ribs from a pig? Since when do Jews eat ribs from a pig.

DICK: It's Chinese food, Mom. Jews can eat it. It's the eleventh commandment. Besides, it's not like you keep kosher.

NETTIE: I don't know why we had to eat out.

CANDY: *(A beat.)* I need to use the little girls room.

(Candy exits.)

NETTIE: What is this about?

DICK: I wanted you to meet her.

NETTIE: You make it up with Doris.

DICK: Mom, I told you.

NETTIE: I don't believe what you told me. Doris was afraid to go to the supermarket. She said they didn't have them in Pittsburgh. Too many choices, she said, she didn't know how to pick. She couldn't see, she said.

DICK: I guess she got her eyes checked.

NETTIE: Someone's telling you a pack of lies.

DICK: No.

NETTIE: At least Doris had a brain. What does this one have between her ears? — Another breast?

DICK: Mom.

NETTIE: She's cheap.

DICK: She's not cheap. You just don't know her. You'll see, she's very nice. Just talk to her.

NETTIE: Hymie, you shoulda finished high school.

DICK: Mom —

NETTIE: You ran away, for three years we didn't hear from you, it broke your father's heart.

DICK: Yeah.

(Candy enters, and sits. Dick gets up.)

DICK: Be right back. You two get to know each other.

(He exits.)

NETTIE: Candy. What kind of a name is that?

CANDY: *(She shrugs.)* My mother liked sweets.

NETTIE: You do your own laundry?

CANDY: No.

NETTIE: You have kids?

CANDY: Three.

NETTIE: From another marriage?

CANDY: Two marriages.

NETTIE: Uh huh. You planning on sending them to college?

CANDY: No. Doug is about to get married so he can avoid the draft, Cheryl has a job, and Susie, well, I don't think she'll go to college.

NETTIE: Listen. Candy. When I was sixteen the Russian army came and killed my father. My mother dressed me up as a peasant girl, so I could sneak into the army camp to find my father's body and bring it back to be buried. I had to wait for hours til the soldiers fell asleep. The next day my mother and I rode in a hay cart to escape to America. Do you understand what I'm saying?

CANDY: Uh —

NETTIE: I'm saying we hid in horse shit and my father's blood so I could have a son. I've worked hard every day I've been here and I'm not gonna let some woman, you, Doris, or anyone else suck the life out of my boy. You understand that, we'll get along fine. He's my son, my only. I only could have one.

(Dick appears in the corner eating a spare rib and smoking a cigarette.)

NETTIE: If it's true about Doris, she's gonna get what she deserves. Which is nothing. And if you're not careful, the same will happen to you. You do anything to take his money or hurt his heart, I will come after you, bury you the way I did my father. Even if it's from my grave. And that's a promise.

CANDY: *(A beat.)* Well, I have a mother, too. And my mother always said "Don't judge a candy by its wrapper." And she raised us on her own, O.K. I love my mother. And all through it, she kept her nails nice, her hair done, and her roots never showed. So. So. You want your son, then we have to get along. The three of us. You and me. Him and me. You and me and him and me. Doris didn't know how to make him happy. Why do you think he had a heart attack? With me he'll be happy. *(Candy eats a rib.)* What'd your first husband die of, Nettie?

NETTIE: Heart attack.

CANDY: Maybe you didn't know how to make him happy.

NETTIE: You want to know what killed my husband? Ask his son.

(Dick enters.)

DICK: So you girls getting along all right?

(Everyone smiles.)

SCENE SEVEN

The present. Outdoors, near the pool at the Gold Sombrero. Doris and Stew are setting up for a game of limbo. Doris wears a tight push-up dress.

STEWART: Hey, va va voom. Move over Marilyn, here comes Doris.

DORIS: Yeah? I think maybe it's a little small.

STEWART: It's not small, it's tight. I like tight.

DORIS: Yeah?

STEWART: Yeah. Turn around. *(She does.)* Saleslady said it was the latest thing.

DORIS: You think I have the figure?

STEWART: You got the kind of figure I want to figure out.

DORIS: It was very sweet of you.

STEWART: It cost mucho dollars, I'll tell you.

DORIS: Thank you, Stew. . . Hey, this'll be fun.

STEWART: You go first.

(*They start a game of limbo, Doris goes under the pole first.*)

DORIS: Your turn.

STEWART: No no no, just you.

DORIS: No, it's a contest. Come on.

(*She drags him to the pole, he goes under, knocks it down.*)

STEWART: I lose. You go.

(*He lowers the pole, Doris goes under.*)

STEWART: Keep going.

(*She keeps going lower and lower during the following.*)

DORIS: Did I tell you? — I lost my job.

STEWART: Uh huh.

DORIS: See, they wouldn't let me take vacation after only working there for a week. So, I quit, cause I wanted to come down here with you. . . (*She stops.*) Did you hear what I said?

STEWART: Yeah, yeah, you lost your job. You didn't like it anyway, right? Keep going.

DORIS: (*She starts again.*) Would you like my hair a different color?

STEWART: Your hair?

DORIS: Yeah.

STEWART: No, I like your hair. Why, you want to change it?

DORIS: You want me to?

STEWART: No.

DORIS: Oh.

STEWART: Your hair is fine.

DORIS: I was thinking maybe when we get back, you'd like to come over for dinner. I could make something: meat loaf or steak. You could get to know the girls a little.

STEWART: Those are some girls. Which one was it, the little one hid behind a chair and gave me the finger?

DORIS: Only cause her sister told her to. (*Doris is bent over backwards, midway under the pole.*)

STEWART: Wait.

DORIS: What?

STEWART: Just stay there a second. *(He grabs her.)*

DORIS: Stew —

STEWART: No one's looking.

DORIS: You are too much.

STEWART: No. You are. Mucho much. *(He growls.)*

DORIS: Maybe if you didn't make that sound.

STEWART: Oh yeah, that's annoying, I won't do that. Hey, you think you could, you know, shimmy a little?

DORIS: Stew —

STEWART: Just a little. I wanna see em shake.

(He shows her how. She starts to shimmy with him. His back goes out.)

STEWART: *(In pain.)* Oh.

(Ben appears with a tray of drinks. He wears a pair of binoculars around his neck.)

DORIS: Oh. Ben, hi.

BEN: Doris, nice to see you.

DORIS: This is my friend, Stewart. Stewart, this is Ben, we met at the pool.

(Ben extends his hand, but Stew is frozen.)

STEWART: Doris —

BEN: Nice to meet you. Would you like a drink? You won't believe it, but this time when I ordered I ended up with three.

DORIS: That's very nice of you. *(Doris takes a drink, hands one to Stew.)*

STEWART: Dor —

DORIS: We were just playing a little limbo. Would you like to join in?

BEN: That's O.K.

STEWART: Excuse me. I gotta go upstairs. You coming?

DORIS: I'll be right there.

(Stew exits.)

DORIS: Can I ask you a question? Maybe this isn't right but. Hell, you're a man. And. As a man. I'm wondering. What would make you propose?

BEN: Hmm?

DORIS: Marriage. If you were with a woman, say, and you liked her, I mean, you seemed to, you were interested and. What thing might she do? Or not do? I mean, what would she have to do?

BEN: Nothing.

DORIS: Nothing?

BEN: Nothing. If I loved her she wouldn't have to do anything.

DORIS: No?

BEN: No.

DORIS: Oh.

BEN: And if I thought she was trying to, I'd ask her to stop.

(She starts to cry.)

BEN: Are you all right?

DORIS: I'm fine.

BEN: Doris.

DORIS: I'm fine. I just — I just — I hate this dress.

(He takes off his shirt, puts it on her, over the dress. A beat.)

DORIS: What what kind of cologne do you wear?

BEN: I don't wear any.

DORIS: You mean that smell, that's you?

BEN: I guess.

(Stew enters.)

STEWART: Doris. *(She doesn't move.)* Dor. I hurt my back.

DORIS: Oh. Well. *(To Ben.)* Good-bye.

BEN: Bye. Nice to meet you, Stew.

(Stew ignores Ben as he and Doris exit.)

(Doris runs back onstage, hands him his shirt, doesn't know what to say, can't speak, then:)

DORIS: I know who you remind me of.

BEN: Who?

DORIS: This man, this man I met before I got married.

BEN: Yeah?

DORIS: He, he wasn't Jewish. But he. He had these eyes. I guess I I made a mistake.

BEN: Maybe you should give him a call.

DORIS: You think? Let's have dinner. The three of us. 8 o'clock. In the restaurant. Thursday.

BEN: That would be nice.

DORIS: And I'll find that woman, Betty. I'll invite her, too.

(She runs off. Ben watches her through his binoculars.)

BEN: Damn it.

SCENE EIGHT

One week ago. Dick's apartment in Brooklyn. Dick and Candy in bed having sex. He kneels behind her, she is on all fours, eating from an oversized platter of smoked fish. The phone rings. She picks up. They don't stop.

CANDY: It's for you.

(He takes the phone. They don't stop.)

DICK: Uh huh . . . Uh huh . . . Uh huh.

(He hangs up. They don't stop.)

DICK: She hired a lawyer.

CANDY: She did what?

DICK: She hired a lawyer.

CANDY: Who?

DICK: Doris. She hired a lawyer.

(She pulls away. They stop.)

DICK: Ugh!

CANDY: I thought you said she wouldn't.

DICK: I didn't think she would. I told her not to.

CANDY: So what happened?

DICK: I don't know. Someone musta talked to her. Maybe it was Boobin.

CANDY: So?

DICK: So she has a lawyer. Now my lawyer tells me he's a loser, a schlemiel, but he is a lawyer.

CANDY: I waited five years for you, Dick. Five long years.

DICK: I know, baby.

CANDY: I've been patient.

DICK: I know.

CANDY: Very patient.

DICK: I know. Let's talk about it later.

CANDY: I've had other offers.

DICK: I know. Now, come here.

CANDY: You want to make me happy, don't you?

DICK: Yeah, I want to make you happy.

CANDY: I make you happy.

DICK: I know you do.

CANDY: I like to do that a lot.

DICK: I like it that you like it.

CANDY: Would you like it right now?

DICK: I'm dying for it right now.

CANDY: Then you better understand this, Dick Goldman, I am thirty-six years old, and I am not going back to being a hatcheck girl.

DICK: Who said? — *(She gets up.)* Where you going?

CANDY: I'm not in the mood.

(Candy gets on an electric waist jiggling machine that makes a loud noise.)

DICK: Candy. Goddamn it Candy, you can't do this! You've never done this. You know how I am. Get over here! . . . Look, it's gonna be fine.

CANDY: How do you know?

DICK: Believe me, she isn't gonna do anything.

CANDY: Except take all your money. There goes our apartment, and our trip to Miami. And my son, Douglas's wedding!

DICK: I know Doris.

CANDY: If you know her so well, how come you didn't know she'd hire a lawyer?

DICK: Hey, you think I like this situation? I waited five years, too. I want what you want too, you know. There's just a lot of elements to consider here. I gotta do things right. Cause there's you, there's my mother, there's Doris, the kids, my money, my health. Just let me figure it out.

CANDY: *(She turns off the machine.)* You want to figure it out? I'll figure it out. You better do something. About Doris.

DICK: Yeah.

CANDY: What are you gonna do?

DICK: I don't know. Something.

(She turns it back on. He stuffs his mouth with some smoked fish. The phone rings. He picks up.)

DICK: *(Distracted.)* Yeah. Oh, hi. Uh huh. Yeah, that's good. Uh huh. Mommy's doing what? *(Interested.)* She's going away with her friend? Do you know when? No? O.K. Do you know where she's going?

(Candy turns the machine off.)

DICK: A place called Al...Ca...Pone Ko? Al Capone-ko. Your mother's going to Al Capone-ko with a man named Stewart Boobin. Oh.

SCENE NINE

The present. In the room at the Gold Sombrero. Doris gives Stew a back-rub, while he lies on the bed.

STEWART: Uhh.

DORIS: Is that good?

STEWART: Yeah. Uhhhhh. Uhhhh. It's good.

DORIS: Good. I'm sorry about your back.

STEWART: Yeah. Ah. This'll fix me right up. Uuuhhh. Thanks, Dor.

DORIS: Stew?

STEWART: Yeah?

DORIS: I made us dinner plans.

STEWART: Uhh.

DORIS: I'm gonna find that woman Betty, that I met on the plane. And being that she's alone and very nice, I thought I'd try to set her up, make a shiddach, you know. So I invited that guy, Ben. Cause he's also alone and very nice. *(Doris stands up and steps on his back.)*

STEWART: Ahh!

DORIS: I figured they'd like each other and they'd go out and maybe he'd propose and then they'd get married cause that can happen, you know. *(She steps again.)*

STEWART: Ahh! What are you doing?

DORIS: I read about this. It'll make you feel better.

STEWART: Uhh. Wait, what did you say, you're inviting who to dinner?

DORIS: Betty and Ben.

STEWART: You mean, the colored guy? The one that gave you his shirt?

DORIS: Yeah.

STEWART: I don't want to have to dinner with him.

(She gets off his back.)

DORIS: What do you mean?

STEWART: I don't like him.

DORIS: You don't even know him.

STEWART: I know how he was looking at you. I'm not blind.

DORIS: Don't be silly.

STEWART: Why'd he give you his shirt?

DORIS: I don't know, I got cold.

STEWART: It's 80 degrees out, how did you get cold?

DORIS: Stew, I already invited him. And I'm going to invite her. Come on, when have you had dinner with a couple of Negroes?

STEWART: Never.

DORIS: Well, there you go. We're in Acapulco, and we're doing things we've never done before, right? It'll be fun . . . A piña colada . . . An enchilada . . . We'll dance the samba.

STEWART: You're not dancing with that guy.

DORIS: Stew, I might dance with him.

STEWART: See? When a guy gives a girl his shirt —

DORIS: — If he asks me, what am I gonna say, no? He'll think we're prejudiced, you don't want him to think that, do you?

STEWART: No. I don't know. I don't care what he thinks. Look, we only have a few days left.

DORIS: I know.

STEWART: So I don't want to share you with anyone. Even dinner.

DORIS: Well, I'm flattered. *(She rubs his back. He moans.)* We could have more than a few days, you know. We could have a lot of days. And I could rub your back whenever you wanted.

STEWART: Yeah?

DORIS: Yeah.

STEWART: Mmmm uuhhh mmmmm . . . Just cancel it, O.K?

DORIS: *(She stops.)* No.

STEWART: What?

DORIS: No, I will not cancel. We are having that dinner. They are going to meet. Hopefully, they will dance with each other. But if he asks me to dance, I will dance with him, and if you ask her to dance, you will dance with her. And that's all there is to it.

STEWART: *(A beat.)* Really?

DORIS: Well. . . Really.

STEWART: Well. And when is this dinner supposed to be?

DORIS: Tomorrow.

STEWART: Tomorrow?

DORIS: Yes, tomorrow.

STEWART: Well. I guess I'll have to see how I feel about it tomorrow.
(She gets off the bed.)

DORIS: Fine.

STEWART: Fine.

DORIS: Fine.
(She goes into the bathroom.)

STEWART: *(After a beat.)* You know, Dor, you mighta asked me before you invited them. I mean, don't you think that woulda been the thing to do?

DORIS: *(Sticks her head out, mascara in hand.)* Well, yeah, I guess. But I haven't invited her yet. And I invited him because I don't know. *(Pulls her head back in, then out again.)* It's just a meal, Stew. *(She goes back in.)*

STEWART: *(After a beat.)* Yeah well. . . *(He tries to get up, but it hurts to move.)* O.K., you wanna have dinner with them, we'll have dinner with them. *(She runs out.)*

DORIS: Oh Stew!

STEWART: Just so long as you dance with me more than with him, O.K?
(She jumps back on the bed.)

DORIS: It'll be fun, you'll see.

STEWART: Whatever makes you happy, Baby.

DORIS: It'll be the four of us.

STEWART: Yeah.

DORIS: In Acapulco!

STEWART: Yeah.

DORIS: Tomorrow.

STEWART: Yeah.

DORIS: What could happen? *(She steps on his back.)*

STEWART: *(In pain.)* Ahh!!

    (She gets off his back.)

DORIS: You're a nice man.

STEWART: I know.

SCENE TEN

    February 6. The day before Doris's trip to Acapulco. Nettie's kitchen in Queens. She is chopping chicken livers in a wooden bowl. Every so often she pours in some schmaltz.

DICK: She's a nice girl.

NETTIE: She doesn't look like a nice girl.

DICK: She is.

NETTIE: A nice girl doesn't go out with a married man.

DICK: Mom —

NETTIE: What are her children like?

DICK: They're a little different.

NETTIE: What do you mean?

DICK: They didn't go to the best schools.

NETTIE: They're dumb.

DICK: No.

NETTIE: You know your father spoke seven languages.

DICK: I know.

NETTIE: A scholar til he came here. A great man. Small, but great.

DICK: I know.

NETTIE: Terrible in business. Pathetic.

DICK: I know.

NETTIE: I loved him like you don't know. When you ran away, it broke his heart. He died before he should have.

DICK: O.K., Mom. Look —

NETTIE: I had plenty of suitors after your father died — wealthy men. But I fell for Sam. And he had nothing. You know his story, he lost his family, he barely survived, but I loved him.

DICK: Uh huh.

NETTIE: So, if there's something going on with this Candy, and it started maybe a little earlier than you're willing to admit, and if this story about Doris is maybe not the truth, then I just want to say — go back to Doris!! Cause if you don't I'll never forgive you!!! Here, try this. *(She feeds him a spoonful of chopped liver.)* How is it?

DICK: It's good.

NETTIE: *(She tastes it.)* Needs more gribbeness.

(Candy enters.)

CANDY: Sam let me in.

DICK: Candy.

CANDY: I've been looking all over for you.

NETTIE: What are you doing here?

CANDY: Hello Nettie, how are you?

NETTIE: All right.

CANDY: I have some news. There was a message from the answering service. It's about Doris.

NETTIE: You should go back to Doris.

CANDY: Over my dead body.

NETTIE: That could be arranged.

DICK: Please. What was the message?

CANDY: She's going to Alcapone-ko.

NETTIE: The gangster?

CANDY: That's what they said.

DICK: It's not Alcapone-ko. It's Acapulco.

NETTIE: *(Gasps.)* That's worse.

DICK: That's what I was trying to tell you, Mom.

NETTIE: What does that mean?

DICK: That's why I came over. She's going to Acapulco with a man named Boobin.

NETTIE: *(Gasps.)* When?

CANDY: The message said February seventh.

NETTIE: February seventh?

DICK: The seventh?

CANDY: Yeah.

DICK: But that's tomorrow.

NETTIE: Ohmigod.

CANDY: What are you gonna do?

NETTIE: I don't believe it.

DICK: Believe it, Mom.

CANDY: You better do something.

NETTIE: If this is true —

DICK: It's true, Mom, it's true.

NETTIE: Then Candy's right. We better do something.

CANDY: See, Dick, I'm right.

NETTIE: Hymie —

CANDY: Dick —

DICK: What?

NETTIE: What are we gonna do?

CANDY: Yeah, what are you gonna do?

DICK: She said tomorrow?

CANDY: She said tomorrow.

NETTIE: Acapulco?

CANDY: Acapulco!

DICK: Acapulco.

   (*Blackout.*)

END ACT ONE

ACT TWO
SCENE ONE

Acapulco. Lights up on a table in the hotel restaurant. Ben and Doris enter from opposite sides.

DORIS: Ben.

BEN: Doris.

DORIS: Nice to see you.

BEN: Same here. You look very nice.

DORIS: Well, thank you.

(They sit.)

DORIS: I'm glad you could make it.

BEN: Me, too. Thank you. For the invitation.

DORIS: Oh, my pleasure. But I have some bad news, that woman I told you about, Betty, I couldn't find her anywhere.

BEN: That's O.K. I don't much care for blind dates.

DORIS: Me neither. I met my husband on a blind date.

BEN: Right.

DORIS: Did I tell you that?

BEN: No, I was just saying, right.

DORIS: Right.

BEN: And Stewart, he's-uh-on his way?

DORIS: To Mexico City.

BEN: Oh.

DORIS: There's a problem at the factory. With the hole. In plastic cigarettes there's a hole, and it seems it's clogged.

BEN: I see.

DORIS: And you can't have a clogged hole.

BEN: No. So, he'll be back — *(Doris shrugs.)* So, it might be —

DORIS: A while.

BEN: Tomorrow? *(Doris shrugs.)* Day after tomorrow?

DORIS: He said he'd call tonight and let me know.

BEN: Oh.

DORIS: He said I'd be better off staying here. I figured, why waste the reservation, why be alone, why not have dinner with you? I hope that's all right.

BEN: Of course.

DORIS: I figured, it's Acapulco.

BEN: It is.

DORIS: Why not have a good time? It's just us. Would you like a drink?

BEN: Waiter!!

(Fast light change.)

(Ben and Doris drinking fancy drinks.)

DORIS: So, tell me about you.

BEN: There's not much to tell.

DORIS: Oh, come on.

BEN: No, really.

DORIS: O.K. then, I'll tell you about you. I have a sense about people.

BEN: Oh, yeah?

DORIS: O.K., so, I see. . . that you're divorced. And you travel a lot. You're handsome. Smart, funny. Um. Oh, you were the one who left the marriage, cause I can see your wife never would have left you. You like to go out. And you're glad that you're single.

BEN: Maybe you need glasses.

DORIS: What was I wrong about?

BEN: My wife left me. I don't go out a lot. I stay home with my kids.

DORIS: Oh. You have kids? How old?

BEN: Todd is seven, James is five, and Nelson is three.

DORIS: Nice. They live with you?

BEN: They do.

DORIS: You mean, you take care of them?

BEN: I do.

DORIS: Wow. That's unusual. A real father. My husband never wanted kids. When Tracy was born, he didn't even come to the hospital, he sent a driver. And with Robyn he was so disappointed that it wasn't a boy, we didn't send out birth announcements. He calls her Bob.

BEN: That's awful.

DORIS: Can I ask, um, about your ex?

BEN: Moved to California with my best friend. My ex-best friend.

DORIS: That's awful. To Todd, James, and Nelson.

BEN: And Tracy and Robyn.

DORIS: Lchaim.

BEN: Salud.

(They toast. Doris spills her drink on Ben.)

DORIS: Oh no, I'm sorry.

BEN: It's O.K.

DORIS: No it's not. I — oh — *(She tries to wipe his pants.)*

BEN: It's O.K.

DORIS: I'll — I'll get them cleaned for you.

BEN: It's fine.

(He stands up, revealing a large wet patch. She laughs. He sits.)

DORIS: I'll make you a new pair. See this, I made it. It's a little uneven but I
like it that way. *(She shows him her poncho; it's wildly uneven.)* You should
see what I've been sewing for my kids. I use all kinds of fabrics I already
have — to save money — like curtains. And I made Tracy a mini skirt
from a bathroom rug — everyone loved it! So, if I spill anything on her
it's fine cause it has a rubber backing. I've learned all kinds of new things.
I moved nine rooms of furniture into a four-room apartment, and there's
so much stuff everywhere, we keep knocking things down like the lamps.
I must have twenty lamps. So now I'm an expert on Scotch Tape lamp
repair. I'm sorry about your wife. Must be hard on your kids, they must
—

BEN AND DORIS: — Miss her.

BEN: Do you have a lawyer, Doris?

DORIS: What?

BEN: For your divorce.

DORIS: Yeah. Stew sent me to this guy Sid Somebody, who said I couldn't afford
him and sent me to someone named Sam who sent me to Bill who sent
me to Phil. Phil's the only one I could afford.

BEN: You should have a good lawyer.

DORIS: Why?

BEN: Just anyone getting divorced should have a good lawyer.

DORIS: Well, he'll have to do. Can I ask you a question? *(He nods.)* Can I touch
your hair? *(She does.)* Do you think I'm too old?

BEN: For what?

DORIS: Just too old. Would you look at me and think, she's too old?

BEN: No.

DORIS: What would you think?

BEN: She isn't too old.

DORIS: And?

BEN: You want to check and see if Stew left that message?

DORIS: It can wait.

BEN: Doris, you're a catch. Don't you know that? He's lucky to have you.
(She holds up her drink.)

DORIS: Acapulco, playground of the world.

BEN: Salud.

DORIS: Lchaim.

(They toast. Ben spills his drink on Doris. They look at each other, surprised. They break out into laughter.)

(Fast light change. They eat.)

DORIS: Hey, this is fun.

BEN: Good.

DORIS: I'm having a great time. I haven't had such a good time in I don't know how long.

BEN: I'm glad.

DORIS: So to hell with my ex and to hell with your ex. What was her name?

BEN: Delilah.

DORIS: Delilah? You married a woman named Delilah? What were you thinking?

BEN: Not much at the time. What were you thinking?

DORIS: When?

BEN: When you married a man named Dick.

DORIS: Not much, I guess. *(She lifts her drink.)* To Dick and Delilah. And what's your ex best friend's name?

BEN: Samson.

DORIS: No.

BEN: No. Jeff.

DORIS: May he get what he deserves.

BEN: I think he already has.

DORIS: To Samson and Delilah. And Dick and Candy. And Stewart. To hell with them.

BEN: Stewart?

DORIS: Yeah, Stewart. I mean, he went off to Mexico City, and day after tomorrow it's back to New York and what has he said about getting married? Bupkes! So.

BEN: So.

DORIS: So, I'm having fun! Let's dance!

(They get up to dance, each with a napkin over their wet spots. They dance to an up tempo song. They look great. While dancing:)

BEN: You're quite a dancer.

DORIS: When I was a kid in Pittsburgh I had a scholarship from Gene Kelly.

BEN: Really.

DORIS: I was good back then.

BEN: I'd say you were still good.

DORIS: I came to New York when I was eighteen to be a dancer, but I had these terrible teeth from a baton-twirling accident and I couldn't afford to fix them and when I went to auditions I didn't smile. Who's gonna hire a girl without a smile? When I got engaged Dick sent me to a dentist in the Williamsburg Bank building. *(She runs her finger along the inside of her teeth.)* All gold. . . *(She smiles.)* Hey, maybe sometime our kids could meet. I just moved to Stuyvesant Town. You know it? I was on the bottom of the waiting list, and I wanted to get in for the school year so I went to the office and cried; and they let me in. It's wonderful: It has playgrounds, security guards. You could come over.

BEN: All white.

DORIS: What?

BEN: It's all white, isn't it?

DORIS: Um, I don't think so.

BEN: Famous for it.

DORIS: That can't be —

BEN: Have you seen any non-whites?

DORIS: Well. . .

BEN: Do you think there aren't Negro families that want to live somewhere that nice? If my sister went to that office and cried like that, they'd tell her she'd have to wait her turn. And her turn would never come. *(They stop dancing.)*

DORIS: Oh, that's terrible. Absolutely terrible. I had no idea. I'm gonna put your sister on the list.

BEN: No, my sister lives in Florida.

DORIS: Oh, well. Still. I mean, I just wanted to do right for my kids. It was one of the few places I could afford. Somewhere they'd be safe.

BEN: I can understand that.

DORIS: They're the most important thing to me. I might not even be here if it weren't for them.

BEN: I know what you mean.

DORIS: Do you?

BEN: Yes. I do. I know just what you mean.

DORIS: They need a father. Believe me, I'm not much good for them on my own.

BEN: Doris.

DORIS: What?

BEN: Forget it.

DORIS: No, what?

BEN: It's none of my business.

DORIS: No come on, we're talking, goddamn it, we're having a real talk, don't stop, please. What were you gonna say?

BEN: I was gonna say I'm sure you're a good mother. And your kids are fortunate to have you. Cause you love them. And you're trying to survive and.

DORIS: What?

BEN: And we all do things for different reasons and maybe it's for our kids and maybe we think it is, but it's really for us and. It gets very confused, I know. Believe me. But the thing is, well for me, see. I don't know, but. What you do matters. That's what you pass on. And Goddamn it sometimes you can't help it, life's not fair and all that. Sometimes you gotta do things that are. But at least you gotta see what you're doing.

DORIS: Oh.

BEN: None of my business. Sorry.

DORIS: No. I just.

BEN: Yeah. I have no right to say —

DORIS: No I.

BEN: I'm sure you'll do what's right.

DORIS: You are?

BEN: Yeah.

(Lights change as they return to the table which has a note on it that Doris reads.)

DORIS: Stewart will be back in the morning.

BEN: Oh? Early?

DORIS: Around ten. Well. It's late, isn't it? I guess I should go. Thanks for the evening. I I really enjoyed it.

BEN: Me, too.

DORIS: I hope I see you again.

(She kisses him lightly on the cheek.)

DORIS: You're a good man.

BEN: You don't even know me.

DORIS: Sure, I do. Genuine. Honest. What we call a mensch. Good night.

BEN: Wait. Doris. I don't know how to say this. Um. I have something to tell you.

DORIS: What?

BEN: Things are not what they appear to be.

DORIS: What do you mean?

BEN: I really can't say.

DORIS: I don't understand.

BEN: I think you should go home.

DORIS: What?

BEN: Before he gets back.

DORIS: What?

BEN: He's. He's not at the factory. He's um, he's with another woman. I'm sorry to tell you this, but it seems the only thing to do. . . Given the situation. I'm sorry.

DORIS: I.

BEN: I ran into him and he uh told me about it. Men sometimes, they do that, they like to uh brag.

DORIS: What?

BEN: Look. *(He pulls out a ticket.)* I know this seems odd, but, I have a plane ticket. Back to New York. It has an open return. And I know there's a 6 AM flight. Will you take it?

DORIS: I can't believe — .

BEN: I know. But um. It happens. Things like this happen. Right? Will you take it? Please? Go home.

DORIS: He told you — ?

BEN: Yes. He's not at the factory. He's with another woman. He's with a young woman.

DORIS: Oh. *(She takes the ticket.)*

BEN: Go home.

SCENE TWO

Next morning. The room at the Gold Sombrero. Stew enters carrying a suitcase.

STEWART: Doris? Dor? *(He looks around, she's not there. He goes to the bathroom.)* Doris? *(Not there. He looks at his watch.)* Damn. *(He picks up the phone.)* Yeah, are there any messages? No?
(He hangs up, looks at his watch again, goes to the door, opens it, and Doris is there, about to enter.)

STEWART: Hey, Doris!

DORIS: Hi, Stew.

STEWART: A sight for sore eyes, look at you, where were you?

DORIS: Just getting some breakfast.

STEWART: Good, that's good, now come in, come in.

DORIS: How was your trip?

STEWART: Lousy, awful, I missed you every minute, baby.

DORIS: Yeah?

STEWART: Yeah. Hey Dor, you believe me, don't you?

DORIS: Sure.

STEWART: I don't know why that guy said that but, I mean I was at the factory, I didn't even leave, I was there all night.

DORIS: I know.

STEWART: I got worried, I came back right away, and when you weren't in the room —

DORIS: It's O.K., Stew.

STEWART: I would never do that. I'm not that kind of guy. Why would I do that when I got a girl like you?

DORIS: Yeah? Thanks.

STEWART: *(They hug.)* Good, that's good. I feel better. Good. Grrr. *(He puts his arm around her.)* Doris. I got something I want to ask you.

DORIS: Oh?

STEWART: It's kind of hard to get the words out.

DORIS: Take your time.

STEWART: No, I gotta do it now. Um. I wanted to ask. . .

DORIS: What?

STEWART: When — when, you know, when we make love —

DORIS: Yeah?

STEWART: Does it — is everything — does it seem O.K?

DORIS: Sure.

STEWART: Nothing unusual?

DORIS: Uh, no.

STEWART: No?

DORIS: No.

STEWART: Good.

DORIS: Why?

STEWART: Well, when I was uh — my mother tells me that uh at the briss — you know —

DORIS: Uh huh.

STEWART: See they didn't have much money, my parents, so they hired a mohel who was young and didn't have alotta experience . . .

DORIS: Uh huh.

STEWART: So he — you know — and it's not terrible I mean it all works, you know that, I got no problem with that, right? But it does look a little — different. And I was wondering if it bothered you. If you'd noticed.

DORIS: No.

STEWART: O.K. Good, great.

DORIS: Is that what you wanted to ask me? Was that the big question?

STEWART: Let me show it to you.

DORIS: What?

STEWART: What we're talking about, you know. I just I just want you to look at it, so you can — you know — make sure.

DORIS: Stew.

STEWART: Please. This is important to me, Doris. I have to be sure it's all right.
(He sits on the bed. She joins him. He unzips his pants. The door flies open, and in walks Ben holding an oversized camera with a large flash. They all look at each other and freeze. Stew can't believe Ben is there, Ben can't believe Doris is there, Doris can't believe Ben is there. Just as Ben is about to turn around and walk away, Dick enters.)

DICK: Take the picture.
(He doesn't. Nettie enters.)

NETTIE: Take the picture.
(He doesn't. The sound of a mariachi band is heard from outside the hall. They all turn and look.)

DICK: What the hell is that?

STEWART: It's the mariachi band I hired. What the hell is this?

NETTIE: Oy, they need a band, they're in bed and they need a band?

STEWART: I'm about to propose.

NETTIE: He's about to propose! She's still married — he's about to propose. Take the picture!!

DICK: You better take the goddamn picture.

STEWART: What the hell is going on here?
(Ben takes a picture. Flash.)
(This moment is then repeated a few times in different ways as if in a bad dream: maybe in silence, slow motion, from different points of view, or with different music. Each time Doris moves further downstage, until she's near the audience, stunned.)
(Another flash and suddenly we bounce back to real time and general pandemonium breaks out: a chaotic overlapping insanity.)

DORIS: Dick, what are you doing here?

STEWART: *Dick?*

(Stew rushes at Dick threateningly. Nettie runs to Dick, and throws herself in front of him, arms outstretched.)

NETTIE: Don't hurt him. He's a sick man!!

STEWART: You better move, lady.

NETTIE: You're gonna have to hit me to get to him!

DICK: Mom —

NETTIE: Get a picture of this, he's gonna hit me.

STEWART: Move —

NETTIE: Call the police!

DICK: Mom —

(As Stew tries to get around Nettie to get to Dick, Ben talks to Doris.)

BEN: Doris, I'm sorry.

DORIS: I don't understand.

BEN: I didn't think you'd be here.

(Nettie takes a swipe at Stewart, perhaps knocking off his toupee.)

STEWART: Sonuvagun.

(Doris, dazed, crosses to Dick.)

DORIS: Are you all right?

STEWART: Doris, get over here.

DORIS: You look pale.

NETTIE: *(To Ben.)* Did you get it?

DORIS: Maybe you should sit down.

NETTIE: *(To Ben.)* Did you get the shot?

DORIS: You want some water?

DICK: For Chrissake, Doris.

NETTIE: If I didn't see it I wouldn't have believed it.

DICK: Believe it Mom!

NETTIE: *(To Doris.)* You better give me back those pearls.

STEWART: *(To Dick.)* You better get the hell outta here.

NETTIE: Take another. For what we're paying, you should take another.

(Stew goes after Ben and grabs the camera, Dick goes after Stew to get it back, Nettie goes after Dick to protect him. Dick gets the camera back, then suddenly grabs his chest in pain, and starts to collapse.)

DICK: Uh!

(Everyone stops and looks.)

DICK: Uh.

NETTIE: Hymie. You all right? Hymie?

DICK: Uh.

DORIS: Dick?

NETTIE: Hymie?

BEN: You all right?

NETTIE: *(To Doris.)* Look what you did. You killed him.

DICK: Uh.

NETTIE: I'll kill you both!

DICK: Let's go Mom.

    (Nettie leads Dick out.)

NETTIE: You all right Hymie? Oy God let him be all right.

    (Nettie and Dick exit.)

STEWART: *(To Ben.)* Out.

BEN: Doris —

STEWART: *Out.*

    (Ben exits.)

STEWART: Jesus H Christ, I swear. Son of a gun! I see that guy, I'll kill him. Heart attack or no heart attack. *(He notices Doris looking stunned.)* Doris. You O.K?

DORIS: Yeah, no, I, I don't, they. That man, Ben —

STEWART: A dick, a private dick.

DORIS: I just, the whole thing —

STEWART: A setup, he was part of the setup: to find out where we were, what our schedule was, everything.

DORIS: I don't understand.

STEWART: What's to understand? He got you Doris. He fucked you up the ass. Both of them. Two Dicks. Right up the ass.

DORIS: He didn't look well. I I thought —

STEWART: He didn't look well? — He's sitting pretty now. He's counting his dollars now. *(Doris shakes her head, not getting it.)* He's got those pictures. Don't you know the law? *(She shakes her head no.)* You're still married, you're his wife, and he's got pictures of you as an adulterer. You're not gonna get a penny.

DORIS: But he's the one who —

STEWART: Do you have pictures of him?

DORIS: How'd he know we were here?

STEWART: I don't know.

DORIS: Are you in on it? Is that what happened?

STEWART: No! Jesus, Doris, you can't tell black from white. I'm on your side and you're running over to him worrying about his goddamn health. Now listen to me, you're in quite a predicament here, and I'll be goddamned if I'm gonna let that bastard ruin my goddamn proposal, so you wanna get married?

DORIS: Oh, Stew. I. I I can't —

STEWART: Damn it, Doris. I'm gonna go look for the sonuvabitch and then I'm going to the bar and have a drink. You consider my offer and and meet me there if you're interested.

(Stew exits. Doris stands there. She notices the door is still open. She closes it, locks it, puts on the chain.)

SCENE THREE

Dick's hotel room. Dick is in bed.

NETTIE: You all right?

DICK: I think so, yeah.

NETTIE: I'll call a doctor, let me call a doctor.

DICK: It's just the ulcer.

NETTIE: That's what you thought last time. *(He drinks some Maalox.)* A shvartze — you hired a shvartze?

DICK: Mom.

NETTIE: What did you — try to get a deal or something?

DICK: No.

NETTIE: Are you crazy?

DICK: I didn't know, O.K? Anthony Caccion, private investigator, highly recommended.

NETTIE: That's Anthony Caccion?

DICK: No, turns out Caccion choked on a calzone, died, so this guy was I don't know, someone who worked for him — just took over the business.

NETTIE: Oy.

DICK: I didn't meet him, Mom, we only talked on the phone. It was the day before, remember?

NETTIE: You know what they've done to my neighborhood?

DICK: He did the job, right? We got the pictures.

NETTIE: Yeah.

DICK: What's the matter, Mom?

NETTIE: The whole thing, it's awful. The food in this place, terrible. Why did we have to come down here?

DICK: You didn't have to come, Mom, I had to come.

NETTIE: Why did you have to come?

DICK: I wanted to make sure it was done right.

NETTIE: And I wanted to make sure you were all right. Are you all right?

DICK: I'm fine.

NETTIE: Listen, I've been thinking. You should make a will.

DICK: Mom —

NETTIE: No one is written into the book of life forever. You can put in all the quarters you want but your cycle's still gonna run out. Now, you've had one heart attack. And I pray to God every night you don't have another one. But you make a will.

DICK: I'm fine.

NETTIE: Will you do it?

DICK: Enough, Mom.

NETTIE: You want to come to my house on Passover?

DICK: Of course I do.

NETTIE: You want to keep bringing the girls over for dinner on Sundays?

DICK: Yeah.

NETTIE: You want me to go to the cemetery and tell your father you did the honorable thing?

DICK: *(Cries.)* Yeah.

NETTIE: Then leave my money and your money to my grandchildren, not to that woman or her stupid kids. And if you don't, think of what you leave your girls: a court battle with Candy and the question, why wasn't my father man enough to make a decision?

DICK: *(Dick grimaces, in pain.)* Uh. Ai.

NETTIE: You all right?

DICK: *(He grabs his chest.)* Yeah. Uh. I don't know.

NETTIE: Dick?

DICK: Ai.

NETTIE: You all right?

DICK: Uhhh.

NETTIE: Oh my God. Dick!

(He groans. Nettie grabs the phone and dials.)

SCENE FOUR

A hospital room in Acapulco. There is a body under a white sheet on a stretcher. Doris enters. She sees the body, peaks at it, cringes. A toilet flushes. Dick enters.

DICK: *(Surprised.)* Doris.

DORIS: Hello, Dick.

DICK: Well.

DORIS: I'm sorry about —

DICK: *(Starts to cry.)* Yeah.

DORIS: I used to think the world of her.

DICK: *(Cries.)* Yeah.

DORIS: That she was a better mother than my own. Stronger, smarter. A good cook. Taught me how to make brisket. Gefilte fish.

DICK: *(Really loses it.)* Yeah.

DORIS: I never cared for her stuffed cabbage, though. Too much vinegar, not enough sweet.

DICK: Prunes. She used prunes.

DORIS: Oh. She never told me that.

DICK: Secret ingredient.

DORIS: How'd it happen?

DICK: I was having some ulcer pain and she had a heart attack.

DORIS: Oh.

DICK: I'm flying back with the body today.

DORIS: When's the funeral?

DICK: Tuesday.

DORIS: I'll bring the girls. *(Dick nods.)* Poor Sam.

DICK: Yeah.

DORIS: His first family in Poland. His second wife in Acapulco.

DICK: Yeah.

DORIS: Tell him I'm sorry.

(Dick nods. Doris pulls out a string of pearls from her purse.)

DORIS: She said she wanted these back. Seems almost like a last request so I figured I should honor it. Unless you want me to keep them for the girls.

DICK: Whatever.

(She puts them on the body.)

DICK: Look Doris, I'm sorry about this whole thing. See, I had to, for my mother, I couldn't let her think —

DORIS: — The truth.

DICK: O.K. fine, I lied to her. A little. And I lied to you. I was trying to not hurt anyone. Or to hurt everyone as little as possible.

DORIS: *(Seemingly sincere.)* That was very thoughtful of you.

DICK: Yeah, well.

DORIS: And now she's gone.

DICK: Yeah.

DORIS: Dead.

DICK: *(Cries.)* Yeah.

DORIS: It's just you now. No mother, no father.

DICK: Yeah.

DORIS: She died knowing what a good son you are.

DICK: Yeah.

DORIS: Mission accomplished.

DICK: Yeah.

DORIS: So now you can give me those pictures.

(Dick stops crying, looks up.)

DORIS: Prove your mother right. That you really are a mensch.

DICK: Sure. I'll give 'em to you. Happy to. I was gonna offer myself.

DORIS: Well. Good.

DICK: Like you said, I got no need for 'em now, right?

DORIS: Right. Where are they?

DICK: Right here. *(He pulls an envelope out from under Nettie's head.)* You want 'em? Or should I just tear 'em up?

DORIS: I'll take them.

DICK: Fine. I'll hand 'em over. All you got to do is go along with our original agreement.

DORIS: Which agreement was that?

DICK: No lawyer.

DORIS: Oh, that agreement.

DICK: That's right. Let me and my lawyer work it out. It's what you said you'd do in the first place.

DORIS: Well, that was before.

DICK: And this is now. And that's my offer.

DORIS: Why don't you just give them to me?

DICK: Why would I do that?

DORIS: Sense of decency.

DICK: I'm a businessman, Doris. Why would I hand over something of value, regardless of how I got it?

DORIS: Why would I forfeit my right to an attorney?

DICK: O.K. You can have an attorney. I'll even pay for him. I even insist I pay for him. As long as I get to pick who it is. No one will see these. And once the settlement is over, I'll tear them up. Final offer.

DORIS: Stewart says you fucked me up the ass.

DICK: He should know. What a loser. You could do better than that.

DORIS: *I* could do better? What do you see in her anyway? I mean I could understand if she were I don't know ten years younger or smart or interesting in some way. But why her? Why did you prefer her over me?

DICK: Candy may not be a genius, but at least she's got a backbone.

DORIS: And I don't? Well. Didn't seem to bother you at first.

DICK: Sure I said "boo" you ran, I said "Marilyn" you dyed it blonde, I said "Put your toes in your mouth," you turned into a pretzel. If I'd wanted a slave I'da bought one.

(A beat. Doris looks toward the body.)

DORIS: How old was she?

DICK: Sixty-five.

DORIS: Your father?

DICK: Forty-eight.

DORIS: I hope your Candy gets stuck in your throat and makes you choke at night.

DICK: It's over, Doris. I got no, I repeat no, reason to give you anything. Hey, she was your only advocate. And she's gone.

DORIS: How'd you find out I was here?

DICK: *(Shrugs.)* What's the difference?

DORIS: Cause I didn't tell anyone.

DICK: *(Shrugs again.)* Can't say.

DORIS: *(A beat. She gets it. Big time.)* Oh, you didn't. Oh. You didn't.

DICK: What?

DORIS: The girls. Ohmigod.

DICK: Who said — ?

DORIS: Your own children. Oh. My. God.

DICK: Hey, we go into court who's gonna get all the sympathy? I should let you wipe me out? Take everything? Because what? Because I stayed in a miserable marriage? Because I supported you? Because I work hard at my business? I don't think so.

DORIS: And the girls?

DICK: I'm sure they'll be fine.

DORIS: That's it?

DICK: That's it.

DORIS: You spied on your own children so you could keep your money —

DICK: *(Overlaps.)* — I didn't spy — they told me — -

DORIS: *(Overlaps.)* — And you think they're gonna be fine? With a father like that?

DICK: They seem fine to me.

DORIS: That's because you're not looking!

DICK: It's over, Doris. You lost.

DORIS: I lost? I don't think so. I have two wonderful daughters to go home to. What do you have, the Whore of Brooklyn?

DICK: You better watch your mouth. Remember there's still dance lessons, piano lessons, private school, college.

DORIS: You're gonna give me those pictures.

DICK: Forget it. Practice your typing. These aren't even them. You think I'm stupid? The pictures aren't even developed yet. The *film* is on its way to my lawyer in New York.

DORIS: You would do that to your own children? You would hurt your own children?

DICK: Did I ever want them, Doris? Did I ever say I wanted to have children?

DORIS: You went along with it, didn't you? You did what was required. And they're here. So it doesn't matter whether you wanted them or not.

DICK: You think I'm a rotten father, fine, O.K. I'm such a rotten father that I will revoke my visitation rights, O.K?

DORIS: *(Stunned. A beat. Then.)* No. No. You will see them. Every Sunday. Because they need you to. And you better appreciate the time you have with them, you better cherish it, cause you're gonna marry that woman, right, and you're gonna give me nothing, and you're gonna give your kids almost nothing, and not long after that Dick, you're gonna die.

DICK: All right —

DORIS: You think you got out of this marriage clean? All you lost was a couple of dollars, but you're wrong.

DICK: O.K. —

DORIS: And I'm gonna be at your funeral, cause the kids, your daughters, they're not gonna be fine, they're gonna need someone, cause they're not gonna understand what happened to their father, where was he, how come he was never around, how come when he *was* around he wasn't around. And when they bury you I'm gonna throw in some sand from the beach in Acapulco, so you'll have to think of this day always. For the rest of eternity you'll have to remember who you were on February 13th, 1966. And when the girls grow up, I'm gonna tell them this story if it's the last thing I do, so that they can recognize, from across a room, and keep away from, *any* man like you.

DICK: You just took the food out of your kids' mouths.

DORIS: My kids'll have enough to eat.

DICK: Well, good luck to you.

DORIS: I'm glad you're with that woman. I'm gonna say my prayers every night and thank God for her. Otherwise, I'd be stuck in that awful house in that awful neighborhood with those awful neighbors waiting for you to come home so I could serve you dinner, and you could take me from behind. So, here's my last offer. Give me the film.

DICK: Fuck you, Doris.

DORIS: You fucked me for the last time.

DICK: Doesn't look that way.

DORIS: You're not gonna even make it to forty-eight. Every lie you've told, has taken a day off your life, so I figure, that's a lot of days. You're halfway in the ground.

DICK: Nice to see you have a voice Doris, too bad it's too late.

DORIS: Good luck with the wedding. Mazel tov. I hope your new marriage gives you everything this one didn't. Enjoy it while you can. Your time's running out.

(She exits. She enters again, grabs the pearls, and exits.)

(Dick, fuming, pulls down the sheet.)

DICK: See, Mom, I told you she was a bitch.

(He puts the sheet back, then storms over to the wall, and kicks it. He goes back to the body, pulls the sheet down.)

DICK: Mom. Could you tell Dad that I'm sorry about when I ran away from home when I flunked outta high school and didn't get back before he died.

(He puts the sheet up, then pulls it back down.)

DICK: And tell him I made it big. O.K? Tell him that I'm a goddamn success.

SCENE FIVE

The bar at the Gold Sombrero. A woman sits on a stool facing upstage, wearing a dress and a hat identical to Doris's. Stewart enters, grabs her from behind, and kisses her passionately. They separate.

STEWART: I'm sorry.

CANDY: Well.

STEWART: I — I thought you were someone else.

CANDY: I thought you were someone else.

STEWART: Terribly sorry.

CANDY: Don't be.

STEWART: You looked just like —

CANDY: It's fine.

STEWART: I'm not myself today.

CANDY: Me neither.

STEWART: I thought I was gonna meet someone here.

CANDY: Me, too. I been waiting here all day. I don't like to be kept waiting.

STEWART: I know what that's like.

CANDY: And I just found out my son, Doug, somehow missed the deadline for getting married to avoid the draft.

STEWART: Oh, sorry.

CANDY: The only good news is my mother-in-law-to-be dropped dead.

STEWART: Oh.

CANDY: So, what brings you to Acapulco?

STEWART: Uh, pleasure and business.

CANDY: What kind of business are you in?

STEWART: I have a factory down here that —

CANDY: Really? Listen, my son, Doug, would be very good in your factory.

STEWART: Well —

CANDY: He'd be perfect. He's very handsome and tall and, what kind of factory is it?

STEWART: Plastic cigarettes.

CANDY: He's very good at that. How bout we go to dinner? The two of us. What's your name?

STEWART: Stew.

CANDY: *(She shakes his hand seductively.)* Hi, Stew. My name is Candy.

STEWART: Candy. Where are you from?

CANDY: Brooklyn.

STEWART: Candy from Brooklyn. What do you know. What brings you to Acapulco?

CANDY: It's a long story.

STEWART: I have time.

CANDY: *(She puts her hand on his thigh.)* So do I. You're a very good-looking guy, Stew. We could get to know each other. I bet we'd find out we have a lot in common.

STEWART: I bet you're right.

CANDY: Why don't we get a room, and I can tell you all about me and my son.

STEWART: I thought you were waiting for someone.

CANDY: I was, but now I met you. And I like you.

STEWART: What room is your friend in?

CANDY: We can get our own room.

STEWART: I'd like to go to his room.

CANDY: Oh? What — what did you have in mind?

STEWART: You bring me there, and then I'll see what I can do for your son.

CANDY: Really?

STEWART: Really.

(Doris enters.)

DORIS: Stew.

STEWART: Hey, I was just talking to Candy from Brooklyn over here, and she was gonna bring me up to her friend's room, right Candy?

CANDY: Well, yeah. Does she want to come, too?

DORIS: No.

STEWART: No, she doesn't want to come, but I'm gonna go, and then I'm gonna see you later. You understand, honey?

DORIS: Stew. We have to talk.

CANDY: *(To Doris.)* Wait a minute, I recognize you. From your picture.

DORIS: And I recognize you from your description.

CANDY: So, you must be Boobin.

STEWART: Rubin, it's Rubin.

CANDY: You knew it was me. What were you gonna do to Dick, huh? I'm gonna tell him.

STEWART: Go ahead. I think you should tell him. Tell him you invited me to be alone with you in his room. That's a very good idea.

(Candy rises and leaves as Stew shouts after her.)

STEWART: And there are a few other things I think you should tell. Tell him to come meet me here at the bar, cause I have a few things I want to tell him!!

DORIS: Stew.

STEWART: Doris, honey I'm sorry I just I — this whole thing. I was just gonna get back at the guy.

DORIS: It's over, O.K?

STEWART: Well yeah, O.K. That sounds good. Listen, I'm gonna make it up to you, all right? We'll do what you said, we'll have a lot of days together.

We'll put the whole thing behind us, how's that? Like it never happened. Like today never happened.

DORIS: Oh today happened, Stew.

STEWART: O.K., today happened. So, we'll start over. We'll extend our stay. We'll have another week, how's that?

DORIS: Oh, I can't.

STEWART: Well, then we'll go home and I can come over for dinner, and we'll have a good time, O.K?

DORIS: I can't.

STEWART: What do you mean you can't?

DORIS: You're a nice man. Really you are. I mean, you've been very nice. It's just. I don't know how to say this. And I'm not sure why, but. I just can't. I'm sorry.

STEWART: What?

DORIS: It's not gonna work out. With us.

STEWART: You mean that's it? Finished? Over? Is that what you mean?

DORIS: Well, yes.

STEWART: Geez, Doris. I thought you wanted to get married.

DORIS: I did. But now. It just wouldn't be right. I am sorry.

STEWART: Yeah. Me, too.

DORIS: *(A beat.)* I'll go upstairs and pack.

(She walks away.)

(Stew grabs a real cigarette from the bar, and lights it.)

SCENE SIX

An airplane in flight. Doris and Betty seated next to each other. Doris has been crying.

BETTY: That's awful.

DORIS: I know.

BETTY: That's one of the worst husband stories I've ever heard.

DORIS: It's not a nice one, is it?

BETTY: I'm so sorry. Here.

(Betty gives them each a tissue. They dab their eyes, blow their noses, reapply lipstick.)

BETTY: I'm glad we were on the same flight.

DORIS: Me, too.

BETTY: So.

DORIS: So, Dick was a rat.

BETTY: Sounds like.

DORIS: I guess you could say I married the wrong man.

BETTY: I think you could. And I guess Stew didn't turn out so great either.

DORIS: Oh, he was all right. He just wasn't for me. And then there's that man, Ben.

BETTY: Oh?

DORIS: Thank God you two didn't meet. He was the worst of them all, a *professional* deceiver. Pretending to be a friend.

BETTY: Shall we have a drink?

DORIS: God, yes.

(They pull out of their bags little liquor bottles, uncap them, and toast.)

BETTY: To um the future.

DORIS: To the future.

BETTY: Salud.

DORIS: Lchaim.

(They drink.)

BETTY: Listen, I know this is none of my business, but I have an idea.

DORIS: Oh?

BETTY: You do the same thing to him.

DORIS: You mean —?

BETTY: That's right. Get pictures of him and that woman.

DORIS: Oh.

BETTY: It would be a clean wash. As if the whole thing never happened, and the court would decide in your favor.

DORIS: Huh.

BETTY: Now, believe it or not, I have a friend who's a private eye, and he's very good. I can set it up for you. And I think as a favor he would do it for free.

DORIS: Free? Why would he do that?

BETTY: Well, because I would ask him, and I think he would see that an injustice has been done, and he would want to uh fix that.

DORIS: He would?

BETTY: If he were here, I'm sure he'd tell you himself, except you'd probably never sit still long enough to talk to another detective after what happened.

DORIS: Probably not.

BETTY: What do you say?

DORIS: How could I turn down an offer like that?

BETTY: Good. Oh my, I think we're gonna land soon. I better get back to my seat. *(Betty stands.)*

DORIS: Wait, I have something for you. *(She gives Betty a small paper bag.)* I saved the pillow mints from the hotel, I thought maybe your boys would like them.

BETTY: What?

DORIS: You know, your sons. Todd, James, and Nelson. Do they know you like to dress as a woman?

BEN: Oh.

DORIS: I don't know what your game is —

BEN: Doris —

DORIS: But don't for a second think I'm playing along.

BEN: You knew.

DORIS: Cause you win, you're the high scorer, you lied as two people.

BEN: I'm sorry. *(Ben sits.)*

DORIS: Who said you could sit?

BEN: *(Stands.)* Look —

DORIS: I have looked. And now I'd like to look away. *(She grabs the bag of mints.)* I'll keep these, cause you probably don't even have kids. You probably made that up so I would trust you and tell you things, right? I hope Dick paid you a lot of money. A whole lot.

BEN: I didn't think you'd be there. Doris. I told you to go. I gave you the ticket, you took it. I thought we'd walk in, and you wouldn't be there.

DORIS: So you told me that pathetic lie about Stew with another woman? Well, it didn't work, did it, cause all I had to do was make one phone call and find out Stew *was* at the factory. Which was the obvious thing to do. Anyone would have done that. So maybe you eased your conscience, but you didn't help me. You were the worst of them all. Cause you knew it was wrong. Goddamn it I liked you. So go away. Go home.

BEN: I'm sorry. I know this doesn't make it better but. I do have three kids and. I didn't think you'd be in the room. I don't know how to say this. I. As soon as we met. And then at dinner.

DORIS: What the hell was all that nonsense you were saying at dinner, you're a good parent, what you do matters, blah blah blah. What are you teaching your kids? How to lie?

BEN: Doris. You have a husband who lied and cheated his way through your marriage, and in the middle of your divorce settlement you went with a man to Acapulco, and you told your children, and you thought your ruthless husband wouldn't find out and wouldn't do anything? And when he walked in on you with a private eye, you ran over to help him?

DORIS: How dare you?

BEN: You went down there wanting to marry a man you didn't even know, saying you were doing it for your kids. Is that the truth?

DORIS: What do you know about it? I'm a single mother with no job and no money —

BEN: And I'm a single father with three kids and a brand-new business that I just put a second mortgage on my home to pay for, and no customers til Dick called. And my kids need winter coats just like yours. And Goddamn it, I liked you too.

DORIS: Well.

BEN: Well.

DORIS: Well, why the hell are you dressed like that?

BEN: Because I didn't have the money to hire a woman for the plane, and that's how it's done: You put a woman next to the wife so she'll open up and spill the beans. And I couldn't pay for it, and I couldn't turn down the account, so I figured it was worth a try.

DORIS: And I fell for it.

BEN: Not this time.

DORIS: No.

BEN: Well, I'll get the pictures like I said. At least you'll get the money you're due.

DORIS: No thanks.

BEN: What do you mean?

DORIS: I don't want you to do that.

BEN: Why not?

DORIS: Because it's not right.

BEN: Oh, it's right.

DORIS: No. What would I tell my kids? Your father was a scum-sucking bottom-feeding water rat so I became one, too? I will get a job. That I like. Eventually. I'm very resourceful. *(She pulls out a bag filled with hotel glassware.)*

BEN: You're something else, Doris.

DORIS: Yeah, well, one day you wake up and nothing's the same.

BEN: I know.

DORIS: Your lipstick's smudged.

BEN: Listen, maybe when this is all over sometime you could maybe, you know our kids could, maybe they could. Maybe they'd get along.

DORIS: I'm sure they would.

BEN: Yeah?

DORIS: I'm sure they'd like you.

BEN: Yeah?

DORIS: Yeah.

BEN: Well, mine would like you.

DORIS: Sounds good, but. *(She shakes her head no.)*

BEN: You're right.

DORIS: Probably not a good idea.

BEN: Probably not.

DORIS: It's just. Everything that's happened.

BEN: Right.

DORIS: So.

BEN: So.

DORIS: Back to New York.

BEN: It ain't Acapulco.

DORIS: No. Back to cold.

BEN: Dirt.

DORIS: Snow.

BEN: Bills.

DORIS: Kids.

BEN: Lchaim.

DORIS: Salud.

SCENE SEVEN

Brooklyn. Dick and Candy enter their new apartment.

CANDY: So, I got the place all fixed up. Ready to move in. You like it?

DICK: Yeah, it's fine.

CANDY: Is it Park Avenue in Brooklyn or what?

DICK: It's nice. My stomach — I gotta lie down.

CANDY: Wait, I want to show you everything.

DICK: Later, O.K?

CANDY: But I worked so hard.

DICK: My ulcer.

CANDY: Just one thing, then you lie down. O.K? Come here. Sit on the new couch.

(She leads him to a plastic-covered couch. They sit, facing the audience.)

CANDY: I hope you're gonna like this, cause you're gonna look at it every day.
(Candy turns on a light switch. The lights brighten as they look at the mural. Candy sees a work of art. Dick sees a big mistake.)

CANDY: See? It's Venice. Isn't it great? I just love it. We're gonna have such a wonderful life together. We get to be with each other every day.
(Dick looks ahead at the mural of Venice seeing — for the first time — into the future with an expression of both horror and resignation.)

CANDY: See, it has the canals and the piazza and the gondolas, those are my favorites. Isn't it great?
(Nettie appears upstage in a striped shirt, rowing as if she's a gondolier. Candy doesn't see her. Dick's jaw drops open.)

CANDY: Dick? You all right? What's the matter?

DICK: *(He groans.)* Nothing. I'm fine.

SCENE EIGHT

Cross fade and voice over announcing Doris's flight arrival to Kennedy Airport. Doris carries her luggage, her souvenirs, her keys. She walks down the hall, gets to her front door, opens it, and steps inside.

DORIS: Robyn? Tracy? I'm home, girls. Mommy's home.
(She wipes her tears, opens her arms, and smiles.)
(Lights fade.)

END OF PLAY

A Shoe Is Not a Question

Kelly Stuart

For my dead cat, Lion.

Kelly Stuart has written more than a dozen plays, including *Demonology,* which was produced at Playwrights Horizons in New York, the Mark Taper Forum, and other theaters across the United States, and won the "New American Play Award" by Sun and Moon Press. (*Demonology* started as a commission and broadcast by BBC Radio in the U.K. and Canada.) Other productions include *Furious Blood,* at Sledgehammer Theatre in California, *The Square Root of Terrible* (a children's musical about girls and math anxiety) that was commissioned and produced by the Mark Taper Forum, *The Interpreter of Horror* at the New York Fringe Fest and the Padua Hills Playwrights Festival, *The Peacock Screams When the Lights Go Out* at Sledgehammer, *Ball and Chain* at the Padua Hills Playwrights Festival and *Taxidance* at the Cast Theatre. As a member of New Dramatists, she participated in exchanges to the Australian National Playwrights' Conference, and the Royal National Theatre in London. As part of an A.S.K. Theatre Projects exchange, *A Shoe Is Not a Question* received a staged reading at the Royal Court Theatre. *A Shoe Is Not a Question* was commissioned by South Coast Repertory. Ms. Stuart has also been commissioned by Sledgehammer Theatre, Playwrights Horizons, the Mark Taper Forum, and A.S.K. Theatre Projects. In the fall of 2000, she received a Whiting Foundation Award. She has taught playwriting at UCSD and currently teaches at Columbia University.

CHARACTERS

SIGGY: A wealthy shoe designer. Sexy, stylish, and smart. Mid to late forties.

TED: A former Yale professor/poet. Siggy's husband. Charming and spoiled. Mid to late forties.

HANK: A composer, down on his luck. Rugged and stoic, a lot going on inside. Mid to late forties.

KALI: A yoga instructor, Hank's new girlfriend. 25 years old.

JEAN: A servant — very cool and always ready to provide what is needed. 30 years old. Speaks with a French accent.

SETTING

Ted and Siggy's cabin in the Adirondacks, and the surrounding woods.

A SHOE IS NOT A QUESTION

ACT ONE

Lights up. A spacious cabin in the Adirondacks. Raw wood planked floor, a hearth, an urn near the hearth. A shelf with several pairs of glossy designer shoes on display. Hank and Ted.

HANK: You told me you scattered them.

TED: I misspoke.

HANK: You told me you took them up in the helicopter.

TED: I . . . We did take them up, but as we passed over, I opened the hatch and this freezing wind . . . invaded my being. I just couldn't do it. What a horrible place, Tibet. The Himalayas. I find them inhuman.

HANK: But that was where she wanted to go.

TED: But in the MOMENT Hank, I felt her want something else. That we find the right way to remember her.

HANK: So, where are the ashes?

TED: Right there in that urn.

HANK: That?

TED: Fabulous isn't it?

HANK: You've kept my wife's ashes in that? All along?

TED: Right here in the hearth. And behind the woodpile sometimes when we had a fire. All along . . . she's been . . . with us.

HANK: Siggy knew about this?

TED: She's the one who found the urn. In a thrift store no less.

HANK: You've had my wife's ashes here for two years.

TED: She was my friend. She was my friend too. Okay . . . We were doing the in-vitro thing, and I hoped if I kept Susie's ashes, her spirit would maybe, you know what they say, that the spirit hovers around near the ashes. I hoped when Sig got implanted, Susie's spirit would . . . get implanted too.

HANK: What?

TED: Reincarnation. She'd make the trip back to us.

HANK: Not to come back is the thing to aim for.

TED: We gave up on in vitro . . .

HANK: You know what I mean?

TED: And everything else. All that's over. Trying to reconcile . . . maybe . . .

HANK: When you go through all that, YOU DON'T WANT TO COME BACK.

TED: . . . Maybe getting one from China, but haven't come to terms on that. *(Pause, Ted sees that Hank is disturbed.)*

TED: I too have been through a lot.

HANK: So that's why you invited me up here. To have . . . what, some kind of catharsis? Some kind of grief therapy?

TED: Believe me Hank, it's not about you. We're up here to work.

HANK: On this . . . what. What's it called?

TED: The Steiner.

HANK: The Steiner. Right. What foundation gives that out?

TED: The Lipshidt Foundation.

HANK: The Lipshidt foundation. I've never heard of that. How do you spell it?

TED: L.I.P.S.H.I.D.T Lipshidt.

HANK: Lipshidt.

TED: Yes. Lipshidt. The Lipshidt Foundation. It's fairly embryonic, we're the first recipients.

HANK: That's a miracle isn't it.

TED: No it's not a miracle.

HANK: At this point . . .

TED: This is completely deserved.

HANK: I mean, only an idiot would . . .

TED: We are entitled to this.

HANK: Who are these people again?

TED: The Lipshidt Foundation.

HANK: Friends of yours?

TED: What the hell is this? You think we don't deserve it? This foundation came to ME. They approached ME. And I've approached YOU.

HANK: It just almost seems to good to be true.

TED: Did you ever see that therapist I recommended? Obviously, you haven't because your sense of self-worth is so low. First of all, I've been a professor at Yale.

I had the Wolfensturn Chair and I won the Amok and Contempt Prizes last year given by the STUDENT BODY. And I am the author of "The Cerulean Bird." Who composed the score for that Hank. Who?

HANK: Me.

TED: What? I didn't hear you. Did you say YOU composed the score for "The Cerulean Bird"? Well I don't think that's been forgotten as yet. And what

awards did that win Hank? Didn't it win a STRING of awards? Answer
me Hank.

HANK: I guess so.

TED: You guess so. And what were those awards? Did it not win AN OBIE?

HANK: Yeah.

TED: And there was Broadway interest!

HANK: Briefly, yes.

TED: Did it NOT win the Outer Fringe Award? And The Lower Borough Critics
Circle Award? So who the fuck are you to think we wouldn't get funding, based on my reputation alone?

HANK: I don't know.

TED: I mean, who the fuck are you?

HANK: Nobody really . . . that's why it's a shock.

TED: You are not a nobody Hank. You're a very important composer. It's just
that you don't remember. I know how you feel. I mean . . . I too have
this feeling of . . . what . . . that I . . . that I don't deserve goodness. Though
I do. Though we all really do. Yet I have this strange and mysterious guilt.

HANK: Of course you do. You didn't scatter her ashes.

TED: It just didn't feel MORALLY right.

HANK: You should've dumped them from the helicopter like she asked you in
the first place.

TED: See, that reminds me of that horrible thing they did to people in Argentina.

HANK: She's not a person anymore. That's the point. She was cremated, Ted.
As in CREAMED. Wiped out. What one does with remains. The point
of it all is to let go.

TED: But memory. Isn't that part of it? There's a place right up here, Falcon
Rock, where it looks over the lake. I've had Travertine marble brought
in, and we got this fabulous stone mason to build this altar to Susie.

HANK: You built her an altar.

TED: I wrote a poem about it. It's inscribed in the marble up there.

(Kali enters.)

KALI: Oh, hi.

HANK: This is Kali.

TED: Kelli?

KALI: No no . . . Kali.

TED: Ted . . . Good to meet you.

KALI: So, what's going on?

TED: Who are you?

KALI: What am I doing here?

TED: I didn't mean it like that. It's fabulous to meet you. I'm pleasantly surprised.

HANK: I told you I was bringing someone.

TED: A friend.

HANK: My girlfriend, Kali.

TED: Oh.

KALI: It's great, isn't it. We are so lucky.

TED: Oh, yeah.

KALI: Excuse me.
(She does a headstand.)

TED: *(Re her headstand.)* Isn't that bad for your brain?

KALI: Oh no. Sirasana is very very healing. It stimulates the immune system.

TED: I see.

KALI: It irrigates the brain cells. Hank can do it. Show him Hank.
(Hank does a headstand. Ted stares in shock. Lights fade out.)
(Lights up. Siggy stands holding a shoe up, examining it.)

TED: You could trample me in that.

SIGGY: I don't need this to trample you Ted.

TED: But you can if you want.

SIGGY: I asked you a question.

TED: If that makes you feel better Siggy . . .

SIGGY: Did I not?

TED: . . . you can.

SIGGY: Is Hank here yet?

TED: Pretend I'm the carpet. I'm the most exquisite silk.
(He gets down on his knees.)

SIGGY: Just answer me please.

TED: I'm a carpet rolling out for you. Step on me Siggy. Step on me. Step on me.
*(He lays down and rolls toward her. She moves back in horror. The follow-
ing dialogue is very fast and overlaps.)*

SIGGY: Don't. Jesus Christ. Get away.

TED: Calm down.

SIGGY: Why is it so fucking difficult to talk?

TED: Don't shout.

SIGGY: You never give me a straight answer.

TED: Calm down calm down calm down calm down.

SIGGY: Why must you do this impersonation of a worm Ted? Do you think I
find it attractive?

TED: That's enough, just calm down.

SIGGY: I'm not the one rolling around on the floor.

TED: I was just being playful.

SIGGY: You think it's the time to be PLAYFUL with me when I've been ripped off? Ripped off by an INTERN. I'm seeing my shoes, shoes I designed which now have her name and are trumpeted as hot. Because she got some STARLET to wear them?

TED: Plenty of starlets are wearing your shoes.

SIGGY: I can't trust anyone now. Everyone I know is a goddamned parasite sucking my blood.

TED: This is the shoe?

SIGGY: Yes, that was mine.

TED: Nothing really special about it. I'd say you haven't lost anything. This is sleek, but it's the same thing essentially. Over and over. The thin supple black, the stealth bomber heel. Don't you get tired? I suppose you're refining. Refining the questions. That's what you do.

SIGGY: A shoe is not a question Ted.

TED: I thought you were going to try something new. The serpent shoes you told me about . . . black and gold. The one's with the snakes' heads glued to the vamp.

SIGGY: That was Feragammo in 1957.

TED: I thought that was you.

SIGGY: You got it confused.

TED: I distinctly remember. You were here. I was standing right there. You were moving your body in subtle undulations.

SIGGY: I'm going to sue her straight into hell where she'll boil alive like a fucking crab.

TED: Maybe we're not up to having guests here.

SIGGY: Hank's not a guest.

TED: He may have someone with him.

SIGGY: Ted . . . Is Hank here now?

(Ted makes a gesture with his head, nodding toward the direction of the tepee.)

SIGGY: I'll go see if he wants a martini.

TED: He's got someone with him.

SIGGY: Oh?

TED: A girl.

SIGGY: Oh . . . I guess he's finally . . .

TED: Getting laid.

SIGGY: I'm sure he's done some of that before now.

TED: I think I'd have known.

SIGGY: You don't know everything Ted.

TED: Hank would have told me.

SIGGY: What do you think of HER?

TED: Who?

SIGGY: Hank's new . . . friend. Is she . . .

TED: Nubile?

SIGGY: You like her?

TED: Jury's still out.

(Hank and Kali enter.)

HANK: Hello Siggy.

SIGGY: Hank . . .

TED: This is Kelli.

HANK: KALI . . . This is Siggy.

SIGGY: Kali? . . . Like the Hindu goddess of destruction?

KALI: Oh she's more really, the goddess of birth.

SIGGY: No dear, death. Anyway. Great name. Let's have a martini.

KALI: No thanks.

SIGGY: Hank?

HANK: Maybe later.

SIGGY: Ted, would you get me one now?

HANK: I'll get you one Siggy.

TED: No, no, no, you relax. Visit. You haven't been here in so long. We thought California had swallowed you whole.

SIGGY: So, Hank.

HANK: How's the shoe business Siggy?

SIGGY: I couldn't make shoes without the Italians, but they lie to me everyday of my life.

TED: Siggy is a shoe designer.

KALI: I've heard so much about you — from Hank. I don't pay attention to fashion, but Hank says your shoes are works of art.

TED: Her shoes are on the cover of *W* this month.

SIGGY: No. Those were Isabella's shoes Ted.

TED: You said they were yours.

SIGGY: Yes they were once. I don't see my name on them now. They trumpet her as new . . . as the new me.

TED: She looks like you, oddly enough.

SIGGY: No she does not.

TED: Just younger than you. Of course she doesn't have your style.

SIGGY: Ted dear, no more shoptalk please.

KALI: It sounds like a stressful business.

SIGGY: It has it's compensations.

(*Kali does a simple forward bend, touches the ground with her palms. Looks through her legs as she speaks.*)

KALI: Whenever I'm faced with a lot of turmoil, I do this pose. It puts things in perspective.

SIGGY: Yes.

HANK: Kali is a yoga instructor.

(*Kali jumps back into Chatarunga, continues to move in various flow series of yoga positions.*)

SIGGY: That's fascinating.

KALI: Actually, I do the more complicated poses, but the utenasana is level one. You get an immediate rush of endorphins. It totally reverses the aging process.

SIGGY: That's good to know. When I get old I'll try it.

KALI: And this position can neutralize anger.

SIGGY: If that's what I wanted dear, I'd do botox.

KALI: Botox? What's botox . . . ?

TED: The toxin produced by the botulism organism.

SIGGY: Hence, it's brand name, BOTOX. It's all natural, injected into the facial muscles it causes paralysis, which makes one beautiful. You can't do this —

(*Smiles.*) Or this. (*Frowns.*) Or this. (*Squints.*) Botox renders the muscles immobile, the face blank, and that is attractive.

KALI: Not to me.

SIGGY: To men. To Men. What they want is that blankness. They find that attractive. That's why they so frequently like young women who haven't yet developed into human beings.

TED: I think I'd better go get that martini.

KALI: Hank, could you get me my carrot juice?

(*Hank and Ted exit.*)

SIGGY: Most men prefer that blank walking cipher, ripe for easy projection of desires.

KALI: Maybe you were like that in your twenties. I'm not.

SIGGY: Oh no. We're both . . . you've got a full life. I'm certain . . . You've got your YOGA.

KALI: And you have your SHOES.

(*Kali does a yoga pose.*)

SIGGY: Where are you from Kali?

KALI: California.

SIGGY: That must have been a fun place to grow up.

KALI: I rarely wore shoes until I was eighteen.

SIGGY: How difficult that must have been for you.

(Kali peruses a row of shoes by the mantle.)

SIGGY: See anything you like?

KALI: Oh, all of them. They're so . . .

SIGGY: Try some on. Whatever you like, it's yours.

KALI: Unfortunately, I don't wear leather.

SIGGY: Those aren't made out of leather.

KALI: What are they?

SIGGY: The hides of some prominent CEO's.

KALI: What are these?

SIGGY: Pony hide.

(Kali draws back from the shoes.)

KALI: Oh, they're all much too big for me anyway.

(Ted and Hank enter with a pitcher and martini glasses.)

SIGGY: Martini?

(Ted pours one for himself.)

SIGGY: Hank? You'll have a martini?

HANK: No thanks Sig.

SIGGY: You're not, "NOT DRINKING" again, are you?

HANK: No, not at all.

SIGGY: That's a relief. I thought you'd slipped and gone back to AA.

HANK: No.

TED: Here you go then.

(Ted hands Hank a martini.)

SIGGY: My therapist says it's a cult.

KALI: Drinking is a cult.

SIGGY: What?

KALI: Alcoholism is a cult. Look at the three of you, identical martinis.

(Siggy pours carrot juice into a martini glass for Kali.)

SIGGY: I wouldn't want you to feel left out. A toast to Kelli.

KALI: Kali.

SIGGY: To Kali. A toast.

(Everyone drinks.)

SIGGY: Welcome.

KALI: Thank you for having me.

SIGGY: You'll be comfortable? Out in the tepee?

HANK: Sure.

KALI: It's the first tepee I've ever seen with a fax machine in it.

SIGGY: I'm sure you've seen a lot of tepees.

KALI: Oh no . . . not really.

> *(Re Susie's urn.)*

> That's beautiful.

SIGGY: There's a story behind it.

HANK: Ted already told me Siggy.

SIGGY: This originally belonged to the Empress Setsuko . . . before she was . . . well, ritually dismembered. She used it briefly, to signal a lover.

KALI: How?

SIGGY: Through a code of flower arrangements. The Calla Lilly meant: Yes, come around. While a stark arrangement of twigs signaled: Caution, her husband was lurking.

TED: That's fascinating Siggy. I never heard that.

KALI: I'm surprised you don't use it as well.

TED: Siggy's social life isn't quite that complex.

KALI: No, I mean for . . . displaying Ikebana. I'd love to give this a flower arrangement. It's such a simple and elegant vase.

HANK: No.

TED: Technically, it's not a vase, it's an urn.

HANK: Those are Susie's ashes Kali.

KALI: Oh. I'm sorry. I didn't know.

SIGGY: So, how did you meet?

KALI: Hank was in my yoga class.

SIGGY: Oh, you take a class together.

KALI: No. I TEACH. That's why I'm always barefoot. I teach about eight hours a day. And Hank, I'll never forget the first time I noticed him. He was doing Virasana One, Warrior Pose. That's this:

> *(She demonstrates.)*

> And his leg was shaking, and tears were running down his face, and sweat. He was reaching up so high it was like he was hanging on to God. But his feet were crooked, so I went to adjust him, and then, just then we looked into each others eyes . . .

HANK: And I fell over.

KALI: He fell down, but after that, he came to my class every day, and he has no trouble staying up now. No trouble at all.

SIGGY: I never knew he had a problem.

KALI: You see, these are the weight-bearing poses. They build up bone density and open the heart. *(She demonstrates an Ashtanga flow series of standing poses.)* Hank can do it, but not when he's drinking. So . . . what is the opera about?

SIGGY: *(Innocently.)* What opera is this?

TED: The Steiner Commission Siggy. The Steiner.

SIGGY: Oh. Right . . . The Steiner. How interesting.

KALI: But how do you . . . do you mind? If I ask? How do you get your ideas? I mean . . .

HANK: He writes the lyrics.

TED: The WORDS.

HANK: I write the music.

TED: And the concept, is usually of my creation. I've got themes. A general sense of the arc of the narrative, and then I want to EXPLODE the conventions. I've grown interested in the way information is disseminated. In the journey of that.

KALI: Uh huh.

TED: How the essence of a thing is obfuscated through language. The exploration of shadow between signifier and sign. Thus exposing a new sense of the signified.

KALI: Is your opera about anything? I mean . . . like people?

TED: You mean . . . like CHARACTERS?

KALI: Right. I hope I didn't inadvertently insult you.

TED: No, not at all.

HANK: Do you have a story in mind, Ted?

TED: You're familiar with the Greek myth of Orpheus?

KALI: Isn't that where Orpheus has a dead wife, and he has to go get her?

TED: Yes. That's right. But he abandons his wife Eurydice . . . in a field . . . and she's stalked, by this . . . Crecion, running to escape him, she steps on the viper and dies. And Orpheus . . . with his lyre . . . with his SONG. GOES to the UNDERWORLD and strikes a deal with Hades — Orpheus can lead Eurydice up from the underworld so long as he doesn't turn back to look at her. And just before they reach the light, something in him, something wonders . . . has she really been there at all. And he turns and looks back.

KALI: And she's gone.

TED: Yes.

SIGGY: And it ends when the Thracyan nymphs tear Orpheus apart because he won't have them.

TED: Yes.

SIGGY: Torn to bits by nymphs. His head floating down the river still singing.

TED: You like it?

SIGGY: It's fabulous. Torn to bits by nymphs. I love it.

TED: Hank?

HANK: Why THIS story Ted.

TED: What . . . you don't . . . (like it?) Orpheus is a classic myth Hank.

HANK: You don't have to do this for me.

TED: We'll talk. Hank. We'll talk. It's okay. It's more . . . than you. It's just . . . a coincidence really. I got the idea from watching Claw to be honest.

SIGGY: Claw was Susie's cat. He lives up here now with Jean.

KALI: Jean?

TED: *(To Kali.)* Jean is the caretaker.

SIGGY: Jean is the chef. And he also does my hair.

TED: There used to be this fabulous songbird, a red-breasted affair. It used to sit and serenade me.

KALI: Does "Claw" come inside? Here? It's just that I'm highly allergic to cats.

TED: And then one day, I looked out the window and there was Claw, with the red-breasted songbird. He had it in his mouth. It went on singing bravely as Claw ran off with it into the woods.

SIGGY: Susie hated that side of Claw, but Claw was her baby. And Hank's as well . . .

KALI: You know, they think they've discovered now, that cat dander may be a source of arthritis.

TED: I have to show you Claw's apartment.

HANK: Apartment?

TED: We had Jean —

SIGGY: Jean is a fabulous carpenter.

TED: We had Jean build Claw a little apartment. Come on, I'll show you . . . Kali?

KALI: I'll stay here thanks.

(Hank and Ted exit.)

KALI: I have a horror of cats.

SIGGY: Susie loved cats.

KALI: I am not Susie.

SIGGY: I know. Susie was my best friend.

KALI: I'm sorry about her. I'm sorry she died. Things work out in very odd ways.

SIGGY: I don't think they've worked out at all.

KALI: Not for Susie, no.

(Siggy pours a martini for Kali.)

SIGGY: You need this in your blood.

KALI: Oh no, I tend to get quickly and easily drunk.

SIGGY: A regular routine of drinking builds up one's tolerance.

(Kali touches the glass to her lips, takes a tiny sip, and grimaces.)

KALI: So, you've known Hank . . .

SIGGY: A long time.

KALI: Probably longer than I've been alive.

SIGGY: Did you really just say what I heard?

KALI: I'm sorry. That came out wrong.

SIGGY: You can't be that stupid.

KALI: No. I just meant . . . You've lived . . . a life. Maybe I don't seem that experienced but I know what disappointment is. I know how things can not work out.

SIGGY: Not as severely as Susie.

KALI: No. But someday, all of us will. It's just a fact of existence.

SIGGY: Kali, is that your real name?

KALI: Yes.

SIGGY: Legally?

KALI: Yes.

SIGGY: That's the name you were born with?

KALI: I'm born again every moment. I'm becoming more myself with time. Don't you find that to be true?

SIGGY: Not when I look in the mirror, no.

KALI: What you see isn't you.

SIGGY: Last time I checked dear, I think it was.

KALI: You're very beautiful. Still.

SIGGY: What do you see in Hank?

KALI: Oh, a lot. Hank is very soulful.

SIGGY: Hank has a lot of connections.

KALI: He does?

SIGGY: He never told you that? He's very connected.

KALI: He just mentioned you.

SIGGY: What did he say?

KALI: He just said you were friends.

SIGGY: What else did he say?

KALI: You seemed really important to him. That phase of his life.

SIGGY: What phase of his life?

KALI: The past, that's all. I mean in the past. He really deeply considered you

238 KELLY STUART

close. A very close friend in the past. He really appreciated you. All your help. But in the end, he just had to get away. Because he associated you with . . . But he's over all that. So we came back here.

SIGGY: Thanks for the information.

KALI: What's wrong? What did I already do wrong?

SIGGY: I don't want him toyed with. I don't want him hurt.

KALI: Then don't hurt him.

SIGGY: What Hank needs is honesty now, from his friends. I owe it to Hank to tell him the truth.

KALI: I think Hank is very sensitive. He has these states of pure raw feeling, like, he's a great big antenna. There's this, rigorous honesty. I want to be like him, pure and true. Lies, you see lies, calcify the spine.

(She does a back bend, flips over to her feet, stands.)

Tell Hank I've gone out to the tepee.

(Siggy drinks.)

(Hank enters as Kali exits. There's an awkward moment where she tries to get him to follow her out to the tepee with a look, though as Siggy looks at him he sees that Siggy expects him to stay with her. He's caught in between. Kali exits with attitude.)

SIGGY: Did you find Claw?

HANK: Oh yes.

SIGGY: You don't think he's gotten too fat?

HANK: He has gotten bigger.

SIGGY: Jean makes a special dish for Claw, but I fear it's too rich.

HANK: He's got a very comfortable dwelling.

SIGGY: We've overcompensated with Claw, I'm afraid, because after you left he just wandered around calling you.

HANK: Now he doesn't know I exist.

SIGGY: Look, I'm glad you brought your friend.

HANK: Good. It's okay then.

SIGGY: Of course.

HANK: It seems awkward.

SIGGY: Why should it be awkward Hank. You came here to work.

HANK: Right.

SIGGY: So, where's Ted?

HANK: He went to look at the moon. I didn't feel like it. Too many mosquitoes.

SIGGY: The heat brings them out.

HANK: Yes, it's hot.

SIGGY: I'd love to slip off for a late night swim.

HANK: We can't do that though.

SIGGY: The mosquito bites would give us away.

HANK: It is really good to see you again Siggy. And Ted.

SIGGY: Ted was very nervous about . . . About Susie's . . . You've been very understanding.

HANK: I don't understand at all.

SIGGY: Believe me it wasn't my idea. Ever since Susie's death I think Ted's gone around the bend. Every day he gets more and more pedantic. He's got delusions of grandeur. I never thought it would end up like this. I suppose that's how husbands are. Like puppies. They're cute when they're young, but they don't stay that way.

HANK: Yeah.

SIGGY: I'm sorry about the film score job. That should have worked out. It's their loss.

HANK: It wasn't a loss after all. It was time I came back.

SIGGY: I think so too.

HANK: So here I am now, working on this opera. I guess I got lucky.

SIGGY: We got lucky Hank. It's lucky for us.

HANK: I didn't mean . . . not that kind of luck.

SIGGY: I want you to know that you're wonderful Hank.

HANK: I'm the farthest thing from wonderful Siggy.

SIGGY: You're an angel.

HANK: I'm a gerbil.

SIGGY: I'll be good for you Hank.

HANK: Be good to Ted. Your husband.

SIGGY: I'm like a spoonful of poison for Ted. I was good for YOU Hank.

HANK: Look, it seemed like you were.

SIGGY: I made you feel . . .

HANK: You know Susie, at the end . . .

SIGGY: Don't talk about Susie now . . . It's time you stopped punishing yourself.

HANK: And I'm . . . I'm WITH her. You know.

SIGGY: Who?

HANK: Kali. I'm WITH her.

SIGGY: Of course you are. It's okay Hank. That had to happen.

HANK: Kali is really . . . she's very smart . . . It's just a different KIND of intelligence. She's . . . she's instinctive. She's a wonderful TEACHER.
(Siggy embraces Hank.)

SIGGY: As far as I'm concerned you deserve a whole harem.

HANK: No . . . I can't have a harem.

SIGGY: A small one.

(They've broken apart. Ted enters.)

TED: We should just be modern.

SIGGY: What?

TED: Orpheus. TRULY POSTMODERN. He journeys to the underworld. He goes through hell to lead her up into the light. In that MOMENT he turns and LOOKS at her, he sees her in all her contradictions. And this vision of her, DISMEMBERS him. Yes . . . This is the PARA-GRAMATICAL moment. He sings calling out to her and each body part in turn sings. It's the perfect metaphor for deconstruction. The deconstruction we all undergo through time.

HANK: That's not the story.

TED: There might be a great many stories Hank. Lurking beneath the surface of perception.

HANK: He looked back and he lost her forever. She doesn't come back.

TED: Perhaps though, perhaps, in embracing the contemporary dialectic . . .

HANK: He tries to lead her into the light and he fails. Because he's a LOSER Ted.

TED: Well, that is one version of the story.

HANK: He can NEVER get her back. I think that's the point.

TED: I want to ask you a serious question. What is the effect of time on the human soul. That's what I'm after. I mean, who are we really?

Did you see the moon? It makes my head swim. You know. We could all do it right now, together, the three of us.

(He puts an arm around both Siggy and Hank.)

SIGGY: Ted . . .

HANK: What are you talking about Ted?

TED: We must create, a MOMENT with the ashes.

HANK: Fine Ted. Fine.

TED: But we must find the right song to sing for her.

SIGGY: Oh, Ted, can't we just drink?

HANK: I don't think she needs a song.

TED: Yes . . . yes . . . she must have a song. She must have, perhaps a whole opera . . . We must work through this process together. She was our . . . she was at least MY inspiration.

HANK: She was my inspiration too, Ted.

TED: She was our greatest collaborator, Hank, and I must still feel the spirit of her, collaborating with us.

HANK: She doesn't exist.

TED: Then we must investigate . . . this moment of fragmentation, deconstruction.

HANK: Music couldn't save her.

TED: Because — parts of Eurydice are lodged within Orpheus, and synthesis, Hank, will . . .

HANK: The point of the myth, is you can't go back.

TED: But you can go back. We've got Susie right here.

SIGGY: Ted, can you get the olives please.

HANK: THAT isn't Susie.

TED: But her ashes may be the KEY.

HANK: Her ashes should've been scattered and gone. Okay? We've got different ideas about this . . .

TED: And we must discover, which idea is authentic.

SIGGY: Ted, can you go get the olives?

HANK: You don't have an idea. You've got postmodern bilge.

TED: And this is our JOURNEY.

SIGGY: Ted. Olives please.

TED: Creatively.

SIGGY: PLEASE get the Olives, Ted.

HANK: I'll get them.

(Hank goes.)

TED: I get the feeling he doesn't like my idea.

SIGGY: So, what's your opinion on HER?

TED: Her? Who?

SIGGY: Bambi. What's-her-name —

TED: Pernicious twit.

SIGGY: She won't last the weekend.

TED: You think so?

(Siggy's cell phone rings. She answers. Hank enters with olives. Ted and Hank watch Siggy.)

SIGGY: Hello? No . . . it has to be a bank draft. It has to be Roberto. Because, we just can't trust these people . . . You'll know how to say it. We can't go there now. No. Can't talk now dear. Because it's my social time. Ted says hi.

(She hangs up.)

SIGGY: That was Roberto.

TED: I find him unsavory.

SIGGY: He's doing some fabulous chopines though dear.

HANK: Chopines?

TED: Essentially it's some — nostalgia for stilts.

SIGGY: No, they're not.

TED: What was it they said about them? Mount on chopines when you go to the ball, 'tis now the fashion to totter and fall?

SIGGY: Well Hank . . . I'm going to bed.

TED: Is that an invitation?

HANK: To you Ted. She was talking to you.

TED: Of course it's an invitation to me you idiot. She's my wife.

HANK: I know. I was joking.

TED: Me too.

SIGGY: Why don't you visit. Don't worry about me.

TED: I won't be long here.

(As she exits he winks at her.)

SIGGY: I might take a Xanex Ted.

TED: Perhaps you'll permit me to wake you.

SIGGY: Not if I'm zonked. Okay Ted? It's so hard to shut off my brain.

TED: What I want from you doesn't involve your brain dear.

SIGGY: Well, good night.

(She exits.)

TED: Have you ever heard of Sonnebend's theory of forgetting?

HANK: No.

TED: It posits that all of our memories, everything we believe our lives are built on, may essentially be fabricated by our own cognition. In other words, none of your memories are real.

HANK: That sounds like a paranoid theory Ted.

TED: Not at all. It's basic neurology Hank. Take for instance what happens in a fight.

HANK: Okay.

TED: I punch you in the eye.

HANK: Yes.

TED: Now you have . . . what?

HANK: I have a punch in the eye.

TED: You have sensory data flooding your system. Imprinting it's energy on your nerves. As the impulses flood and pass through you and die, all those sensations are LOST. FOREVER. And to protect ourselves from the pain, the loss of all these irretrievable moments. The human mind invents a memory.

HANK: What are you trying to tell me Ted?

TED: Everything we think we know about ourselves may be untrue, may have never happened at all. Orpheus may have faced this question.

HANK: What question is this Ted?

TED: Did Eurydice love him at all? Or was she someone else entirely . . . Because, my sense of that girl out there is that she's going to put the knife in your back. You wait.

HANK: I thought we were talking about Orpheus.

TED: I realize I just made a leap of cognition.

HANK: You don't even know her. Kali, is a TEACHER. She's HELPED me a lot. In fact I wouldn't be here if it weren't for Kali. I had no money coming here. Kali paid for our plane tickets, Ted. Kali rented the car we drove up in.

TED: What?

HANK: I told you, I don't have any money.

TED: I'm sorry . . . that can mean a lot of things. I thought it was a metaphor.

HANK: No.

TED: I mean, . . . "I" . . . don't have any money. Of course I can always get some but "MY OWN" personal accounts may be empty.

HANK: I have no money. Literally. That's why I was so grateful for this OPERA thing Ted. I mean . . . will we have a check soon?

TED: Uh, the contracts are on their way.

HANK: But how long will it take.

TED: Oh, you know how bureaucracies are.

HANK: Can I read the letter you got from them?

TED: Tell you what, I'll write your check. Better yet, I can just give you cash . . . You can pay me back later.

(Ted exits. He returns with a bundle of money.)

TED: Here you go. Five thousand now and the rest when we finish. It should all be there. That way you can pay her back for the plane ride. You know, for Orpheus . . . we need a song that expresses . . . I have this thought. We can only understand our lives looking backwards in time, but the paradox is, we're forced to live it going forward.

HANK: Actually, that was Kierkegard's thought.

TED: Well, there's no ownership of thoughts. And if I happen to SHARE a thought with Kierkegard, so much the better, right?

HANK: Why not?

TED: So, this is the first set of lyrics, the song of the snake as it slithers toward Eurydice. This demands an intense sonic vertigo. I'll give you my approximation.

HANK: I'll read it.

TED: No, Hank. I think I should read it out loud so you can get the rhythm.

HANK: I'm sure I'll get the rhythm.

TED: My rhythm I mean. The rhythm I intend.

HANK: Well, you don't really have to sing it Ted.

TED: But, to hear it in my voice. Something is communicated . . .

> GLOWING EYED GLITTER GREEN
> SNAKE SNAKE SNAKE
> SNAKE SNAKE SNAKE
> TITANIUM FANG IN
> THE DANDELION DAWN
> SLITHER ALONG. SLITHER ALONG.
> OH WHOM PA WOOMP. COMBUSTIBLE HEART
> TO MIMBRE LAND YOU WILL GO
> OH WE ARE FOOLS OF STRIPEY WICKEDNESS
> SEETHING BELOW, SEETHING BELOW
> SNAKE SNAKE SNAKE
> SNAKE YOU DOWN TO SHANNANGO
> SPUN GLASS SPROCKET
> FLIM FLAM IN DEATH'S POCKET

And then, fading out, the refrain:

> SNAKE SNAKE SNAKE
> SNAKE SNAKE SNAKE
> SNAKE SNAKE SNAKE
> SNAKE SNAKE SNAKE

And at that point, Eurydice is dead.

HANK: She gets bitten by the snake.

TED: That's right. What do you think?

HANK: Oh . . . Yeah.

TED: Ça Va?

HANK: Yes. Yes.

TED: Fab. Get to work.

(The two men embrace. Ted exits. Hank sits there holding the money and looking at Susie's urn. Kali enters.)

HANK: You should see the apartment they built for my cat.

KALI: Were you touching the cat?

HANK: It's bigger than our apartment in L.A. It's got three levels and oriental rugs. Ted said Siggy found them used. They're better rugs than I'll ever have.

KALI: Did you wash your hands?

HANK: Of course I did.

KALI: I'm sorry. I'm really allergic to cats. If you touch the cat, and then you touch me . . .

HANK: I washed them okay. You told me before.

KALI: So now you can put them wherever you want.

(Hank puts his hands in his pockets.)

KALI: On me Hank . . .

HANK: Let's go out to the tepee. This isn't a good place to —

KALI: They've gone to bed.

HANK: I don't know.

KALI: There's too many mosquitoes out there Hank. Let's just do it here fast.

HANK: No, come on.

KALI: *(Re the Urn.)* It's not because of that is it?

HANK: Of course not. No.

KALI: It's not like she's in there watching you.

HANK: No.

KALI: Not like "I Dream of Jeannie" or something.

HANK: She'd be happy for me.

KALI: Would she? She wouldn't be jealous?

HANK: No. She wasn't that way.

KALI: Maybe she didn't really . . .

HANK: What?

KALI: Take very good care of you.

HANK: She was —

KALI: Yes. You've told me.

HANK: She was the smartest person I knew.

KALI: Okay. That's right. I forgot.

HANK: What?

KALI: I'm being very patient, Hank, I think I should get some credit for that.

HANK: Sure. It's just . . .

KALI: Still too soon for you.

(Fighting tears she goes into twisting triangle.)

Twisting triangle. It's three things at once Hank. It's balance, it's breathing and a spinal twist. The twisting action wrings out the toxins, it flushes them out, and it lubricates the spine.

(She falls over.)

HANK: Kali.

KALI: I don't think your friends like me at all.

HANK: There's a lot of tension in that marriage. It has nothing to do with you.

KALI: Ted is so, full of himself.

HANK: That's because he has weak sperm.

KALI: Weak sperm?

HANK: Weak sperm. They can't have a baby.

KALI: But there are exercises he could do, to promote his yang . . .

HANK: Do me a favor, don't mention it Kali.

KALI: How do you know? He told you?

HANK: Siggy did . . .

(Jean enters, an acoustic guitar strapped to his back. He speaks in a French accent.)

JEAN: Hello. Forgive me if I interrupt you.

HANK: No not at all. Kali, this is Jean.

JEAN: Mademoiselle. Charmed to have you . . . as a guest.

KALI: Hi.

JEAN: While you are here, if you require, anything, please, let me know.

KALI: Okay.

JEAN: I will live for your satisfaction.

HANK: No thanks Jean. Everything's fine.

JEAN: By the way, have you seen Madame?

HANK: Siggy? Not here. I thought she went to bed.

JEAN: Perhaps it seems I am mistaken. I thought I was, paged.

KALI: Paged?

JEAN: My pager went off. Perhaps is . . . how you say, a malfunction.

KALI: Why would she page you?

JEAN: *(Trying out her name.)* Kali . . . Kali?

KALI: Yes.

JEAN: Kali is . . . how you say, new?

KALI: Yeah, I'm new.

HANK: Kali came up with me to work on Ted's opera.

JEAN: Oh. You are a singer?

KALI: No, I'm not a singer.

JEAN: You look like a singer. Perhaps you have hidden talent. Very well. It seems I am not needed here. Excuse moi.

(Jean exits. Beat.)

KALI: Why did he say that?

HANK: What?

KALI: Susie was a singer. Why did he say that.

HANK: He thought you'd be helping us with the opera, singing the parts for us.

KALI: Is that what Susie did?

HANK: She . . . She used to improvise and we'd just write down what she did.

(Siggy enters.)

SIGGY: Oh . . . You're still up.

KALI: I hope you don't mind.

HANK: We were just going.

SIGGY: Don't go if you're up.

KALI: No, we were just going. TO BED.

SIGGY: I just thought . . . I might've left something down here.

KALI: What?

SIGGY: My *anti-aging* cream. Dear.

HANK: Jean was here.

SIGGY: Oh?

HANK: He was looking for you. Good night.

SIGGY: Good night.

(Hank and Kali exit. Siggy is left alone. Off, sound of a guitar strum. Siggy looks off towards it, listens then exits.)

(Ted enters. Guitar music from off. Intensifies. Ted stands there listening. Guitar music stops. Ted stands there looking out. A sound that seems sexual, a moan, is heard. Lights fade.)

(Lights up. Next morning. A table has been moved into the space. Ted and Hank sit at the table.)

TED: So, you've got something for me?

HANK: Already? No.

TED: But I heard your guitar. You were playing at first. Then you stopped Hank. You completely stopped working.

HANK: But I didn't bring a guitar.

(Siggy enters. Begins setting the table.)

TED: All I can say is it was a hot night in the Adirondacks.

HANK: Yeah, it was hot.

TED: You were really going at it Hank.

SIGGY: Really Ted. Please.

TED: Darling. I'm surprised you didn't hear them.

HANK: I don't know what you're talking about.

TED: She sounded like a wild animal Hank. I mean, the grunting and moaning and thumping . . . the screaming. Like someone being torn asunder.

SIGGY: Jesus Ted.

(Siggy exits.)

TED: Nice guitar work though, for a moment. Pretty smooth FINGERING action I'm sure.

HANK: I told you. I didn't bring my guitar.

TED: What?

HANK: I had to sell my equipment.

TED: I swear I heard you playing.

(Jean enters. He puts fresh flowers on the table.)

TED: Weren't you playing music Hank?

HANK: No.

(Siggy enters with a tray of food. Jean exits.)

TED: You must've worked yourselves through the entire Kama Sutra. I mean, there were these sucking sounds Siggy . . . these great slobbering sucking gulps, and great SQUEALS of delight. Like a stuck pig Siggy . . . And then this banging and knocking. The whole forest was trembling with the vibrations.

HANK: I don't know what you're talking about.

TED: Don't try and pretend you didn't give it too her good. I mean, those were the sounds of some pure Tantric ecstasy.

(Jean returns with a plate of sausages.)

SIGGY: Oh, look at these lovely sausages.

(Siggy and Jean serve plates of food.)

SIGGY: Is SHE coming to breakfast? Or is she off somewhere levitating.

(Kali enters.)

KALI: (Looks at the food.) Oh.

SIGGY: Sausages dear?

KALI: I'm sorry. I'm not very hungry.

SIGGY: Hard Night? They're delicious. Please, just have a little taste.

KALI: I . . . I . . .

SIGGY: Oh. You're not a vegetarian are you?

KALI: Yes, I am.

SIGGY: Well, don't worry, this is all tofu dear. Isn't it incredible?

KALI: Tofu?

SIGGY: Yes. Jean is an expert vegetarian chef.

HANK: I don't think this is really, are you sure?

(Siggy looks to Jean.)

JEAN: Oh yes, it is, very, the finest tofu.

SIGGY: Try it.

KALI: It smells good.

HANK: This can't be tofu.

SIGGY: Yes it is Hank.

(To Kali.)

Sit down.

KALI: I haven't eaten meat in like, my whole life.

HANK: Don't eat this, Kali.

KALI: Oh.

SIGGY: Why? What's wrong? She's a big girl. She's a teacher Hank. Let her do what she wants.

HANK: You know this isn't tofu.

SIGGY: Jean? Is this tofu or not?

JEAN: Tofu. Of course.

SIGGY: Well, maybe it's got some wheat gluten in it. Are you allowed to have wheat gluten?

KALI: Yes.

SIGGY: I recently had to cut out meat. You must know a lot about HEALTH, right Kali? I was found to have high cholesterol. Ted thinks it's funny to tempt me. But it won't be funny when I have a heart attack. It won't be funny when I have a stroke. You get the age of Hank and I . . . We've got to take care of ourselves, and if you've got a fabulous cook like Jean, you never know the difference. This is just delicious Jean. You'll never guess, Kali where we got these recipes.

KALI: No.

SIGGY: You know Michael Milken, Kali?

HANK: Michael Milken?

KALI: No.

TED: Michael Milken . . . Isn't he . . .

SIGGY: Michael Milken. We met recently.

TED: On the board of the Lipshidt Foundation.

SIGGY: He had prostate cancer, so he hired a chef, an expert vegetarian chef to create various dishes with soy.

KALI: Who's Michael Milken?

SIGGY: Soy-based products. Explain Michael Milken to her Hank.

HANK: In the eighties. He was the Junk Bond King.

SIGGY: Junk bonds Kali. You know about those.

TED: His name's on their stationery.

KALI: What are junk bonds?

SIGGY: She doesn't know what JUNK BONDS are.

KALI: What are they.

HANK: Well, it's hard to explain . . . Junk bonds were these bonds . . .

SIGGY: Anyway he's writing a book, a collections of recipes, he had his chef e-mail them to me. He wants to do some good in the world. He's trying to atone for —

TED: Getting caught.

SIGGY: He got caught for some, economic improprieties . . . but that's petty really, compared to this vegetarian-lifestyle cookbook. Right, Kali. It's going to be fabulous.

TED: You didn't influence him, did you Siggy?

HANK: Don't eat this Kali.

TED: Siggy?

SIGGY: Let her do what she wants Hank. You don't have to take orders from him, do you? She's a big girl. How old is she? She's . . . She is at least over eighteen. We're women Kali. We must think for ourselves.

TED: Because, I'd like to think . . .

SIGGY: We can't always be trying to please some man.

KALI: That's so true.

TED: Because I'd like to think . . . I got this commission on my own merit.

SIGGY: You don't have to eat if you're at all unsure. Not to please me. We all please ourselves here.

TED: I did get this commission on my own merit.

SIGGY: Of course you did dear.

(Everyone watches Kali. She eats.)

KALI: This is delicious.

SIGGY: Oh yes. It is isn't it.

KALI: Michael Milken was right. Whoever he was.

SIGGY: Tasty?

KALI: Oh. Mmmm.

SIGGY: Susie would have loved this recipe.

TED: Susie loved to eat sausage, she did.

SIGGY: So you like it?

KALI: I've never tasted anything like it.

SIGGY: That's because it's meat dear.

KALI: What?

SIGGY: It's VEAL. VEAL SAUSAGE. Delicious.

KALI: Oh! Oh my god.

(She spits out a chewed bit of sausage.)

HANK: I told you . . .

KALI: I TRUSTED you.

SIGGY: It was just a little bite.

KALI: Oh!

SIGGY: Just a joke.

(Kali is gasping and spitting into a napkin.)

HANK: Okay Kali.

KALI: Oh my god I can't believe it!

SIGGY: Can a little piece of sausage MEAN so much?

HANK: Are you happy now Siggy?

KALI: Oh . . . I feel sick.

SIGGY: I'm sorry. One bite completely unravels her!

HANK: You got her to eat sausage. Quite an accomplishment.

KALI: OH! I'm poisoned.

HANK: Okay. It was just one bite.

KALI: I'm going to be sick.

SIGGY: You'll be alright dear.

KALI: Excuse me.

(Kali exits.)

TED: Hank, I've been thinking of Orpheus. The dichotomy of the Orphic situation.

HANK: What the hell are you talking about.

TED: The fragmentation of narrative.

HANK: This is the story of a man who fails. He can't protect the person he loves, from snakes, from death, from people, from sausages.

TED: This is interesting Hank. We have parallel ideas. My Orpheus doesn't fail Eurydice and visa versa.

HANK: This is MY story as much as yours Ted.

TED: And that's why I picked you —

SIGGY: You PICKED HIM Ted?

TED: There may be multiple realities Hank.

HANK: There's one reality. I know it too well.

TED: We may have invoked THE DOPPELGANGER HERE.

HANK: The DOPPELGANGER?

TED: Yes. The Doppelganger. Yes.

HANK: This isn't the story of a DOPPELGANGER Ted. It's the story of a man in terrible agony.

TED: Over what Hank? Articulate.

HANK: I can't say . . . But this idea of the D —

TED: DOPPELGANGER. It was something that Susie was endlessly intrigued with.

HANK: I never heard her mention it. EVER.

SIGGY: I thought the Lipshidt people picked both of you.

TED: *(To Siggy.)* You're mistaken.

(To Hank.) Susie and I talked at length about the Doppelganger. Didn't she talk about that to you?

HANK: Susie didn't go in for that hogwash.

TED: No wonder she didn't talk to you Hank.

HANK: She TALKED to me Ted. But not about the —

TED: DOPPELGANGER DOPPELGANGER DOPPELGANGER She never said a word about it Hank? Are you sure? Not even at the end?

SIGGY: Ted!

HANK: No Doppelganger NO.

TED: I understand now.

HANK: I was there Ted.

TED: I've learned to embrace the complexities Hank, the myriad realities . . . The DOPPELGANGER is revelatory in it's INQUISITION of MEMORY.

HANK: You sound as if you've escaped from the asylum of the criminally pretentious.

TED: *(Irritable, to Jean.)* Is there a guitar laying around somewhere Hank could use?

JEAN: Oui.

TED: And the mini moog, with the laptop please.

JEAN: Oui Monsieur.

TED: Could you locate those items for us? Right away?

JEAN: Oui Monsieur.

(Jean exits.)

SIGGY: You don't have to treat him like that.

TED: He gets what? Twenty-two thousand a year, for sitting on his ass most of the time.

HANK: That's all he gets? How does he live?

SIGGY: Don't worry dear, he gets plenty of extras.

(Kali comes in.)

KALI: You know what EATING MEAT does to you Siggy? Dead animal flesh activates the free radicals. It starts off a deadly reaction . . . the pesticides the hormones, the invisible toxins.

TED: Perhaps. In your head.

KALI: And what about the FEET! What do you think constriction of the feet does to the brain?

SIGGY: What?

KALI: YOU create implements which bind the feet and force the pelvis into an unnatural angle. What does that do to mental development, of WOMEN?

TED: The Chinese believed it was good for the vagina.

HANK: How was that Ted?

TED: It stimulated vigorous blood circulation. Upward . . . upward . . . That's what they believed. I don't think there were studies.

KALI: There are studies that prove it causes arthritis in the knees.

SIGGY: What does?

KALI: High heels.

SIGGY: I thought we were talking about foot binding.

KALI: No, I'm talking about high heels, the knee and hip joints . . . how you're part of the system that coerces the body mutilation of women.

SIGGY: I wear high heels, am I sexy? Or mutilated?

KALI: Tell me in twenty years. That's the difference between us Siggy. In twenty years, I plan on being around. Alive and unchanged.

TED: You won't be unchanged. You'll be Siggy's age then. At best you'll be mildly decayed.

SIGGY: Who knows if you'll be here in twenty years Kali. Who can say if you'll even last out the weekend.

KALI: I have determination.

HANK: She does . . . She's been through a lot.

KALI: In the Northridge earthquake my apartment collapsed.

HANK: She was nearly crushed to death.

SIGGY: That would've been a shame.

KALI: When things started falling on me I went limp.

SIGGY: Ted can do that.

KALI: The whole roof came down on my head. But I told myself I've got to survive. This is not gonna kill me, I'm going to survive. I will survive Siggy. I will survive.

TED: Oh my god . . . the most terrible Déjà vu.

SIGGY: Ted.

TED: Susie once . . . she was sitting right there and she said exactly the same thing.

(Siggy gets up.)

HANK: Ted, don't do this.

TED: I'm sorry. It's just that we've been having a cycle of these sort of Déjà vu moments. Time is crushing us here.

SIGGY: Time isn't what's crushing us Ted.

TED: We must do something new.

SIGGY: What's CRUSHING — Ted is your GARRULOUS BOMBAST.

TED: The thought that it's all been done. There's nothing new left.

KALI: That's a deep realization.

TED: As if we've become a repetitive sequence in a pattern already degraded.

KALI: That's exactly what Karma is.

TED: As if the greatest gift mankind has is the gift of forgetting.

HANK: That was Neitcheze's thought too.

TED: Because it's all been thought before. We're caught in a cycle of thoughts not our own.

SIGGY: Speak for yourself Ted.

TED: But I long to find some ORIGINAL thought. To CEREBRATE my way from the paper bag of history. Yes. Here it comes. The IDEA. I think there are TWO ORPHEUSES HANK. There must be TWO.

HANK: Two Ted?

TED: And only the one with an AUTHENTIC memory can summon Eurydice. Which Orpheus had a REAL life with her. And which was the impostor. And they must do battle.

KALI: Why all this conflict? Why can't you just make it a happy ending?

TED: What? What did she say?

KALI: Make it a happy ending.

TED: Why?

KALI: Why? I think it sounds good. Hank likes it, don't you Hank. He does. I can tell. He's got that expression. Hank's so cute when he likes something but doesn't want to admit it . . . aren't you Hank?

HANK: No.

KALI: Oh come on Hank. People would like it. You get to have all the good parts. The romance, and the singing part.

HANK: Orpheus is a TRAGEDY.

SIGGY: Well, as someone famous once said. Artists talk about money. Amateurs talk about art.

TED: And airheads talk about "HAPPY ENDINGS." Nobody wants to feel BAD anymore. We just want to feel good. All the time.

HANK: Well, I think I'm done eating. Thank you Siggy, this was just wonderful.

SIGGY: Jean! Can we get some Irish Coffee?

HANK: I'm going for a run.

TED: What?

HANK: I have to go jog.

TED: I thought we were going to talk about this.

KALI: Hank? Did I just embarrass you Hank?

HANK: I just need to run about twenty-six miles. I won't be long.

> *(Hank exits. Jean enters with whiskey, coffee, and cream. He fixes Siggy an Irish coffee, pouring a generous portion of whiskey then loudly squirts whipped cream into Siggy's coffee.)*

TED: Must we squirt that cream at the table?

JEAN: I am sorry Monsieur.

TED: Don't call me Monsieur, please. Call me SIR.

JEAN: But of course. SIR. As you wish.

TED: No, no, no worry Jean. It's me who's been rude. I've . . . I've just been deprived of . . . sex. That's all. Of sex, and it's making me addled.

JEAN: But of course.

> *(Jean exits.)*

TED: That's it you know Siggy. That's my problem.

SIGGY: Ted, please stop.

TED: I offended my friend. My deep and dear friend.

KALI: No, it was me. I was so stupid.

TED: Oh, you're not stupid. Not by a mile.

KALI: I know you care about him.

TED: He seems to be stronger now. You've obviously been good for him. Don't you think so Siggy?

SIGGY: I think we got off to a bad start that's all.

KALI: I do to. I'll try and do better.

SIGGY: You've obviously been good for him.

KALI: I try to . . . just to restore.

TED: It takes time.

KALI: Yes it does. It takes time, but I give. I give freely. I've never met anyone like Hank. He's special.

TED: Yes. We all feel that way.

KALI: Hank and I are very lucky. To find each other.

TED: Yes you are. Congratulations.

KALI: You mean that?

TED: I'm happy for you.

KALI: Oh good, because I thought . . .

SIGGY: What dear?

KALI: I thought you couldn't stand me.

SIGGY: Of course not.

TED: We adore you.

KALI: Really?

TED: You're absolutely a charming young girl.

KALI: That's a — gosh . . . that's a relief. Because I really think . . . I like you
both too. And thank you for choosing Hank for this opera. I know he's
going to do a good job. I think I'll go meditate now.
(*She exits.*)

SIGGY: That was vapidly hyper sincere.

TED: "Thank you for picking him." Cloying airhead.

SIGGY: Narcissistic monster.

TED: Does she think those abnormal displays of flexibility qualify her as being
someone worthy of interest?

SIGGY: You really . . . you picked him Ted?

TED: I'm loyal. I'm loyal to Hank. Not like that.

SIGGY: Ubiquitous mouthpiece of banality.

TED: Yeah. You're talking about her . . . right?
(*Lights fade out.*)
(*Lights up. Later. Ted stands reading Ovid out loud. Kali enters watching
him, waiting for a chance to break in and ask a question. He doesn't notice
her.*)

TED: And when at last the bard
Had mourned his fill in the wide world above.
He dared descend
through Taenaruss's dark gate.
To Hades to make a trial of the shades.

KALI: Um . . .

TED: And through thronging wraiths.
and grave spent ghosts.
Hmmm.

KALI: Ted?

TED: One moment. Concentrating.
Lord of the Shades.
I have come down.
Not with intent to see the glooms of hell.
Nor to enchain the triple snake haired necks of Cereberus.

KALI: I'm sorry.

TED: Yes?

KALI: Have you seen Hank?

TED: Hank? I'm sure he's with you. I mean . . . I thought.

KALI: No.

TED: Oh.

KALI: I just wondered if you'd seen him.

TED: I've been reading Ovid.

KALI: I see.

TED: I'd really like to go through the mirror of time. If you know what I mean.

KALI: Oh yeah. Maybe Siggy's seen Hank.

TED: Hank is probably off working. That's all.

KALI: He's been gone for over four hours.

TED: And SOMEONE has taken the guitar. A sign that he's working. And should be left alone.

KALI: What if something happened to him? That's all. I'm just worried.

TED: The struggle, the struggle I'm having here is that . . . I mean . . . I have to make this my own.

KALI: Yes.

TED: *(Reading.)* But for my dear wife's sake.
    In whom a trodden viper.
    (Looking at Kali.)
    Yes. Viper.
    (Again reading.)
    Trodden viper poured it's venom.
    Now by these regions filled with fear,
    by this huge chaos. These vast silent realms.
    (Looks up.)
    This is a really lousy translation.

KALI: Where is she?

TED: Who?

KALI: Siggy. Your wife.

TED: Siggy? She's here.

KALI: No she's not. I've looked everywhere for both of them.

TED: Oh.

KALI: What if they . . . Or something.

TED: Oh, they're not together.

KALI: Where are they then?

TED: *(Calling out.)* SIGGY!!? SIGGY?
    (Lights out.)

END ACT ONE

ACT TWO

Lights up in the woods. Sound of guitar music. A few strums — from off. Siggy enters. She carries a quilt. As she walks, the heel of her shoe breaks. She takes it off, limps along holding the broken shoe. The music stops. She's obviously looking for its source. She goes off.
Hank enters with guitar. A few frustrated strums. Then he sings:

HANK: You should cry
    all the way to hell
    for leaving me with nothing
    but a lousy song to sell
    Goddamn this thing.
    (He tunes a string. It twangs up and down. Siggy enters.)
SIGGY: Oh.
HANK: Siggy?
SIGGY: So, I found you.
HANK: Siggy, come on, you were looking for Jean.
SIGGY: Not this time Hank. Not this time. Jean is gathering mushrooms for dinner.
HANK: You broke your shoe.
SIGGY: Help me with this.
    (She kicks off her shoes . . . spreads out the quilt. He helps straighten it, nervously.)
HANK: Jean should be along in a minute then.
SIGGY: No, really, he's forbidden to come.
HANK: It's nice you've got someone who follows your orders.
SIGGY: Yes. I made him learn the guitar. I paid for his lessons.
HANK: That's generous.
SIGGY: No Hank. I pretend that he's you.
HANK: Well, I'm sure he's a fine musician.
SIGGY: Oh my god. I really missed you Hank. I'm so happy you finally came back.
HANK: I had to —
SIGGY: I know. We had to see each other. I can talk to you, Hank. We have something in common. With Ted . . . it's all about sex. You *listen* to me. He doesn't. And when we don't . . . because I don't want to . . . He gets so angry. He's livid. You can practically see his balls turning blue. It's not my fault he turned out mediocre.

I thought he was going to be fun. He doesn't excite me and then he gets mad. It's not my fault that he isn't exciting. He's not like you. You're a real man Hank. Play me a song will you?

HANK: No, I can't.

SIGGY: Come on, I've missed hearing you play.

HANK: I can't. It's been a while. My fingers are really not working right now. *(She takes his hand, puts his fingers in her mouth, sucks on them.)*

HANK: I really like you Siggy. You're a good person. You're beautiful too. You've helped me a lot. Your friendship has meant a lot to me . . . I really need my fingers back please.

SIGGY: We can get away with anything we want Hank. Carpe Diem.

HANK: That's no way to live.

SIGGY: How are we to live Hank. With some teenager?

HANK: She's more than a teenager. She's . . . twenty-five.

SIGGY: She's a birdbrain.

HANK: Well if she's a birdbrain, she's a very nice birdbrain.

SIGGY: What can you possibly have in common?

HANK: She's got a good soul. We're honest with each other.

SIGGY: Hank, you're a liar.

HANK: No, we really are, we try to be.

SIGGY: Does she know about us?

(Pause.)

HANK: No.

SIGGY: You and I have something real . . . not like with Miss Pigeon-head. You came to me, remember? At the lake. You needed me. And I was there for you.

HANK: I know.

SIGGY: And I was there. I've always been there for you. Was that so bad?

HANK: No. It was good.

SIGGY: It was good wasn't it. You and I understand each other Hank. We really KNOW each other.

HANK: I care about you.

SIGGY: You see what my life has become? You came to me once, now I'm coming to you. You're the only one who can save me.

HANK: I'm not capable of saving anyone.

SIGGY: If we were swimming down at the lake, and I went under . . . You'd pull me to shore . . .

HANK: Siggy . . .

SIGGY: If I was sinking to the bottom, with my clothes falling off . . . you'd swim down and rescue me? Wouldn't you Hank? . . . You wouldn't let me just sink to the bottom? I'm suffocating Hank. I'm gasping for air. I'm going down. Down to the bottom. And all around me the sound of bubbles. My clothes floating up above in water. Come on Hank.

(She moves closer to him . . . seductively, she pulls him near her. They kiss.)

SIGGY: Let's go for a swim. Just a swim that's all. We'll be perfectly chaste. Just, swim, like old friends. There are swans, it's very beautiful. You imagine it can't you? Me and the swans?

HANK: Siggy, I . . . We better talk about this.

SIGGY: In the water, with the swans . . . come down to the lake. Just one little swim? You can think about taking a swim with me. Can't you? I need to talk to you too. There's something I have to tell you Hank. Something you should know.

HANK: What?

SIGGY: I'm not going to tell you about it unless you come swimming with me. It's got to be the right place, with the swans, where it's beautiful.

HANK: Is this about Susie?

SIGGY: Come on Hank . . . O.K. I'll give you a minute, you know where I'll be.

(She exits. A beat. Hank stands staring out after Siggy.)

(Kali enters.)

KALI: Hank? Are you aware it's been four hours?

HANK: I . . . I've been trying to work. To work something out.

KALI: Where did you get this blanket?

HANK: I don't know. It was here.

KALI: It just happened to be here?

HANK: It's true.

KALI: With these shoes.

HANK: Those . . . those look like Siggy's shoes don't they.

KALI: The heel is broken.

HANK: Yes. Yes it is.

(He absently twists the heel, and twists it back in place.)

KALI: Is there something you need to tell me Hank?

HANK: No. Why would I lie to you?

(Hank chucks the shoes into the trees.)

KALI: About what? I never said you were lying. Look at your shoulders . . . how tight you've gotten.

(She takes his arms behind his back in a stretch that looks more like an arm-lock.)

HANK: Oh.

KALI: Too much?

HANK: *(In pain.)* No.

KALI: This . . . really opens the shoulders Hank. Opens the chest, lets the blood feed the heart.

HANK: Yes.

(Ted enters. Stands watching for a moment.)

TED: That's quite S&M Hank.

KALI: It's just a shoulder opener Ted. I can do it for you.

TED: No thanks.

HANK: *(In pain.)* It really feels good.

KALI: It's helpful for people with weak sper —

TED: What?

KALI: Weak spines.

TED: As far as I know . . . my spine is quite solid. Why is this quilt out here?

KALI: I don't know.

TED: It's antique, from Virginia. It's two hundred years old.

KALI: Wow, really?

TED: It was sewn by slaves.

KALI: Oh.

TED: There's mud.

KALI: Here . . . you better take it. Here. I'm sorry.

TED: I'm sure you didn't know any better. For all you know this could have come from Kmart.

KALI: Sure.

TED: This is genuine. I can hear the voices of the slaves still wailing in this fabric. I think about the people who made this, and what must've happened to them. It's horrible really. This is all that remains. And here it is now, surrounded by all this opulence. It puts me on edge, that TRANS-HISTORICAL edge.

KALI: It's not good for your immune system to be so on edge.

TED: I don't see the value in being IMMUNE. Conflict is GOOD Hank. We can't run away. We must use the FIERY FORCE of our friction . . . By the way, have you seen Siggy?

HANK: No.

TED: All right . . . Will you FINISH THIS UP? SOON?

HANK: Sure.

TED: I'd better go find Siggy.

(Ted turns. Exits.)

HANK: Why did you say that about his sperm?

KALI: I'm sorry. It just came out.

HANK: I told you not to say anything.

KALI: I could help him.

HANK: People don't always want help.

KALI: He's suffering.

HANK: Weak sperm is the least of his problems. Believe me.

KALI: It may be a serious energy imbalance.

HANK: It may be he's a cuckold.

KALI: What makes you think that?

HANK: Something Siggy said.

KALI: She told you that?

HANK: Uh, yeah.

KALI: Why would she tell you?

HANK: I guess she needed to confess.

KALI: Why to you?

HANK: Maybe I was just there at the time.

KALI: Where? Hank? Was she here? Who is she fooling around with, Hank?

HANK: It's really not my business.

KALI: Well, who else could it be? It's isolated here. The only other men around are you and Jean.

HANK: Yeah, so it's Jean.

KALI: Jean.

HANK: Yeah.

KALI: So what are you going to do?

HANK: Nothing.

KALI: Ted is your friend.

HANK: They're both my friends.

KALI: They've been good to you.

HANK: It's just a phase she's going through.

KALI: If I was your friend and you didn't tell me, it wouldn't feel good.

HANK: It might feel worse to know the truth. I need to get along with Ted, to do this opera. I need to do this.

KALI: Why?

HANK: We've gone through all of your money. I need this . . . I need to do this opera Kali.

KALI: So, is it just about money?

HANK: I really need to start something for myself. I need to start working again.

KALI: There's something else you need to start again Hank.

HANK: I will.

KALI: This would be a good time. You're so . . . hot Hank and you don't even know it. I just want to make you feel good.

HANK: Believe me, you do.

(She sinks down on her knees. He remains standing. Her face is near his zipper.)

HANK: You don't like Ted.

KALI: You always do this Hank, you want to avoid . . .

HANK: I don't know what you see in me besides someone broken you can practice repairing.

KALI: I'm learning a lot from you Hank.

HANK: About what?

KALI: About how to live with death. Which is central to my practice.

(She puts her arms around his legs, tries to pull him down. He remains standing.)

KALI: How can you not fall down with me Hank? It's beautiful here, the grass is so soft . . .

HANK: You're very pretty down there on the ground, but when you've done all this work of STANDING UP at my age Kali . . . standing up is not so easy so once you get up you don't want to get down again.

KALI: Hank, you're only as old as your spine. That's the secret of youth. The spine is everything.

HANK: Umm, not really.

(Hank walks off. Shocked at being abandoned. Kali stands up, emits a little sob. Goes into the bushes, retrieves Siggy's shoes. She holds them, pondering them for a beat, then puts them on the ground and gingerly slips them onto her feet.)

(Cross fade. The cabin. Late afternoon. Ted and Siggy. He is holding the quilt.)

TED: What the hell were they doing with this? Fine if she wants to suck his cock, she doesn't need an antique to kneel on, does she?

SIGGY: She was sucking his cock?

TED: Among other things.

SIGGY: Jesus.

TED: She said something odd as well.

SIGGY: What?

TED: Something odd about my spine. But I don't think that was what she meant at all. What could Hank have said about us? Maybe it's not a good idea to tell Hank things.

SIGGY: Obviously.

TED: Fortunately, I have no secrets, but if I did, one would expect that to be honored and not broadcast into the ear of something he picked up in

California. We should've been working today but she kept him out in the woods somewhere sucking his cock.

SIGGY: You don't have to keep saying it.

TED: Why not? They're probably doing it right now. I'll bet she's got a pretty strong suction action going on him. Night and day.

SIGGY: Shut up.

TED: Night and day suction.

SIGGY: You're so crude.

TED: Show me how crude you can be.

SIGGY: Not right now Ted.

TED: Show me how crude.

SIGGY: I said STOP IT. QUIT PAWING ME.

TED: Pawing you?

SIGGY: You slobber on me like a dog, you paw me. You have sharp little claws Ted. It's annoying. Try being a little more gentle.

TED: Don't tell me how to be.

SIGGY: You're making me nauseous.

TED: I know. I seem to make you nauseous lately. I'm irritated with Hank. That's all. We must agitate from the essence, together. The heat of our conflict . . .

SIGGY: Quit masturbating Ted. Just do your part.

TED: First of all, I've done my part. I got him the grant.

SIGGY: What grant was this Ted?

TED: The Steiner. The Steiner, The Steiner I told you, from the Lipshidt Foundation.

SIGGY: The Lipshidt Foundation.

TED: I got him the grant. It's my concept, my idea. I'm the one who brought Hank in.

SIGGY: Really.

TED: Why do you ask? Why do you care?

SIGGY: Curious. Just curious, that's all.

TED: About what?

SIGGY: About your work Ted.

TED: This is a very prestigious honor you know.

SIGGY: Really? That's wonderful Ted.

TED: Yes. They have a very strict criteria. Expertise, innovation in one's field. The sphere of influence likely outside the field. And . . . They have beautiful letterhead. What a great organization, The Lipshidt Foundation, really visionary people.

SIGGY: And when did you meet them?

TED: What?

SIGGY: You say they're visionary, have you met? Or is it just because they picked you and Hank.

TED: Actually Siggy. They picked ME. And I was free to choose my collaborator.

SIGGY: You're a liar Ted. You know that don't you.

TED: What's the agenda here dearest.

SIGGY: They wanted Hank and they wanted you. They wouldn't have one without the other.

TED: Hank really needs this, but he's so obstreperous and sour. I'm talking and I look at his face and he's not there. He's not fucking there for me. It's incredible, how, self-destructive.

SIGGY: Why don't you stop PROJECTING on Hank, all your own neurotic tendencies . . .

TED: His reputation is terrible now. Nobody, nobody wants to work with him. You know why? He's so negative and difficult. Bogart won't work with him. Neither will Woodruff. You know what Andre said about him? He said he'd never work with him again. And that thing with George . . . I mean it was BAD. When we were doing THE CERULEAN BIRD, he was considered a HOT composer, but no more. I mean, I love Hank.

SIGGY: And you loved Susie too.

TED: Of course . . . I mean . . . We all loved Susie. But this woman, this woman, this woman he's with. She's a fake little cocksucker. She'll justify him in his bullshit, "Oh Hank, that's okay, let me just suck your cock."

SIGGY: Ted.

TED: I'd like to see him put himself on the line before he looks at me with that sneer of blasé, detached superiority. What's his sense of the sonic milieu? God damn it. What I do is very complex.

SIGGY: No Ted. What you do doesn't earn any money. You suck me dry.

TED: There's a deep creativity involved. That's why I got the Steiner, didn't I?

SIGGY: Of course. Of course you GOT THE STEINER. And these visionary people of the Lipshidt Foundation . . . Who do you think those people are Ted? Who the hell would want to give you a dime. They must be VISIONARY all right.

TED: What . . . like YOU? Is that what you mean? Like YOU Siggy? I see what you do, of course. Of course. It's an art, but it's a utilitarian art, it has it's utilitarian functions that determine certain certainties of form. There are only so many variations of a shoe and you recycle those year after year.

You can't really create something new, it's more about, sampling now, historical sampling. I see what you do, it's very astute. Of course I admire what you do, my god. You're the most astute woman on the planet. I'm just saying the utilitarian demands of your discipline determine a certain narrowness of form. Of course you can push it, and you do. But the parameters can only be pushed so far. Because most of all, we are still human beings, our bodies retain basically the same skeletal structure. . . and although, I believe . . . I believe I have suffered through some of the same problems as you, artistically speaking, in my discipline, it's possible, there is hope for new forms. Because, the human mind, dear, the mind. The mind dear may be more amenable to change, to change dear, more than the human foot. I create for the mind, you create for the foot. That's the difference dear. Between our two disciplines. Do you think you should be drinking so early?

(They look up to see Kali watching. She is wearing Siggy's shoes but only Siggy is aware of this.)

TED: Hello.

KALI: Hello.

TED: Something different about you.

KALI: Stuff happens, things change a lot.

TED: Hank out in the Tepee?

KALI: Sure. Go ahead.

(Ted exits.)

KALI: Take me under your wing.

SIGGY: What?

KALI: Take me under your wing.

SIGGY: That's a bit strange.

KALI: You've had so much History with Hank. I know you know things about him I'll probably never know.

SIGGY: We all know different things about each other.

KALI: Yes.

SIGGY: I know things about you.

KALI: Yes, and I know a few things about you and Hank.

SIGGY: We're both women. We have that in common.

KALI: And that's deep.

SIGGY: Yes it is deep. Our intentions are . . . similar.

KALI: What intentions?

SIGGY: We both want . . .

KALI: Hank.

SIGGY: To be free . . .

KALI: Yes.

SIGGY: To free himself from . . .

KALI: Susie.

SIGGY: That's right. To free himself from Susie.

KALI: The idea of her death.

SIGGY: Well, she did actually die Kali. It wasn't just an idea.

KALI: But now she's gone and he wants to be free.

SIGGY: I agree with you there.

KALI: My guess is you are the one who brought Hank up here. No, your generosity.

SIGGY: And you must be very perceptive to have guessed that.

KALI: It's probably due to a lifetime of yoga. I have intuition.

SIGGY: I'm going to tell you something in confidence.

KALI: Yes . . .

SIGGY: This is just between us. Two women.

KALI: Hank and I don't have any secrets.

SIGGY: Then maybe you don't want to know. But you could help Hank, if I told you. You want to help Hank don't you?

KALI: Yeah.

SIGGY: Can you keep this just between you and me then?

(Kali nods.)

SIGGY: I'm the one funding the opera.

KALI: The Steiner.

SIGGY: Actually, it's the Lipshidt Foundation, which administers the Steiner.

KALI: But really, it's your money.

SIGGY: Yes.

KALI: Hmmm.

SIGGY: So you have a choice here. Hank really needs this, he needs the work Kali.

KALI: I don't want to lie.

SIGGY: What Hank needs right now, is to work. To work and break free. To start a new life. Maybe with you Kali. But Hank is very proud. He won't take money from me. Who can say what he'd do if he knew. So you have a choice. You can help Hank start working, or you can shove his face down in the mud. Which do you choose. Because I . . . actually, I want to help you.

KALI: Really?

SIGGY: Yes.

KALI: Okay then, I won't tell Hank. And you'll help me.

SIGGY: We've got a deal. In some ways, Kali, Susie's death is the best thing that happened to Hank. And maybe to all of us.

KALI: I think so too.

SIGGY: Then we're on the same page. Together.

KALI: Yes.

SIGGY: You shouldn't be afraid to assert yourself Kali. Hank's . . . Hank's OBSESSION with Susie isn't healthy. And you should put a STOP to it.

KALI: Really? You think so? How?

SIGGY: I'd be firm.

KALI: It's hard cause I see that he's in so much pain.

SIGGY: Aren't you in pain, Kali? Isn't this causing you pain as well? You have to think about your feelings too. Those ashes don't challenge him Kali.

KALI: No, they don't.

SIGGY: Those ashes are easy to get along with.

KALI: Easy.

SIGGY: They don't talk back. But you can.

KALI: But what do I say?

SIGGY: You say how you feel.

KALI: I might be afraid.

SIGGY: It's time that you make a big ugly scene.

KALI: A scene?

SIGGY: A scene. It's time for some drama. Some drama, Kali. Hank has always responded to drama.

KALI: Has he?

SIGGY: Oh yes.

KALI: What if I say things that make him hate me?

SIGGY: If you speak sincerely from your heart, how can he hate you? How could anyone hate you Kali? Trust me.

KALI: I wish you could like . . . uh . . . give me a sign.

SIGGY: You want me to coach you?

KALI: Yes.

SIGGY: Like . . . this means . . . go for the throat . . . and this means . . . intensify . . . and this means back off?

KALI: Yes.

SIGGY: I can do that.

(Hank and Ted enter mid conversation. Hank carries a large self-satisfied orange cat.)

TED: You're desperate in your desire not to feel.

SIGGY: Be fierce, Kali.

HANK: Some things I don't want to feel, Ted, NO.

KALI: Hank, can you get rid of that CAT?

> *(She sniffs/sneezes.)*

TED: Lay your hands on the urn here, Hank.

HANK: I TOLD YOU. I don't have the right to touch that.

KALI: Hank! THE CAT!

> *(He moves to put the cat out. Ted blocks him.)*

TED: Why not, Hank? Tell me. You touch this urn, the music will flow, music and words joined by the muse.

HANK: There's no more muse. I FAILED HER. SHE'S GONE.

KALI: Hank can you get rid of that THING.

TED: It's not a THING. It's Claw.

KALI: It's a toxin-producing carnivorous pest.

TED: It lives here, you don't. Tell me about how you failed her, Hank. Explain it to me. I've never understood it.

HANK: I JUST FAILED HER OKAY.

KALI: I'm going to break out in a rash. I can't breathe —

TED: We can use this Hank. For the Battle of Orpheus.

HANK: The Battle of Orpheus. Jesus . . .

KALI: Hank! Cat. Hank!

HANK: Can we put the cat out?

SIGGY: Here. I'll take him. Come on Claw. Come on Baby.

> *(She takes Claw off.)*

TED: When the AUTHENTIC vanquishes the FAKE —

KALI: Oh!

TED: He needs to discover,

HANK: Can we get her some —

TED: How she really felt.

HANK: Water, some —

KALI: Oh . . . *(Gasping.)*

SIGGY: *(Entering.)* Vodka.

> *(She gives Kali vodka. Kali drinks.)*

TED: The REAL Orpheus rescues Susie.

HANK: SHE'S GONE. SHE CAN'T —

TED: But the IMPOSTOR must be drowned in the waters of Lethe.

HANK: I can't drown myself, Ted.

TED: Of course not no. That's how impostors are. Someone must always do their work for them.

> *(He takes up the urn. Approaches Hank.)*

TED: *(Overlap with Hank.)* Jube weiss, und Sehnsucht ist gestandig, nur die Klage lernt noch; madchenhandig Zahlt sie nachtelang das alte Shlimme.

HANK: Get the hell away from me, Ted.

TED: Sonnets to Orpheus! The Rilke. What a meditation of grief!

SIGGY: He wants you to think he speaks German, he doesn't.

TED: My pronunciation may not be on the mark. If SUSIE were here, she'd understand. Susie's German was perfect. Fluent.

HANK: No Ted, she didn't speak German.

TED: Of course she spoke German.

HANK: She sang in German. But she couldn't speak it.

TED: We had intimate conversations in German.

KALI: Susie spoke German?

TED: When she was on tour, she wrote wonderful letters to me IN GERMAN.

HANK: She never wrote me in German.

TED: Because you were with her Hank. You were dragging along at the hem of her skirts. She wrote what a helpless baby you were IN GERMAN.

KALI: She liked to control you, Hank.

HANK: No she didn't. You didn't know her.

TED: She was . . . she was . . . too perfect for this world. Yes.

KALI: But that's not important, in the big picture. None of this "perfection" matters.

TED: Someone's life and death matters.

KALI: It's all just SAMSARA. Everything. This.

TED: I've done TAI CHI. Tai Chi you know, so don't throw your Sanskrit terms at me. I can match you reference for reference. PERNICIOUS INFLU-ENCE. Let's talk about that.

KALI: Tai Chi is just derived from Yoga, as are all the Martial Arts. All deriv-ative.

TED: I took Susie to my teacher, this eighty-year-old man. He looked at her and said "This one, I can't help. She's beyond my help. I can't help you he said. You should go now, because I can't help you I'm sorry." And you should have seen her face.

KALI: Maybe it helped her to know.

TED: And where the hell were you then, Hank?

KALI: Leave Hank alone.

TED: You were her husband. I'd just like to know. Why weren't you with her.

HANK: I was with her at the end

TED: Easy thing to come in right at the end isn't it, Hank. To come in at the end. But in the last year it was me. It was me. I took her to doctors, and healers and quacks. And where the hell were you?

HANK: In agony, Ted. That's where I was.

TED: You used to be gone for days at a time . . . Where? What's the longitude and latitude of agony exactly?

HANK: Failure, betrayal, and fear. All right Ted? It's failure, betrayal, and fear.

KALI: That's all over now.

TED: No. We're just getting started.

HANK: What are you trying to do to me, Ted? I failed her okay? I did not make her happy. There was always something just . . . something not there.

TED: Details Hank. I need details.

HANK: I betrayed her. I did that. I probably . . . in the end. I caused her death. Okay? I'm the one responsible for her . . .

TED: DEATH.

KALI: No, you're NOT responsible, Hank.

HANK: I take responsibility. That's what I have to do.

TED: We can use all of this. All of this. Yes. This is good Hank. And what did she say at the end?

HANK: Fuck you. I can't exploit her death for this CRAP.

TED: If you perceive feeling as exploitation, no wonder you never knew about the doppelganger.

HANK: What's that supposed to mean?

TED: Just tell me what she said in the end.

HANK: Nothing. She didn't get what she deserved.

KALI: Maybe that was her Karma.

HANK: What the fuck did you say?

KALI: Who knows what she was getting. And from Whom.

HANK: Susie was GOOD. She wasn't like me.

TED: She was far beyond good. Susie was perfect.

KALI: It's easy I say, it's easy to be perfect when you're DEAD. Because that's what death is. It's perfection. Perfection is death. Only life is imperfect. Hank. Life.

TED: Then my dear, you are all too alive.

KALI: I can't compete with a dead woman, Hank.

HANK: It's not about competition.

TED: It's truth.

KALI: You wouldn't know the truth if it bit you in the ass.

TED: What truth, Kali. Is there some great truth you've come to impart? What is your truth. I'm ready to hear it.

KALI: No, Ted. You're not strong enough yet.

TED: Give me the truth Oh Great Sanctimonious.

KALI: If you knew, you'd be pulverized, Ted.

TED: By all means I'm curious now. What is your TRUTH Oh Great Holy Gumby.

KALI: I can't say.

TED: Why not?

KALI: Because I am trained not to harm.

SIGGY: I admire the discipline there.

KALI: There was a reason Susie died. It happened for a reason. We have to accept. That we choose our reality.

HANK: I didn't choose this.

KALI: I think you did.

HANK: There are some things you just can't know when you're twenty.

KALI: I'M TWENTY-FIVE!! I'M TWENTY-FIVE, HANK!.

HANK: But sometimes Kali, it's like talking to a parrot.

KALI: *(Softly.)* I can't . . . I thought that you loved me.

HANK: Okay, well, I FEEL like . . . I've felt love. It's been a long time. But I'll try. That's all I can say is I'll try.

KALI: LOVE ISN'T A FEELING, ASSHOLE. LOVE IS A VERB! IT'S SOMETHING YOU DO.

HANK: Okay, well, I guess I'd be willing . . .

KALI: YOU DO IT HANK. YOU JUST DO IT, ASSHOLE. THERE'S NO "WILLING." THERE'S NO, "I'LL TRY." YOU DO IT. YOU EITHER LOVE ME OR NOT. YOU DON'T SOAK AND STEW IN THE PAST. I'M HERE. GET IT. HERE I AM NOW. LOVE ME NOW OR ELSE FUCK YOU. FUCK YOU, HANK. FUCK YOU. FUCK YOU. I'm leaving now. If you love me you'll follow.

SIGGY: No dear . . . you don't have to do that.

KALI: I do. Yes I do.

(Siggy shakes her head, signals.)

I can't. I can't bear it Siggy. I hope you get over your pain and your guilt. But I'm driving . . . I'm driving back to the city. I can't . . . I've just got to drive.

(Hank stands there paralyzed. Kali walks out.)

HANK: What was that? What did you say to her?

SIGGY: She misunderstood me. That's all.

TED: Siggy.

HANK: Kali!!!

(Hank exits.)

TED: What a piece of work.

SIGGY: Her?

TED: Her, right, her.

(Siggy's cell phone rings. She answers.)

SIGGY: Bueno . . . No Roberto. Not now. I asked you not to call me here. Forget the FedEx now. We don't need it now. Yes. I said cancel it. Ciao. I said Ciao. Did you hear me? Ciao. Ciao dear, that's better.

(She hangs up.)

TED: Honey? What did Roberto want?

SIGGY: A big barbed dildo rammed up his ass.

TED: Roberto is gay?

SIGGY: All the men I know are gay.

TED: Well, not Hank.

SIGGY: Not Hank, but, Hank doesn't count. Hank is our friend, Ted.

TED: Jean is gay?

SIGGY: Flaming.

TED: If you betrayed me. If you lied and made me a fool, Siggy . . . that would be devastating.

SIGGY: You're really enough of a fool without that aren't you Ted.

TED: I love you, Siggy.

SIGGY: I love you too, Ted.

(Jean enters.)

TED: Did you clean the bird shit off the Ferrari?

JEAN: Yes of course . . . but if I may, sir . . .

TED: Did you cover it? Because I noticed it sat there for twenty-four hours uncovered last time. Uncovered . . . save for the bird shit that is.

JEAN: If I may, SIR. there has been a terrible accident.

TED: What?

JEAN: A car accident. Mademoiselle Kali . . .

SIGGY: She's not . . . hurt is she?

JEAN: Not her, but . . .

(Hank enters with a bundle wrapped in his jacket.)

HANK: Claw.

TED: What happened?

JEAN: Miss Kali was driving away when Claw.

HANK: He ran right in front of her.

SIGGY: She ran over Claw!?

JEAN: It would appear the death was instantaneous.

TED: Oh, I can't look. I can't look Hank.

HANK: FUCK!!! Claw. Stupid Claw.

(Lights fade out.)

(Lights up. The woods. Hank is digging a hole with a heavy square-bladed shovel. Claw lies in a bundle nearby. Kali approaches.)

KALI: I've never taken the life of anything.

HANK: Well, now you have Kali. Now you have.

KALI: He ran right for me. His eyes were glowing.

HANK: You stepped on the gas.

KALI: I swerved.

HANK: You swerved toward him!

KALI: Oh! I'd rather be boiled alive in lava than see you hurt, Hank. And I know Siggy feels the same way.

HANK: What does that mean?

KALI: I really can't say.

HANK: What do you mean, you can't say. What is it?

KALI: I promised her I wouldn't tell. Except, certain things she said, certain things Ted said . . . I mean where were you?

HANK: Don't believe everything they tell you.

KALI: That's why I . . . It's yours to tell if you want. I wouldn't believe it coming from them.

HANK: What?

KALI: Whatever you need to tell me Hank. Just be honest.

HANK: Honest. You want me to be honest. O.K. I don't think I can have a relationship ever. With anyone. I can't. You want to know why?

KALI: You think you caused you wife's death. But you didn't.

HANK: You don't know.

KALI: Why do you think that? You can tell me, Hank. You can tell me anything.

HANK: I can barely say this out loud. I was a bastard. I had an affair with my best friend's wife. With Siggy, in the last year while Susie was dying. And I'll never get past this: At the end. She asked if I'd always been faithful to her. I told her yes. And I saw, one tear fall down her cheek. That was her gift to me. That simple goodness. At the moment of her death I LIED to her.

KALI: Every day I know you Hank, you reveal more of yourself to me. You reveal these great expanses of you, like a mountain side exposed to the moonlight. You're like this amazing mountain to me and I am just in awe of you.

HANK: I'm an idiot, Kali, and you're an idiot too.

KALI: Have you ever thought maybe Ted . . .

HANK: Ted doesn't know. You can't tell Ted this.

KALI: Haven't you ever thought . . . Ted . . .

HANK: What?

KALI: All this . . . all this TWO ORPHEUS stuff, this German stuff . . . what he's telling you about Susie?

(Jean appears.)

JEAN: There will be a light memorial supper shortly, if you would like to go in. Does that sound ridiculous? I am tired of being ridiculous. Let me finish with dignity. For among these people, I know what I am. Give me the shovel.

(He takes the shovel from Hank, puts Claw in the hole, kneels down as in prayer over the grave.)

JEAN: I have prepared a saute of green, red, and yellow bell peppers, roasted eggplant, wild mushrooms. There is also a tricolor salad served with a dressing of creamed goat cheese and chives. And for desert, yellow custard.

Monsieur Claw had a very good life. A very good life, Miss Kali, but everything ends. You must go inside now, have a beautiful meal. I will take care of everything here.

HANK: Thank you Jean.

KALI: I promise you I won't tell. I would never let on what I know. Especially to Ted . . .

(They exit. Jean continues to fill in the hole. Lights fade.)

(Lights up. The cabin. The dinner table. Kali, Hank, Siggy, Ted sit around the table eating. Everyone has a martini. Siggy appears to be quite drunk.)

SIGGY: Well, fuck the olives. A toast. To Claw.

(Siggy drinks.)

KALI: I am so, sorry for Claw.

(Kali drinks.)

SIGGY: Yes dear, to sorrow, remorse.

(Siggy and Kali drink.)

KALI: I didn't mean to do it.

TED: It just goes to show how unaware one can be.

KALI: Well, there's a lot of suffering here, at this table. I'm all too aware of that.

SIGGY: To suffering!

(Siggy drinks.)

Suffering Kali. It's good.

(Siggy and Kali drink.)

HANK: *(Pointedly, to Siggy.)* To friendship, which eases this suffering.

KALI: *(Drinks.)* Oh, you aren't really suffering, Hank.

SIGGY: *(Drinks.)* You don't even know what suffering is.

KALI: *(Drinks.)* Yet.

SIGGY: To passion!

TED: To the Susie nobody knew.

KALI: What's that supposed to mean?

HANK: To water under the bridge.

SIGGY: Susie Susie Susie.

TED: To Mental Clarity. Rigor.

KALI: *(Drinks.)* Is anyone listening to him?

SIGGY: His bombastic proclamations. His obsession with Susie. He never shuts up.

KALI: Get honest, Ted. TO HONESTY!!!

SIGGY and KALI: To honesty.

HANK: I think you've had enough to drink, Kali.

SIGGY: Oh Hank, don't be a "Ted."

> *(Kali laughs at this and drinks.)*

HANK: She can't take it. I mean it, you can't handle it Kali.

TED: What did she say?

KALI: She said, "DON'T BE A TED."

HANK: You'd better stop drinking.

KALI: I'm sure SUSIE could drink me under the table.

TED: *(To Siggy.)* I've been nothing but supportive to you. And all your shoes, even though they've walked all over me.

SIGGY: I think there's something that you should tell Hank, Ted.

TED: There are many things one Orpheus should say to another . . .

KALI: There's something I want to say about pain. You think that by hanging onto the pain you hang onto the person. I've learned to let go. SO GET HONEST, TED.

HANK: Is there something you want to say to me Ted? About all of this? About this whole weekend?

TED: I think you're the one who has something to say.

KALI: I let go of you, Hank. So forget it.

HANK: What is it you want out of me!?!

TED: Tell me. At the end.

KALI: Woo! Tilt a wheel.

> *(Hank takes Kali's drink away.)*

HANK: You've had ENOUGH.

TED: At the end. What did she say?

KALI: I'm drunk, oh my god.

TED: I know there was a message.

KALI: The room is spinning.

SIGGY: That's what I like to see. A sloppy little bimbo losing her lunch.

KALI: I've lost a whole lot more than my lunch here Siggy. So fuck you.

HANK: I want to know why are you so obsessed with my wife, Ted?

KALI: Dead wife. She's dead. Your goddamn dead wife.

TED: She is going to come back.

HANK: In the opera, Ted? And why the two Orpheuses . . . this whole idea of authentic and fake?

KALI: Are you saying — like, you're the real Orpheus, Ted?

SIGGY: I think it's time you level with Hank about Susie.

TED: She is going to come back. I'm going to save her.

SIGGY: Since when did you turn into Jesus, Ted?

TED: She wrote me at the end . . . in German. She said she would come back . . . to look for a sign.

HANK: And what else was this letter in German about? Can I see it?

TED: It was all about longing. Her loneliness. Verlassenheit!

SIGGY: Liar! You're lying.

KALI: Let's see the letters.

HANK: Can I see the letters, Ted?

TED: I burned them all. They're mixed with her ashes.

HANK: They're mixed with her ashes? The letters she wrote?

KALI: That's FREAKY, Hank.

TED: This is not about me. It's about how HE'S withholding. He won't tell me what she said at the end. The Sign. Her Message.

KALI: There isn't any message.

TED: What do you know, you turnip.

SIGGY: Who'd leave a message for you, Ted?

TED: You vegetable. Carrot brain. I'm trying to get an answer from my friend.

HANK: What message are you expecting, Ted?

TED: The ritual manner of her return.

KALI: That's crazy. You're quite a fruit loop.

TED: Will you SHUT THE FUCK UP! You potted plant. There is a price to self-knowledge, Miss Gandhi.

KALI: Hank has paid, and paid through the nose.

TED: What could you possibly know about Hank. Really.

KALI: I know a few things.

TED: About Fellatio perhaps. That's a blow job dear, in case the word is unfamiliar. You're blowing him full of a false sense of comfort.

KALI: To give comfort, Ted, is human and warm.

TED: I prefer the comfort of true pure honesty. You said you betrayed her. How was that exactly? Why can't you at least give us details on that?

KALI: Okay, Ted. If you want to get honest.

HANK: NO.

KALI: You want to get honest. You're ready for that.

HANK: No, Kali. Don't. You promised.

SIGGY: Let her go.

TED: What could you possibly say to me, that could cause the slightest RIPPLE on my surface?

KALI: You'll find out. I need a breath of fresh air. Accompany me to Claw's grave and you'll get the message you've been waiting for. Excuse me, I may just have to puke first.
    (She exits. Sound of puking offstage.)

TED: *(Gleeful.)* It seems I made her sick.

HANK: Lay off, Ted.

TED: She wants to show me Claw's grave.

SIGGY: Let her be sick in peace now, Ted.

TED: Perhaps I was wrong about her. Perhaps she and I were meant to be friends.

HANK: No you weren't.

TED: Jealous, Hank?

HANK: No.

SIGGY: Oh really, Ted.

TED: I'm not going to try and steal your girlfriend, so don't worry Hank. She isn't my type. She just wants to give me a message at Claw's grave.
    (He gets up to go.)

HANK: Why don't you wait till tomorrow Ted, and we'll put some nice marble around it?

KALI: *(From offstage.)* OKAY TED! I'M READY.

TED: If she is really your friend, Hank. . . I must deign not to despise her.
    (Ted exits.)

HANK: This is bad. This is bad. She's telling him, Siggy. Ted was my friend. Twenty years is about to end, Siggy.

SIGGY: Oh, you have the most wonderful mouth. And your tongue, my god. I will never forget it.

HANK: It's the end of the opera. The Steiner. The money. It's finished.

SIGGY: Well —

HANK: We'll never work together again.

SIGGY: I'm leaving him.

HANK: No.

SIGGY: I'm leaving him, Hank, I want you.

HANK: She's telling him Siggy and it's going to be hell.

SIGGY: Oh well, then let hell reign down. Let it come, Hank. Bring on hell.

HANK: I don't want hell, I don't want hell.

SIGGY: I'd like to think I'm worth a little hell. I'd like to think I'm expensive Hank, and hell is the price for me.

HANK: That would kill Ted. He was my friend.

SIGGY: Ted never gave a shit about you. All he cared about was Susie. All his CRAP about Susie. She wasn't LONELY. She was THINKING OF HIM. There wasn't a mystery. She was GETTING IT elsewhere. So give the guilt a fucking rest.

HANK: WHAT!!

SIGGY: Ted had her first, before you and me. Susie. He had her, so don't feel so guilty.

HANK: How long?

SIGGY: What?

HANK: How long did they — .

SIGGY: From the beginning. And maybe before

HANK: From the beginning of my —

SIGGY: Marriage. He had her the whole time.

HANK: Why didn't you tell me?

SIGGY: I can make you happy.

HANK: You can make a lot of people be a lot of things, but HAPPY isn't one of them.

(Beat. Siggy surveys the scene.)

SIGGY: If this isn't a maggot's picnic.

(Kali and Ted enter.)

SIGGY: That was a quick little trip to the grave site.

KALI: Can I have a napkin, please?

SIGGY: By all means, dear. There's a little putrid dribble at the corner of your mouth. You look green, Ted. Did you step on a snake? Did a cobra spring from her cute little mouth and bite you in the brain? Are you feeling sick, Ted?

TED: So you two had a little conversation just now? A little talk about old times?

HANK: Actually we were just discussing hell.

TED: Hell. Ah, hell. One day you can go there together. You can fuck each other in hell you ravenous bloodsucking poisonous cunt. I think hell might suit you just fine, you and —

SIGGY: Don't be a broiling mediocrity, Ted.

HANK: Is it true about you and Susie, Ted?

TED: I now understand the Lipshidt Foundation.

SIGGY: What about it, Ted?

TED: Why they had to have Hank. Why they had to have Hank, because frankly, Hank wasn't my first choice.

HANK: The Lipshidt Foundation?

KALI: It's Siggy, Hank.

TED: I was hoping to work with . . . If not Sondheim, then Randy Newman, he might have been good. You've got all that money you hire the best. But they insisted. They had to have Hank. They wanted him, Siggy. They insisted on Hank. I thought the Lipshidts were trustworthy people.

SIGGY: Get a grip, Ted. We came up with The Steiner TOGETHER. I'm the Lipshidt. You're so goddamned delusional . . .

TED: I knew that all along. I had to believe it for Hank's sake . . . for Susie.

HANK: Answer me Ted. You and Susie . . .

TED: The Steiner . . . The Steiner. The Steiner. The Steiner . . . The Steiner . . .

  (Jean enters.)

JEAN: Do you require anything here?

HANK: Just the Truth. The truth would be good.

KALI: I'd like a glass of cold water. No ice.

JEAN: A glass of cold water it is.

  (Jean exits.)

HANK: You and my wife . . .

TED: I had her. That's right. She was my wife, really. In the eternity.

HANK: Susie . . .

KALI: She could not have been worth all this.

TED: When Orpheus turns back he sees Susie. We must bring her back. This deserves full orchestration.

HANK: There's not going to BE orchestration, Ted.

TED: This blackness . . . this void must be sonically filled. The dissonance. The dissonance. The dissonance.

SIGGY: YOU ARE A CUCKOLD, TED. YOU'RE AN IDIOT. SO HOW DOES IT FEEL.

HANK: You were my friend. Twelve fucking years —

TED: That's the terrible trick Hades has played on all of us. Because . . .

SIGGY: Susie knew what she was doing.

TED: When you look back, you're left with what, Hank?

HANK: Fucking hypocrites.

TED: The Causality? Hank? Cause and effect? Chance? Or chaos, or sin? Or anarchy?

SIGGY: I had Susie's number. It was a good routine.

TED: You never knew Susie at all. None of you did.

HANK: Oh, only you, Ted?

KALI: I understand who Susie was more and more.

TED: UNDERSTAND THIS: We all wish it were YOU in that urn instead of her.

(Kali goes and gets the urn.)

KALI: Hank doesn't want that now. Do you, Hank?

TED: Give me that. You have no right to touch it.

KALI: Answer me, Hank! Do you want me or her?

TED: Give me that.

(Ted goes for the urn. Kali holds on.)

KALI: Me or Her, Hank.

TED: Mine! Mine! She was mine!

KALI: This Susie! This Susie you thought was so great. How could she do this to you?

HANK: Let's stop this please.

(Siggy pulls at the urn.)

SIGGY: Did you know about me and Hank, Susie?

TED: I know she had a message for me. What was it, Hank?

SIGGY: Did you get a big thrill when you croaked on him Susie?

HANK: STOP!

KALI: Do you think this is what she wanted to happen?

SIGGY: Manipulating bitch. Miss Perfect. Miss Pure. Miss SONGBIRD.

TED: Why were you there at the end and not me? Why? WHY? I had the right.

SIGGY: Everything she ever said was a lie.

TED: Why didn't she tell you . . . what did she say?

HANK: She just gasped. She just gasped.

TED: Liar Hank! Liar.

HANK: She was MY WIFE.

KALI: Me or her, Hank.

TED: WHAT DID SHE SAY! SHE MUST'VE SAID SOMETHING.

(Hank dumps the ashes out onto the table:)

HANK: ASK HER! ASK SUSIE! ASK HER YOURSELF. HERE SHE IS! MAKE OF HER WHAT YOU WILL. ASK SUSIE. GO ON. I DIDN'T

KNOW HER. NOBODY HERE DID. SO GO ON ASK HER! ASK
SUSIE! GO ON. (*Everyone stares at the ashes all over the table. A long beat.
Jean enters. He stares at the mess. A long beat.*)

JEAN: What is the word . . . how you say . . . Grow up? When does this happen. In America.

(*Jean has a little tablecloth brush. He begins cleaning up the ashes as everyone watches. Lights fade out.*)

(*The cabin. The mess is cleared away. Jean works packing a thickly wrapped
parcel into a backpack. Hank and Kali look on.*)

JEAN: So . . . you are getting the plane to Tibet. No? At last . . . where she
wanted to go.

HANK: I hope that's where she wanted to go.

KALI: I've always wanted to go there.

HANK: She could've been just saying that. She could've said the East River for
all I care. She's going now. She'll get what she asked for.

KALI: Hank . . . stop.

JEAN: One thing you must know. This is human remains . . .

HANK: Yeah.

JEAN: This must be smuggled on board. The plane.

KALI: We can't just declare it?

JEAN: Declare? No no no. Declare as what?

KALI: Declare. As ashes.

JEAN: Human remains is not approved. No . . . these you can't take on the
plane like Ham Sandwich. There is so much red tape. And perhaps customs will seize Miss Susie's . . .

KALI: So what do we do?

JEAN: You must lie. Can you lie? For Hank? And for her . . . You must smile
at the man in customs and lie. Make him think you have feeling for him.
Lie and flirt with the man in customs and you will get through. Can you
do this?

KALI: Yes. I can do it for Hank.

JEAN: Good then. I zip this up now for you.

(*Jean zips up and gives her the backpack.*)

HANK: Ready?

KALI: Uh huh.

(*Ted enters, sees them. Turns and exits quickly.*)

TED: (*From offstage.*) They still haven't left.

SIGGY: Oh, Ted. Don't be a baby.

(*Siggy enters, followed by Ted.*)

TED: So, all set? Got everything?

HANK: Yes thanks.

TED: You have a nice drive back to the city then.

SIGGY: *(Kissing Hank.)* Good-bye, Darling.

HANK: Good-bye Siggy.

> *(Siggy kisses Kali.)*

SIGGY: *(To Kali.)* Nice to have met YOU, dear.

KALI: Okay . . .

HANK: Good-bye, Ted.

KALI: Bye.

> *(Kali and Hank exit. Jean goes after them carrying a suitcase. Ted and Siggy look at each other. A beat.)*

SIGGY: I hope Susie won't mind.

TED: What?

SIGGY: The yellow custard she's all mixed up with.

TED: No. I don't think so.

SIGGY: Ted?

TED: Yes dear.

SIGGY: Let's have a martini. That would be fun, don't you think?

> *(Ted looks at her. Lights fade out.)*

END OF PLAY

PERMISSION INFORMATION